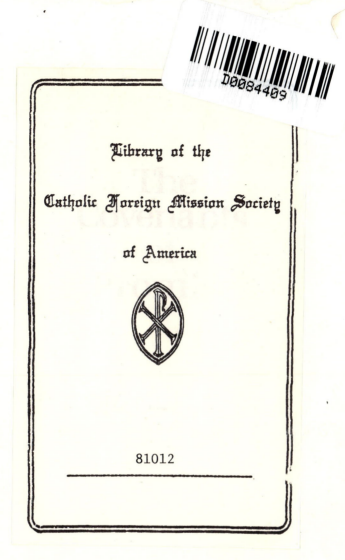

The
Covenants
of
Promise

A Theology of the Old Testament Covenants

Thomas Edward McComiskey

BAKER BOOK HOUSE
Grand Rapids, Michigan 49506

To My Beloved Wife Eleanor
whose love and understanding have
contributed more than she knows
to the writing of this volume

Contents

Introduction

T he Bible is a book of history. It weaves a tapestry of events that stretches from the creation to the end of time. But the Bible is concerned with more than human events, for the history of the Bible is redemptive history. Even the cursory reader of Scripture soon realizes that God is at work in the affairs of mankind. It is God alone who gives meaning to history.

It is sometimes easy to lose sight of that fact when reading the Bible, particularly when we see Israelite pitted against Canaanite in the choking dust of battle, or when we read of the devious machinations of kings of the divided monarchy. It is then that we may conclude that the history of the Bible is an all too human history.

However, the writers of the Bible do not let us think that for long. They have a unique way of bringing us back to the fact that the events of history—even those that are darkest—are related to the centrality of God in human affairs. We soon learn that the Israelite incursion into Canaan was in fulfillment of the divine promise, and the moral weakness of kings was really rebellion against the divine law. Thus, events as mundane as these are re-lated to the fact that God has entered the sphere of human history to proclaim his purpose and will and to carry out that purpose within his created world.

Several events stand out above others in the history of redemp-tion as it unfolds in the Old Testament. These are the statement of the promise to Abraham, the giving of the law at Sinai, and the restatement of the promise to David in the Davidic covenant. The importance of these events is underscored not only by the dramatic way in which they are presented in the narratives, but also by the fact that the Old Testament writers—particularly the prophets—appealed to them frequently in their pronouncements of hope and doom.

Each of these events involved the establishment of a covenant. Thus, the history of redemption in the Old Testament is marked by the ratification of covenants in which God affirmed his will for his people. A covenantal structure underlies the program of redemption.

This structure is not unique to the Old Testament, for when we turn to the New Testament we read in the Gospels of the ratification of a new covenant. Like the covenants of the Old Testament, the new covenant is underscored by its dramatic presentation and its importance in the theology of the New Testament. This covenant was instituted when Jesus lifted the cup in the dim interior of the upper room. Thus, the major periods of redemptive history are governed by great covenantal institutions.

The purpose of this volume is to examine the theological importance of the covenantal structure of redemptive history. The central thesis is that the major redemptive covenants are structured bicovenantally. The promise covenant, made with Abraham and his offspring, is an eternal covenant that never loses its force or integrity. Its elements are explicated in several covenants, called in this work administrative covenants. These covenants govern human obedience. Both types of covenant must function together for the successful administration of the inheritance.

Each of the major redemptive covenants will be studied from two perspectives: its content and its relationship with the other covenants. Because of the importance of the promise covenant the first chapter of this volume deals with the nature of each element of the promise expressed in that covenant. The promise of land and the promise of offspring receive the greatest amount of attention in the first chapter because of the prominence they are given in both testaments and because they are controversial subjects in current theological dialogue. If other elements are not given as much attention in the discussion it does not mean that they are considered to be of less importance. Indeed, the promise that the

Lord would be God to his people, the promise from which the others spring, is given considerably less space in the discussion only because its meaning is clear and it has not engendered great disagreement in the history of its interpretation.

In the second chapter the relationship between promise and covenant is considered. This is foundational to the discussion that follows, for it establishes the relationship between the promise covenant on the one hand and the law and the new covenant on the other. The writer hopes that the excursus on the law in the New Testament will be regarded as an essential part of the argument. It is not an incidental section in the book. It is an integral part of the discussion.

In chapter 3 the bicovenantal structure of the covenants is considered; the remaining chapters deal with the theological and hermeneutical implications of the study. One of the major theological implications of the bicovenantal structure is that it provides a theological function in which the unity of the testaments finds expression, but at the same time, the discontinuity apparent in the flow of redemptive history through the testaments may be given theological definition and exegetical authority.

In recent years several works have dealt with some of the issues discussed in this volume, such as the theological implications of the promise and the nature and content of the covenants. It will be apparent to the reader, however, that the thesis of this volume is quite different from the basic conclusions of other works. The author has attempted to give a fresh discussion of the promise and the covenants. As to how successful he has been, only the reader may judge.

The Davidic covenant is discussed at several points in the book, but because it is considered a restatement of the promise given to Abraham it is viewed as a refinement of the Abrahamic covenant and thus an integral part of the continuum of promise and its covenantal expression. For this reason it is not commented upon extensively in the work. Again, this is not intended to diminish its importance.

This book is the result of a decade of teaching Old Testament theology. It was written with the hope that the reader will share some of the profound blessing that has come to the author in his exploration of the great covenantal expressions of God's will. It is not intended to set forth a moderating position between dispensationalism and covenant theology. It is a theology of the Old Testament covenants. It is not a criticism of any theological system. It is an effort to utilize modern principles of exegesis and biblical theology in the quest for continuing refinement and precision in our theological categories.

The reader may wish that certain concepts had been given fuller treatment in the discussion. But this is one of three works in preparation which are prolegomena to a larger theology of the Old Testament projected by the author. The concepts set forth here will be treated more fully in that volume.

introduction

Abbreviations

ARV	American Revised Version
AV	Authorized Version
BA	*Biblical Archaeologist*
Bib	*Biblica*
BS	*Bibliotheca Sacra*
CBQ	*Catholic Biblical Quarterly*
CJT	*Canadian Journal of Theology*
ET	*Expository Times*
Interp	*Interpretation*
ISBE	*International Standard Bible Encyclopedia*
JAOS	*Journal of the American Oriental Society*
JBL	*Journal of Biblical Literature*
JETS	*Journal of the Evangelical Theological Society*
JQR	*Jewish Quarterly Review*
JSOT	*Journal for the Study of the Old Testament*
LXX	Septuagint
MT	Masoretic Text
NASB	New American Standard Bible
NEB	New English Bible
NIDNTT	*New International Dictionary of New Testament Theology*
NIV	New International Version
PTR	*Princeton Theological Review*
Rest Q	*Restoration Quarterly*
RSV	Revised Standard Version
RV	Revised Version
SJT	*Scottish Journal of Theology*
ST	*Studia Theologica*
TDOT	*Theological Dictionary of the Old Testament*
TZ	*Theologische Zeitschrift*
VT	*Vetus Testamentum*
WTJ	*Westminster Theological Journal*

Remember that you were ... strangers
to the covenants of promise. ... But now in
Christ Jesus you who once were far off have
been brought near in the blood of Christ. [Eph. 2:12 — 13, RSV]

1

The Promise

One of the most foundational aspects of Old Testament theology is the promise that was given to Abraham and reiterated to his descendants. The theme of promise is interwoven throughout the Old and New Testaments. It is appealed to in the New Testament especially by the apostle Paul, who based much of the argumentation of the epistles to the Romans and to the Galatians on events in Abraham's life (Rom. 4; 9:6 – 13; Gal. 3; 4:21 – 31).

The promise is not an incidental theme that appears from time to time in the Bible when the writers wished to use an interesting illustration from history. Its theological implications reach far into the future. The promise touches lives today and provides the foundations of redemption for all who by faith are the descendants of Abraham.

The Nature of the Promise

The first statement of the promise to Abraham followed the Lord's command to him to remove from Ur of the Chaldees and to set out for the land of Canaan (Gen. 12:1). The people of Abraham's day probably took little note of the family-clan that journeyed from Ur to Haran and then to Canaan, but the events surrounding that journey were to mark one of the most monumental periods in human history.

The terms of the promise given in that first statement are found in Genesis 12:2 – 3:

> "I will make you into a great nation
>   and I will bless you;
> I will make your name great,
>   and you will be a blessing.
> I will bless those who bless you,
>   and whoever curses you I will curse;
> and all peoples on earth
>   will be blessed through you."[1]

The promise relates not only to Abraham but also to all mankind. The terms that relate specifically to Abraham are that he will become a great nation (v. 2), that he will be blessed (v. 2), and that his name will become great (v. 2). The elements of the promise that extend beyond Abraham are that he will be a blessing (v. 2), that the Lord will show favor to those who favor Abraham and disfavor to those who do not (v. 3), and that all peoples of the earth will be blessed through him (v. 3).

This last element does not teach a universalistic concept—that all mankind are included in the saving benefits of the promise. The fact that God blesses some and curses others (v. 3a) precludes that possibility, and faith is clearly the prerequisite for receiving the benefits of the promise. Rather, those benefits extend beyond the Jewish people to include Gentiles as well.

When Abraham's pilgrimage of faith took him on to Canaan, an aspect of the promise was refined and amplified for him in the words "to your offspring I will give this land" (Gen. 12:7). This was implicit in the earlier words "I will make you into a great nation" (Gen. 12:2). It served to refine that earlier statement by more narrowly defining the "great nation" as Abraham's offspring and it amplified the statement by designating the land of Canaan as the country in which his posterity would become a nation.

Later, in Abraham's ninety-ninth year, the promise was again affirmed to him (Gen. 17:1 – 8). It was in this restatement of the promise that Abraham's name was changed from Abram (v. 5).

---

1. The last clause is also translated "by you all the families of the earth shall bless themselves" (RSV) or "all the families on earth will pray to be blessed as you are blessed" (NEB). The translation of this clause will be considered in the subsequent discussion.

There is a significant concept in the statement in Genesis 17:1 – 8 that does not appear in the earlier statements. It is the concept of divine-human relationship inherent in the words "to be your God and the God of your descendants after you" (v. 7). This concept occurs also in the summary statement of verse 8, "I will be their God." It is in this context also (17:6) that Abraham was told that kings would descend from him.

In its totality, then, the Abrahamic promise includes the promise of the offspring, the promise of blessing for Abraham, the promise that Abraham's name would be great, the promise of blessing for those who favor Abraham and disfavor for those who do not, the promise that Abraham's descendants would occupy the land of Canaan, the promise of divine blessing for Gentiles, the promise that the Lord would be the God of those who comprise Abraham's offspring, and the promise that kings would be descended from Abraham.

It is important to note that the promise given to Abraham is an eternal promise (Gen. 13:15; 17:7 – 8, 13, 19; 48:4). It was not to find its fulfillment only in Isaac, but it would be administered forever, extending its blessings to all the people of faith throughout the ages.

To grasp the full significance of the covenantal idea that lies at the heart of Israelite religion it is essential to understand the elements of the promise and their relationship to the covenants that secured them.

The Promise of the Offspring

The Complexity of the Concept

The first element of the promise to be considered is that of the offspring, or "seed," as the word *zera'* is translated in several versions.[2] This element was particularly significant in view of the fact that Abraham and Sarah were too old to have children at the time the promise was given (Gen. 17:17). The earnest of this aspect of the promise was given to them by God in the birth of their son Isaac (Gen. 21:1 – 3).

2. AV; ARV; RV.

The concept of the offspring is given prominence in the subsequent restatements of the promise in Genesis as well as in its first statement. The offspring are promised the land of Canaan (13:14 — 15, 15:16, 18 — 21; 17:8; 22:17; 26:3 — 4; 28:4; 35:12; 48:4), they are to be very great in number (13:16; 15:5; 22:17; 26:4; 28:3; 35:11 — 12; 48:4), they are to include kings (17:6, 16), the Lord is to be their God (17:7 — 8), and they are to be a medium of blessing to others (22:18; 26:4).

Thus, the promise given to the patriarchs, a promise that involves the blessing of multitudes, was to function through Abraham's offspring, and through them that promise would be realized. This is emphasized particularly in Genesis 22:18, "and through your offspring all nations on earth will be blessed. . . ."

It may seem unnecessary to ask at this point who the offspring are. They seem clearly to be the physical descendants of Abraham. Yet, when the concept of the offspring is traced through the Old and New Testaments it takes on a complexity not evident in the cluster of statements made to the patriarchs. For example, in the New Testament the word *sperma* (seed, offspring) refers to the physical descendants of Abraham (Luke 1:55; John 8:33, 37; Acts 7:5 — 6; Heb. 11:18), but the apostle Paul included within the concept those who are Abraham's offspring by faith (Rom. 4:13 — 18; 9:6 — 8; Gal. 3:7, 23 — 29). He added a dimension to the promise not explicit in its occurrences in Genesis. The concept is expanded still further in the New Testament by strong messianic motifs. In Acts 3:25 — 26, Peter affirmed that Christ is the offspring (*sperma*) through whom the blessing of the promise is mediated, and in Galatians 3:16 Paul argued that the word *seed* (*zera'*), used in the Genesis accounts of the promise, is not a grammatical plural and thus refers to Christ. He said, "The promises were spoken to Abraham and to his seed. The Scripture does not say 'and to seeds,' meaning many people, but 'and to your seed,' meaning one person, who is Christ."

These New Testament passages raise serious questions concerning the approach of the New Testament writers to the Old Testament. Did they see more than is warranted in the simple statements of the Genesis narratives? Are they vulnerable to the objections often leveled against early rabbinic interpretation of Scripture? In their zeal to promote the Christian faith among the

Jews did they paint their picture of the fulfillment of the promise with too wide a brush?[3]

These questions are of greatest concern to those who hold to a unity of revelation between the testaments, but they hold an interest for all who are concerned with the development of religious thought in this period and the biblical hermeneutic that formed it.

We have observed two dimensions in the way in which the New Testament understands the Genesis accounts of the promise of the offspring: the concept of the individual offspring, who is Christ; and the concept of corporate offspring, which includes, along with the physical descendants of Abraham, all the people of faith. The individual dimension will be considered first.

The Individual Offspring in the Old and New Testaments

The Pauline concept of the offspring against the background of the Old and New Testaments

Commentators have struggled with the hermeneutical methodology underlying Paul's identification of zera´ with Christ in Galatians 3:16.[4] The word is a grammatical collective and refers most naturally to the descendants of Abraham in its occurrences in Genesis. But it should be noted that Paul did not apply the concept of the offspring only in an individualistic way. He applied it corporately as well. He stated, "If you belong to Christ, then you are Abraham's seed" (v. 29). The same concept obtains in Romans 4:13 – 18 and 9:6 – 9. To Paul, the concept of the seed allowed for a reference to one individual as well as to many.[5] He was writing

3. For extensive discussions of the way in which the New Testament interprets the Old Testament see Richard N. Longenecker, *Biblical Exegesis in the Apostolic Period* (Grand Rapids: Eerdmans, 1975); E. Earle Ellis, *Paul's Use of the Old Testament* (Grand Rapids: Eerdmans, 1957).

4. Donald Guthrie, *Galatians* (London: Nelson, 1969), p. 107, writes, "There is no denying that there is a touch of Rabbinical method in Paul's argument ..."; E. D. Burton, *A Critical and Exegetical Commentary on the Epistle to the Galatians* (Edinburgh: T. and T. Clark, 1921), p. 182, says, "He doubtless arrived at his thought, not by exegesis of scripture, but from an interpretation of history ..."; J. B. Lightfoot, *The Epistle of St. Paul to the Galatians* (1865; Grand Rapids: Zondervan, 1962), p. 142, comments, "The question therefore is no longer one of grammatical accuracy, but of theological interpretation."

5. William Hendriksen observes that the word *seed* refers to individuals alone in Gen. 4:25; 21:13; 1 Sam. 1:11; 2 Sam. 7:12; 1 Chron. 17:11. *A Commentary on Galatians* (London: Banner of Truth Trust, 1969), p. 135.

to common people, and if he did not explain the collective in Galatians 3:16 in sophisticated linguistic terminology he should not be faulted. He observed that the word *zera'* is not plural.[6] This is important, for if it were plural, the promise would be unintelligible because of the ambiguity involved in determining its recipients. The collective function of *zera'* allows the writer to refer to the group or to a representative individual of that group. One must ask whether Paul was on good ground in interpreting the whole range of the concept of the offspring as it unfolds in the Old Testament. Does that concept allow for a single representative individual who is the offspring of Abraham and who mediates the blessing of the promise?

Paul stated in this passage that there were two heirs of the promise, Abraham and Christ. Thus, Paul gave to Abraham, along with Christ, the role of principal heir to the promise. R. C. H. Lenski says, "He [Abraham] is here not named as a mere individual, as one of many beneficiaries of the testament. Even Isaac, Jacob, and the patriarchs could not be named here as Abraham is. Whatever promises God spoke to them were entirely Abraham's. He was the heir. All others only share in his inheritance. They inherit only as spiritual 'sons of Abraham' (v. 7)."[7]

Paul's argument is that the promise reigns from Abraham to Christ (v. 16); the law did not nullify it (v. 17). Christ is heir to the promise along with Abraham (v. 16) and only those who are united to Christ by faith may share those blessings (v. 29).

Since Paul attributed to Christ the role of principal heir, every theological system that gives credence to Paul must acknowledge Christ's participation in the promise as its recipient and mediator. At some time in the progress of God's redemptive activity the terms of the promise were guaranteed to Christ as the offspring, and since the offspring is also the mediator of the promised blessings (Gen. 26:4), he was given the privilege of granting those blessings to all who share its benefits. This participation by Christ in the promise is often used as proof of the existence of the covenant of grace or the covenant of redemption by covenant theologians.[8] Its

6. The word *zera'* occurs in the plural only once in the MT (1 Sam. 8:15).

7. R. C. H. Lenski, *The Interpretation of St. Paul's Epistles to the Galatians, to the Ephesians, and to the Philippians* (Minneapolis: Augsburg, 1961), pp. 158–59.

8. See, for example, Hermannus Witsius, *The Economy of the Covenants Between God and Man,* trans. William Crookshank, 2 vols. (1677; Edinburgh: Thomas Turnbull, 1803),

importance in the program of redemption is acknowledged by dispensationalists as well.[9]

Since the concept of the offspring in Pauline theology includes more than is evident in the statements of the promise to the patriarchs, we must ask whether Paul was in agreement with the broad range of Old Testament revelation in his understanding of the promise of the offspring. To answer this question it is necessary to examine the references to that promise in the Old Testament.

The Davidic covenant (2 Sam. 7). The first of these contexts is 2 Samuel 7. Here the promise was reiterated to David. The background against which this reaffirmation was given was David's desire to build a house for the Lord (vv. 1–3). The prophet Nathan approved at first (v. 3), but he later received a revelation from the Lord in which it was announced that David would not build a house for the Lord; rather, the Lord would build a house for him (v. 11). The house of the Lord that David wished to build was the temple. This work, he learned, would be accomplished by his offspring (vv. 12–13). The house that the Lord would build for David is a dynasty (vv. 16, 19). This promise thus secured a line of kings, who were descended from David and who would rule over the kingdom established by him.

The elements of the Davidic promise are strikingly similar to those of the Abrahamic promise. Like Abraham, David is promised that his name would be great (v. 9; cf. Gen. 12:2). The nation is promised security in its own land (v. 10; cf. Gen. 12:7). David is promised offspring (vv. 11–12; cf. Gen. 12:2). Kings are to descend from him (vv. 12–16; cf. Gen. 17:6, 16). David is conscious of the Lord's blessing (v. 29; cf. Gen. 12:2, "and I will bless you"). God is the Israelites' God and they are his people (v. 24; cf. Gen. 17:7–8). Like the Abrahamic promise, the Davidic promise is eternal (vv. 13, 16, 24–25, 29; cf. Gen. 17:7). The only element of the Abrahamic promise that seems to be lacking in 2 Samuel 7 is the extension of divine blessing to Gentiles. However, it is quite possible that this concept is to be found in the phrase *wĕzō't tôrat hā'ādām* (and

vol. 1, pp. 170–71. Charles Hodge distinguished between the covenant of grace and the covenant of redemption. *Systematic Theology,* 3 vols. (1871–73; Grand Rapids: Eerdmans, 1952), vol. 2, pp. 357–61.

9. Lewis Sperry Chafer refers to "The Before-Time Covenant." *Systematic Theology,* 8 vols. (Dallas: Dallas Seminary Press, 1947–48), vol. 5, pp. 27–28.

this is the law of mankind, v. 19).[10] Unfortunately this phrase has been obscured in most English versions.[11] The interpretive problems here are formidable, but they must be considered.

The word *tôrāh* (law) is best understood to refer to an established body of teaching.[12] In this context it finds its referent in

10. This statement occurs in somewhat different form in 1 Chron. 17:17, *ûr'îtanî kĕtôr hā'ādām hamma'ālâ*. Here *tôr* may be a contracted form of *tôrāh*. Willis J. Beecher translates the phrase, "And thou art regarding me according to the upbringing *torah* of mankind. . . ." *The Prophets and the Promise* (Grand Rapids: Baker, 1963), p. 237. See the fuller discussion on pp. 237 – 40. See also Walter C. Kaiser, Jr., "The Blessing of David: A Charter for Humanity," in *The Law and the Prophets: Old Testament Studies Prepared in Honor of Oswald Thompson Allis*, ed. John H. Skilton (Nutley, N. J.: Presbyterian and Reformed, 1974), pp. 298 – 318.

The LXX translates the phrase in 2 Sam. 7:19 (2 Kings 7:19, LXX) *houtos de ho nomos tou anthrōpou, Kurie mou Kurie* (And is this the law of man, O Lord, my Lord?).

11. "And is this the manner of man . . . ?" (AV); "and this too after the manner of men" (ARV); "and hast shown me future generations" (RSV); "this is the custom of man" (NASB); "such, O Lord GOD, is the lot of a man embarked on a high career" (NEB); "Is this your usual way of dealing with man . . . ?" (NIV).

12. The basic meaning of the verb (*yārāh*) from which the word *tôrāh* comes is "to direct." This meaning is evident in the uses of the word that denote shooting arrows (1 Sam. 20:36 – 37; 2 Kings 13:17) and in the less frequent sense of throwing (Exod. 15:4; Josh. 18:6). In both instances an object is directed toward a particular point. The word occurs with the connotation of giving directions in Gen. 46:28, where Judah, Jacob's son, went before Jacob to obtain directions to Goshen and to direct the family there. The word is used in a somewhat similar sense in contexts where it means "to point out" or "to show."

It is not difficult to see how the connotation *to teach* was derived from this concept, for teaching involves giving direction.

The noun *tôrāh*, in its basic sense, connotes a body of teaching. The word occurs in Gen. 26:5 in association with the words *requirements, commands,* and *decrees,* connoting the body of truth to which Abraham was obedient. In the vast majority of cases the word denotes the legal material given by God to Moses. The word may apply to individual laws (Lev. 6:9 [2], 14 [7], 25 [18]; 7:7, 11, 37) or to the whole body of legislation (Exod. 16:4; 18:16; Lev. 26:46; Deut. 17:19; Josh. 1:7; Ezra 3:2).

It occurs in a more general sense in Job 22:22, where Job is enjoined to accept instruction from the mouth of God. It is paralleled by the phrase *lay up his words in your heart.*

In the Psalms, the word is frequently used of the body of revealed truth (1:2; 19:7 [8]; 89:30 [31]; 94:12).

In Proverbs, the word occurs in the general sense of instruction, as well as in the more technical sense of God's law. It is used of the teaching of one's mother (1:8; 6:20), the teaching of Wisdom (3:1), and the teaching of the wise (13:14). It is used of the law of God in 28:4, 7, 9.

In the Prophets, the word is used almost invariably of the body of revealed truth by which God made known his will to man. Only in Ezek. 43:11 – 12; 44:5 is there the possibility of a somewhat different meaning. There the word seems to be used of the regulations which govern the temple that Ezekiel envisioned.

The word *tôrāh* clearly reflects its verbal root and in each case denotes an identifiable body of teaching.

David's thankful praise (vv. 18 — 19). It cannot be divorced from the reference to the perpetuity of David's house: "Moreover, you have spoken concerning the house of your servant for a long time to come" (v. 19, author's translation).

The phrase *this is the* tôrāh *of mankind* has been interpreted in various ways. The majority of interpreters and translators understand the word *tôrāh* in the sense of custom or manner. They take it to refer in some way to the manner in which God has dealt with David. But in no clear instance does the word have that meaning in the Old Testament.[13]

Taken in its simplest and most literal sense, the phrase may denote that the promise that David's house would continue is the established body of teaching for mankind. There is only one body of teaching that relates the concept of the offspring to the destiny of mankind, and that is the promise given to Abraham.[14] This understanding of 2 Samuel 7:19 emphasizes the continuity between the offspring of the Abrahamic promise and the offspring of David. Both are viewed as mediating the divine blessing to all mankind (cf. Gen. 22:18).

Not only is a continuity maintained in this view, but there is a sharpening of focus as well, for in 2 Samuel 7 the emphasis is on the Davidic dynasty, not the descendants of Abraham as a whole. In some way, the dynasty of David bears a relationship to mankind. This prepares us for the great prophetic pronouncements about the Messiah, the Davidic king par excellence.

Another problem in this passage is found in the references that describe the Davidic dynasty as everlasting. In what way could David's dynasty be an everlasting dynasty? This concept is expressed in the constructions *'ad 'ōlām* and *lĕ'ôlām*. There seems to be no great distinction in meaning between the two. Both express the concept of unbroken duration. Only the context can

13. The view of Carl F. Keil and Franz Delitzsch is more in keeping with the meaning of *tôrāh*: "This—namely, the love and condescension manifested in Thy treatment of Thy servant—is the law which applies to man, or is conformed to the law which men are to observe towards men, i.e. to the law, Thou shalt love thy neighbor as thyself. . . ." *Biblical Commentary on the Books of Samuel* (reprint; Grand Rapids: Eerdmans, 1969), p. 350. However, the application of *zō't* (this) to a previously unexpressed attribute of God is somewhat abstract and vague, particularly since the preceding use of *zō't* in verse 19 refers to a historical fact (v. 18).

14. For a similar interpretation of this passage see Kaiser, "The Blessing of David," pp. 313 — 15; *Toward an Old Testament Theology* (Grand Rapids: Zondervan, 1978), pp. 152 — 55.

determine whether the connotation is eternality in the strict sense of the word or duration within a fixed time. For example, the phrase connotes limitless duration in Genesis 3:22, Exodus 3:15, and Psalm 146:6, 10. It connotes unbroken duration within a fixed span of time in Exodus 21:6. It is difficult to argue for the eternality of David's dynasty solely on the basis of these expressions.

However, two important traditions in the Old Testament support the possibility that these words connote infinite duration in 2 Samuel 7. One of these is Psalm 89, where the reiteration of the promise to David is celebrated by the psalmist. The psalm is difficult to date, but the evidence points strongly to the post-Davidic monarchy.[15] This psalm affirms that David's line will be established for "as long as the heavens endure" (v. 29 [30]), and his throne is to last as long as the sun and the moon (vv. 36 – 37 [37 – 38]). It is difficult to understand this to mean anything other than unending duration. The other corpus of material that supports this concept is the Davidic theology in the Prophets. The prophets envisioned a messianic king whose kingdom is described in obvious Davidic motifs. The eternality of his kingdom is set forth in various ways. Isaiah said there will be no end to "the increase of his government and peace" (9:7 [6]). Jeremiah stated that David will never lack a man to sit on his throne (33:17 – 22). And Ezekiel affirmed, "David my servant will be their prince forever" (37:25).

This material does not let us apply the term 'ôlām in 2 Samuel 7 in a restricted sense, that is, only to the historical Davidic monarchy. That application of the word may be within the semantic range of 'ôlām, but its implications are profound, for the end of that monarchy would have meant the end of the promise. The prophets envisioned a continuing Davidic dynasty that found its expression in a king whose eternal reign will bring universal peace and justice. The interpretation of 'ôlām in the strict sense of limitless duration is thus in keeping with some of Israel's early traditions.

Even if one should not accept the solutions proposed for these problems one cannot deny the monumental importance of 2 Samuel 7 in the historical outworking of the promise. It rivals in grandeur the first majestic statement of the promise to Abraham as well as the impassioned messianic predictions of the prophets.

15. M. Dahood, *Psalms II*, the Anchor Bible (Garden City, N. Y.: Doubleday, 1966 – 70), p. 311.

It is a mountain peak in redemptive history. Surely Isaiah viewed that peak in the distance when he spoke of the "unfailing kindnesses promised to David" (55:3), and Amos too, when he talked about the restoration of David's house, which he described as a fallen hut (9:11).

This restatement of the promise in 2 Samuel 7 affirmed that God was continuing to operate on the basis of his promise long years after the time of Abraham. The numerous references to the everlasting nature of the promise attest to God's continuing resolve to honor his pledged word.

This discussion has attempted to show that although 2 Samuel 7:19 is not without its exegetical problems, there is a literal interpretation of the verse that is linguistically and theologically feasible. The theological feasibility lies in the agreement of the concept with the patriarchal material and the theology of hope in the Prophets.

If 2 Samuel 7:19 is not understood to refer to the mediatorial function of the offspring, there exists no bridge between the patriarchal and prophetic expressions of the promise of offspring relative to that mediatorial function. There is no clear written revelational material upon which the prophets could have based the concept of the mediatorial function of the Messiah relative to the promise. There is much in 2 Samuel 7 to indicate that the Davidic offspring will receive the promises, but there remains nothing to indicate that the offspring will mediate them. Yet there is a strong corpus of material in the Prophets that assumes the mediatorial office of Messiah. This will be considered in the subsequent discussion.

In the promise given to Abraham, the concept of the offspring appeared to have only a national perspective, referring to the Hebrew people. The administration of the promise through a royal dynasty was hinted at only vaguely in the reference to kings who would descend from Abraham (Gen. 17:6, 16). But in the solemn moment in Israel's history when God established the Davidic dynasty by his inviolable promise to David, the reference to kings among Abraham's descendants was given greater clarity and meaning.

The prophetic corpus. As we continue to pursue the questions raised by Paul's use of "seed" in Galatians 3:16, we must bring our discussion of 2 Samuel 7 to the Prophets, for it is in the reiteration

of the Davidic promise there that we find the bank of material in
the Old Testament that is most consonant with Paul's theology of
the offspring. Before the relevant passages are considered we must
examine first those passages that stress the enduring nature of the
promise. The perpetuity of the promise is foundational to the messianic theology of the prophets, for if the promise ever came to an
end, the messianic hope would die.

The redemption of Abraham from Ur of the Chaldees is a part
of Isaiah's affirmation of hope for Israel: "Therefore this is what
the LORD, who redeemed Abraham, says to the house of Jacob: 'No
longer will Jacob be ashamed...'" (29:22 – 24). In 41:8 – 10, Isaiah
appealed to Israel's relationship with Abraham to affirm that the
Lord had not rejected his people: " 'But you, O Israel, my servant,
Jacob, whom I have chosen, you descendants of Abraham my
friend, . . . do not fear, for I am with you. . . .'" The continued
operation of the Abrahamic promise is strongly affirmed by Isaiah
when he pointed out that God made Abraham a great nation. This
is the basis of his assurance that the Lord would continue to bless
the nation. He said in 51:2 – 3, "Look to Abraham, your father. . . .
When I called him he was but one, and I blessed him and made
him many. The Lord will surely comfort Zion. . . ." Hosea said that
"the Israelites will be like the sand on the seashore, which cannot
be measured or counted" (1:10). This statement clearly reflects the
language of the Abrahamic promise (Gen. 22:17). Micah concluded
his prophecy with the assurance that the Lord would again "show
mercy to Abraham" and fulfill his oath to the fathers (7:20).

A number of the prophets who proclaimed that the promise
would never be nullified also predicted the demise of the kingdom
of Judah. This, of course, meant that the Davidic monarchy would
collapse. But the theological emergency posed by the doom of the
two kingdoms was met by the prophets in their affirmation that
the Davidic dynasty would not fail, for a scion of David would
mediate the eternal promise for the people of God. It is this prophetic concept that finds consonance with Paul's theology of the
offspring in Galatians 3:16.

Isaiah spoke of this figure as a child to be born, whose government will have no end. His connection with the Davidic line is
established by the association of his kingdom with the throne of
David (9:7 [6]). His mediatorial function with regard to the promise
is observable in his restoration of the land (9:1 [8:23]) and the

security he gives his people (9:7 [6]). In 11:1, Isaiah spoke of the shoot from the stump of Jesse. This firmly establishes the Davidic origin of this figure who brings security to his people.

The prophet Jeremiah saw the fulfillment of the Davidic promise in a "righteous Branch" raised up by the Lord to David (23:5).[16] The "Branch" is connected with the Davidic dynasty in Jeremiah 33:20−21,[17] where the prophet says that if God's covenant with day and night may be broken, "then my covenant with David my servant ... can be broken and David will no longer have a descendant to reign on his throne" (v. 21; cf. v. 15). Jeremiah established the theological continuity between the Abrahamic and Davidic covenants: "I will make the descendants of David my servant and the Levites who minister before me as countless as the stars of the sky and as measureless as the sand on the seashore" (v. 22). The enduring nature of the Davidic dynasty is expressed in the words "David will never fail to have a man to sit on the throne of the house of Israel ..." (v. 17), as well as in the guarantee that the Davidic covenant will never be broken (vv. 20−22). The mediatorial function of the Branch may be seen in the security he achieves for Israel (23:6).

Amos envisioned the restoration of the dynasty of David which would result in the return of Israel to their land, "never again to be uprooted" (9:11−15).

16. The emphasis on the righteousness of the Branch places the quality of his reign in sharp contrast with that of the earthly Davidic monarchy. Note the oracles beginning at 21:11, where Jeremiah asserted the responsibility of the Davidic monarchy to administer justice. He concluded that it had not; therefore, it was doomed (see, for example, Jer. 21:11−14). John Bright comments on Jeremiah's denunciation of the Davidic monarchy: "If it discharges this obligation, its existence is justified and it will endure; but since it has not done so, it is under judgment." *Jeremiah*, the Anchor Bible (Garden City, N.Y.: Doubleday, 1965), p.145. The righteousness of "the Branch" assures the perpetuity of the Davidic monarchy.

However, the word ṣaddiq (righteous) may be used here in the sense of true or legitimate. J. A. Thompson notes the use of a similar formula which means "legitimate scion" in Phoenician inscriptions and Ugaritic texts. *The Book of Jeremiah*, New International Commentary on the Old Testament series (Grand Rapids: Eerdmans, 1979), p. 489. See also James Swetnam, "Some Observations on the Background of צדיק in Jeremias 23:5a," *Bib* 46 (1965): 29−40, and Bright, *Jeremiah*, p.144.

In the oracle in Jer. 23:5−6, the expectation of an individual king, rather than a dynasty, is supported by mālak melek (he will reign as king, v. 5) and the clear use of the term *Branch* with reference to an individual king elsewhere (Isa. 11:1; Zech. 3:8; 6:12).

17. Joyce G. Baldwin argues that the term *Branch* or *Shoot* is used when the Old Testament writers "wish to bring together the offices of both priest and king." "ṢEMAḤ as a Technical Term in the Prophets," *VT* 14 (1964): 93−97.

Micah spoke of a ruler from David's birthplace in Bethlehem whose "origins are from of old, from ancient times" (5:2 [1]). The precise meaning of the word *origins* (*môṣā'ōtâyw*) is difficult to determine because of the lack of definitive context. Most modern commentators see in the word a reference to the ruler's Davidic extraction.[18] If the word refers to the origination of a child in the loins of the father, as James Luther Mays suggests, then Bethlehem is regarded "as the parent of the ruler. . . ."[19]

One of the strengths of this view is that it maintains a connection between the word *môṣā'ōtâyw* (goings out) and the verb *yāṣā'* (go out) in the same verse. But one may wonder why the word *môṣā'ōtâyw* is plural. If the ruler goes forth from Bethlehem, why are there many goings forth?

It is possible that the word *môṣā'ōtâyw* is used here in the sense of going out on military expeditions. Forms of the verb *yāṣā'* are used in that way in the Old Testament.[20] This connotation is particularly appropriate to the preceding reference to the ruler (*mōšēl*). If this suggestion is valid, it is difficult to understand the word to refer to a human king, because his regnal activities are placed in the remote past. There may be a strong sense of eternality here. However the word is understood in this passage, the Davidic roots of the coming ruler are emphasized by the prophet Micah. This figure mediates the promise to his people in the security he guarantees (5:4 [3]).

Ezekiel affirmed the close association of the Messiah with the Davidic dynasty by applying the name *David* directly to the Messiah (37:24−25). Zechariah applied the Davidic motif of the Branch to the Messiah in 3:8 and 6:12.

There are two important lines of thought in these passages. There is first the enduring nature of the Davidic dynasty. By stressing this, the prophets established a vital connection between the Abrahamic promise and their own messianic expectation.[21] In this

18. Leslie C. Allen, *The Books of Joel, Obadiah, Jonah, and Micah,* New International Commentary on the Old Testament series (Grand Rapids: Eerdmans, 1976), pp. 343−44; D. Bryant, "Micah 4:14−5:14: An Exegesis," *Rest Q* 21 (1978): 222−23; James Luther Mays, *Micah: A Commentary* (Philadelphia: Westminster, 1976), pp. 115−16.

19. Mays, *Micah,* p. 115.

20. Judg. 2:15; 4:14; 1 Sam. 8:20; 17:20; 2 Sam. 5:24.

21. For a discussion of the way in which the perpetuity of the Davidic dynasty is expressed in the Psalms, see John Bright, *Covenant and Promise: The Prophetic Understanding of the Future in Pre-exilic Israel* (Philadelphia: Westminster, 1976), pp. 58ff.

way they met the theological emergency posed by the impending demise of the monarchy, and in this way they preserved hope and nurtured faith. The second line of thought is the relationship of the Messiah to the terms of the promise. This striking fact sheds light on Paul's application of the word *sperma* (seed, offspring) to Christ in Galatians 3:16.

In this corpus of prophetic material the Messiah is pictured as sustaining a relationship to the promise that involves not only his mediation of the terms of the promise, but his reception of them as well. He thus stands as recipient and mediator of the promise, just as did Abraham. This relationship of the Messiah to the promise may be observed in these passages in the way in which each element of the promise finds expression in the regnal activity of the Messiah.

In Isaiah 9, the promise of the offspring applies to the Messiah in the relationship he sustains with David's line. He belongs to David's dynasty (9:7 [6]). He is a shoot from the stump of Jesse (Isa. 11:1). The use of the term *Branch* by Jeremiah speaks of one who will emerge from David's line (23:5). He is the offspring of David.

The promise of the land is inherent in the assurance of national security under the aegis of the Davidic king (Isa. 11:12−16; Jer. 23:6; 33:16; Amos 9:14−15; Mic. 5:4).

The royal aspect of the offspring, a concept that figured in both the Abrahamic and Davidic statements of the promise, is found in the motifs that relate him to David's royal line (Isa. 9:7 [6]; 11:1; Jer. 23:5; 33:15, 17, 21; Mic. 5:2 [1]).

The extent of the beneficial rule of the Davidic king to Gentiles as well as to Jews is found in Isaiah 11:10, Amos 9:12 (cf. Acts 15:15−21), and possibly in Micah 5:2−3.[22]

The concept of a great name or enhanced reputation found in both the Abrahamic and Davidic expressions of the promise was made only to the immediate recipients, that is, to Abraham and David, not to their descendants. If Paul's assertion that Christ is heir of the promise is correct, we should expect to find some

---

22. Some scholars understand the phrase *the rest of his brothers* (Mic. 5:3) to refer to Gentiles. See Theodore Laetsch, *Bible Commentary: The Minor Prophets* (Saint Louis: Concordia, 1956), p. 273; E. B. Pusey, *The Minor Prophets*, 2 vols. (Grand Rapids: Baker, 1950), vol. 2, pp. 72−73. Others understand it as referring to the exiled northern kingdom. Allen, *Joel, Obadiah, Jonah, and Micah*, pp. 345−46; Bryant, "Micah 4:14−5:14: An Exegesis," p. 224.

reference to the renown of the Messiah. These instances are not numerous but they exist in the passages cited. Isaiah described the repute of the Davidic king in the names *Wonderful Counselor, Mighty God, Everlasting Father,* and *Prince of Peace* (9:6 [5]). His great renown is inherent in the universal scope of his regnal activity (11:11 – 12). The prophet Micah spoke of the greatness of the figure born in Bethlehem—greatness that will reach "to the ends of the earth" (5:4 [3]). Zechariah said of "the Branch" that he will "bear royal honor" (6:13, RSV).

The promise that the Lord will be God to his people also finds fulfillment in the role of the Messiah, for in Ezekiel 37:27 we find that God will be their God and they will be his people. The realization of this promise occurs when the everlasting covenant is established by God with his people (v. 26) under the aegis of the scion of David who will reign forever (v. 24; cf. v. 25).

This expression of Davidic theology in the Prophets is the culmination of the development of the promise of offspring in the Old Testament. Without it the affirmation of 2 Samuel 7 would remain only a vague promise that David's dynasty will continue—a promise ultimately threatened by historical circumstances. The major contribution of the prophetic theology to the concept of the offspring is in its exposition of the role of the individual offspring in the history of salvation.

We may now view Paul's statement in Galatians 3:16 in a broad perspective. When he affirmed that Christ, along with Abraham, was a participant in the promise (Gal. 3:16), Paul was not on tenuous theological ground. His belief that Christ was the Davidic king enabled him to affirm that Christ shared and mediated the blessings of the promise. It is possible that Paul saw much more in the promise than Abraham would have known, but Paul was writing at a much later stage in the progress of revelation and saw the development of the concept of the offspring in its totality. If the promises made to Abraham and to David are also part of the regnal prerogatives and privileges of the Messiah, there is no reason why one who acknowledges Christ as Messiah may not affirm with Paul that the promises were made to Christ.

The concept of the offspring in Acts 3:25 – 26
against the background of the servant songs (Isa. 41 – 53)

The apostle Peter also affirmed the participation of Christ in the promise. In Acts 3:25 – 26, Peter quoted from Genesis 22:18,

" 'Through your offspring all peoples on earth will be blessed' "
(v. 25). He then went on to say, "When God raised up his servant,
he sent him first to you to bless you by turning each of you from
your wicked ways" (v. 26). Peter understood Christ to be the mediator of the blessings of the promise.[23] This is clear from his
ascription of the blessing cited in Acts 3:25 to the work of the
servant (v. 26).

The identification of the servant.   The connection of the servant
role of Christ with the Abrahamic promise seems anomalous. No
hint of such a motif can be found in either the Abrahamic or
Davidic statements of the promise. We wonder again if the New
Testament writer inferred too much from the Old Testament.

The servant concept is taken from Isaiah 41 – 53. Isaiah began
that section with a deep consciousness of the relationship of the
servant to the Abrahamic promise. He said, "But you, O Israel, my
servant, Jacob, whom I have chosen, you descendants (*zera'*, offspring) of Abraham my friend ..." (41:8). The servant concept is
unequivocally tied to the Abrahamic promise by Isaiah. Peter did
not distort the theology of the Old Testament when he connected
the work of the servant to the promise.

It may be argued that although Peter was on good ground in
identifying the servant concept with the Abrahamic promise, he
was not on good ground in identifying that concept with Christ.
Yet an examination of the servant songs of Isaiah reveals an un-
usual complexity that makes it difficult to maintain that all of
them refer to the nation of Israel.

To be sure, the servant is to be identified with Israel in a number
of passages (Isa. 42:18 – 22; 44:1 – 2, 21; 49:3), but in Isaiah 49:5 the
servant is pictured as acting upon Israel to restore her to God.
The verse states, "And now the LORD says—he who formed me in
the womb to be his servant to bring Jacob back to him and gather
Israel to himself. . . ." It is difficult to posit an absolute identification of the servant with the nation of Israel in this passage, for the
servant is distinct from the nation.

The view that the servant in Isaiah 49:5 represents the righteous
remnant of Israel is also difficult because in verse 6 the servant's

---

23. F. F. Bruce says, "In the present passage the 'seed' of Abraham is interpreted of
Christ, through whom the blessing was being offered, as in the similar quotation in Gal.
iii.8." *The Acts of the Apostles* (Chicago: Inter-Varsity Christian Fellowship, 1952), p. 114.

work is connected to the restoration of "those of Israel I have kept" (RSV, "preserved of Israel").[24] The description of this group is consonant with the material about the remnant in the Prophets. The construct relationship (něṣyyrê yiśrā'ēl, the preserved of Israel) lends support to the idea that these are a portion of the nation, hence a remnant. This group is not simply those who returned to the land after the exile, for they are to be restored to God (vv. 5 – 6) as well as to the land (vv. 8 – 9); they are a redeemed people. Their restoration is concurrent with the conquest of the nations (vv. 18, 22 – 23) and is described with an ultimacy that bespeaks the triumph of God's people (vv. 24 – 26a), the end of oppression (vv. 25 – 26), and the beginning of an era when Gentiles will recognize the might of Yahweh (v. 26b). These magnificent concepts are all consonant with the Old Testament material concerning the redeemed remnant and its ultimate glory (cf. Mic. 2:12 – 13; 5:7 [6], 8 [7]). The figure of Isaiah 49:5, then, may be understood to be separate from the nation of Israel, as well as from the remnant to whom God faithfully fulfills the terms of his promise and shows his redemptive love.

The complex nature of the servant concept in Isaiah is seen further in the terminology used of the servant.[25] He is called a man ('îš) in Isaiah 53:3. He is distinguished from the nation in Isaiah 53:8, where we read that he was stricken "for the transgression of [his] people." In the same verse he is described in terms

---

24. The view that the servant is the remnant or a pious minority in Israel may be found in S. R. Driver and A. Newbauer, "The Fifty-third Chapter of Isaiah According to the Jewish Interpreters," *Translations*, vol. 2 (New York: Ktav, 1969), pp. 44, 116, 150; C. R. North, *The Suffering Servant in Deutero-Isaiah: An Historical and Critical Study* (London: Oxford University Press, 1956), pp. 19, 20, 35, 36, 62, 63; O. Thenius, "Neue Beleuchtung des leidenden Jehova-Dieners (Jes 52, 13 – 53, 12)," *Zeitschrift für Wissenschaftliche Theologie*, 2 Bd. 1 Heft, pp. 1105 – 30; C. F. Burney, "The Book of Isaiah: A New Theory," *Church Quarterly Review* 75 (1912): 99 – 139. Franz Delitzsch observes a threefold structure in the concept of the servant that allows for its application to the nation, the "true people of Jehovah," and a single person. *Biblical Commentary on the Prophecies of Isaiah*, trans. James Martin (reprint; Grand Rapids: Eerdmans, 1969), vol. 2, p. 258. In more recent years this view has been set forth by G. A. F. Knight, *Deutero-Isaiah: A Theological Commentary on Isaiah 40 – 55* (New York: Abingdon, 1965), pp. 184 – 85; James D. Smart, *History and Theology in Second Isaiah: A Commentary on Isaiah 35, 40 – 66* (Philadelphia: Westminster, 1965), pp. 152 – 54. See also C. G. Kruse, "The Servant Songs: Interpretive Trends Since C. R. North," *Studia Biblica et Theologica* 8 (1978): 3 – 27.

25. Harry M. Orlinsky argues that the servant in Isa. 53 is Second Isaiah. "The So-called 'Suffering Servant' in Isaiah 53," in *Interpreting the Prophetic Tradition*, ed. Harry M. Orlinsky (Cincinnati: Hebrew Union College, 1969), pp. 227 – 73.

that could never be applied to Israel, for he suffers for the transgressions of the people; Israel is always pictured in the second part of Isaiah as suffering for her own sin (40:2; 42:24 − 25; 43:24 − 25; 44:21 − 22; 48:1 − 8; 50:1).

The task of the servant to bring salvation to the ends of the earth (Isa. 49:6) is apparently accomplished by his redemptive work, for Isaiah 53:11 says, "After the suffering of his soul . . . my righteous servant will justify many." It is not difficult to understand how the similarities between the role of the servant in the prophecy of Isaiah and the ministry of Christ would have led the early church to affirm the identification of the servant with Christ.

Since the servant concept admits of an individual as well as the nation, and since Isaiah identified the servant concept with the offspring of Abraham, it is possible to conclude that the individual servant in Isaiah is also the offspring of Abraham. The complexity within the concept of the offspring in the Old Testament is reflected in Peter's statement, as well as in other portions of the New Testament. The proclamation is that the individual offspring has appeared and in him the promises are fulfilled. A figure who comes out of the nation rises far above the nation to effect its restoration and glory.

The servant and the terms of the promise.   Like the Davidic king, the servant is both the mediator and recipient of various terms of the promise. The servant mediates the promise of divine blessing to Gentiles (Isa. 49:6), but he is the recipient of a number of terms of the promise as well. He is promised a great name or reputation: "Therefore I will give him a portion among the great, and he will divide the spoils with the strong . . ." (Isa. 53:12). He is promised offspring, for "he will see his offspring and prolong his days" (Isa. 53:10). The royal aspect of the servant is not stated in so many words, but he will be granted a universal reign, for "he will not falter or be discouraged till he establishes justice on earth" (Isa. 42:4). In 49:7, Isaiah said of the servant who was despised by the nations, "Kings will see you and arise, princes will see and bow down. . . ." And Isaiah 52:15 says, "Kings will shut their mouths because of him."

J. Morgenstern argues for the royal nature of the servant from the application of the term *Israel* to him in Isaiah 49:3. He compares this with the use of the name *Judah* in Malachi 2:11, where it designates the king of Judah. Morgenstern holds that the occurrence of "Israel" in verse 3 "is the name or title of the Servant in his role as a king of the people, Israel. This conclusion, that the Servant is an individual rather than the people Israel, that he is a royal figure, a king of Israel, finds strong support in the Servant's statement in lxi. 1, that God's spirit rested upon him because He had anointed him, and thereby had endowed him with superhuman powers; for, as we have learned, anointing, with resultant possession by the divine spirit and consequent endowment with superhuman powers, was the prerogative of the kings of early Israel and of subsequent Judah, and particularly those of the Davidic line . . . it suffices to have established beyond any possibility of challenge, so we believe, that the Servant is not the people, Israel, but is rather an individual figure, one of royal character, a king of Israel."[26]

Morgenstern concludes that the servant songs comprise a drama based on Greek dramatic forms. The servant is "a member of the Davidic family, a potential king of Israel, who offers himself as a sacrifice, the sacrifice regularly offered in ancient times during the course of the festival for the physical salvation of the nation, in order to guarantee the renewal of their food supply during the new year just beginning, but here the self-sacrifice is for the salvation of all mankind."[27] Although the conclusions of Morgenstern differ from those of this work, his observations have a bearing on our present discussion in their emphasis on the royal nature of the servant.

Only the promise of the land lacks emphasis in the servant songs, but it may be that this concept has been expanded to include the whole earth.[28] Isaiah said that Israel's future dominance over the nations is a direct result of the promise given to David (55:3 – 5). This expansion of the promise of the land to include the whole world is similar to Paul's application of the same concept in Romans 4:13.

26. J. Morgenstern, "The Suffering Servant—A New Solution," pt. 1, *VT* 11 (1961): 307 – 8. See also "The Suffering Servant—A New Solution," pt. 2, *VT* 11 (1961): 406 – 31; "The Suffering Servant—A New Solution," pt. 3, *VT* 13 (1963): 321 – 32.

27. Morgenstern, "The Suffering Servant—A New Solution," pt. 2, p. 420.

28. George W. Buchanan argues that the "land of life" in the Old Testament refers to the Promised Land. The cutting off of the servant from the "land of the living" (Isa. 53:8) refers not to an individual but to the first generation of Jews exiled to Babylon. *The Consequences of the Covenant* (Leiden: Brill, 1970), p. 129.

It is clear from this discussion that the servant of Isaiah's prophecy shares in the promises. He is a recipient of certain terms of the promise, and he mediates certain terms as well. Thus, when Peter attributed a mediatorial function to Christ in his servant role, he was not out of keeping with the Isaianic materials cited.

These observations shed light on the earlier discussion of Paul's concept of the "offspring" in Galatians 3:16. In the servant songs we have another bank of material in which Christ functions as both mediator and recipient of important elements of the promise. He is heir of the promise in the same sense that Abraham was.

The promise of the offspring forms a strong bond between the Old and New Testaments. There is a theological continuum inherent in the promise that spans these two periods of redemptive history. This continuum exists because of the anticipatory nature of the promise in the Old Testament and the sense of fulfillment of the promise that permeates the New Testament. One comes to the end of the Old Testament era with a sense of failure and frustration mingled with hope and expectation. The people had returned to the land in the postexilic period. Zechariah, a leader in that time, predicted a dark period for Israel when she would again be subjugated to foreign powers (11:4 – 17), but Israel was to be delivered by a king who came into Jerusalem riding on a donkey (9:9 – 10). At the end of the Old Testament period the Gentiles had not yet come in significant numbers to the Lord and the promise of an eternal Davidic monarchy had not been realized, but the writers of the New Testament were deeply conscious of the promise and affirmed that the offspring had come and that the terms of the promise are still in effect.

The Corporate Concept of the Offspring in the Old and New Testaments

To this point the discussion has centered only on the individualistic aspect of the offspring. But we have observed a corporate aspect of the concept as well. This aspect of the offspring of Abraham is obvious in both testaments and will be considered only briefly.

It has been observed that Paul identified the body of believers with the offspring of Abraham (Rom. 4:13 – 18; 9:6 – 8; Gal. 3:7, 23 – 29). He did not limit the concept only to Christ. His identification of the offspring with the people of faith seems to broaden the concept beyond the scope of the promise of offspring in the patriarchal accounts. There it connotes the physical descendants of Abraham.

It is clear that the offspring of Abraham are primarily a spiritual community in the Pauline writings. Paul did use the concept in a more nationalistic sense on occasion (Rom. 11:1; 2 Cor. 11:22), but these usages were only incidental to his main purpose. Paul defined the true offspring of Abraham as a community of faith (Gal. 3:7, 29) producing a positive righteousness which is not the result of legalistic adherence to the law (Rom. 4:13–15).

In Galatians 3:7, Paul said, "Understand, then, that those who believe are children of Abraham." In the previous verse he supported his premise by appeal to Genesis 15:6. He wrote, "Consider Abraham: 'He believed God, and it was credited to him as righteousness.' " Paul affirmed the primacy of faith in the administration of the Abrahamic covenant by pointing out that faithful obedience on Abraham's part was the ground of his participation in the benefits of the promise.

Jesus also affirmed this in his denunciation of the notion that those who were descended from Abraham were automatic recipients of God's favor. In Matthew 3:9–10, he asserted that if all God wanted were physical descendants of Abraham, he could raise them up out of the stones on the ground. God wants the fruit of repentance (v. 10; cf. v. 8).

The Book of Deuteronomy

This same principle obtains in the Old Testament as well. It begins to become apparent in the Book of Deuteronomy, where faithful obedience is set forth as an important characteristic of the descendants of Abraham. Deuteronomy 4:37–38 states that because the Lord loved their forefathers and chose their descendants (zera', offspring), he brought the Israelites into the land of Canaan. But verse 40 makes it clear that continued appropriation of the promise of security in the land was not a national privilege free of obligation. It was dependent on faithful obedience to the "decrees and commands" of the Lord. The people were to keep the "decrees and commands" that they might live long in the land the Lord their God gave them.

In Deuteronomy 10:16 the command is given to the Israelites to circumcise their hearts and not be stiff-necked. As is the case in the previous passage cited, they are referred to as descendants (*zera'*, offspring) of the forefathers (v. 15). Because they are the chosen offspring they are to reflect the very nature of God (vv. 16 – 19). This is done by maintaining the purity of heart and deep sensitivity to the will of God reflected in the concept of ethical circumcision (v. 16). The offspring are seen here as a people with a spiritual responsibility. They are not only a national entity in Deuteronomy, but also a people who, by virtue of God's faithfulness to his promise (v. 22), owe to God the debt of obedience to his commands.

A similar concept is reflected in Deuteronomy 11:8 – 10, where the promise of the land to the offspring of the forefathers is cited. The possession of the land (v. 8) and continued security in the land (v. 9) are based on faithful obedience to the Lord: "Observe therefore all the commands I am giving you today . . ." (v. 8).

The prophetic corpus

The prophets set forth the same principle. One cannot read far in the prophetic corpus without realizing that national privilege alone is not the guarantee of continued existence in the land. The sovereignty of the kingdoms of Israel and Judah was wrenched from the grasp of the ancient Hebrews because of their failure to reflect the ethical demands of the law (Jer. 29:17 – 23; Ezek. 5:5 – 12; 6:8 – 10; Dan. 9:4 – 16).[29] The promise of the land was temporarily interrupted, not because of the weakness of Israel's God nor the fortuitous course of national events, but because of the failure of the people to trust God and respond to him in humble obedience. The prophet Amos stands far above his fellows in those troubled times, crying out against the popular belief that because Israel was an elect nation established by God, the people would be protected in spite of their hardness of heart (2:6 – 16; 3:2, 9 – 11; 7:7 – 9; 9:7 – 8).

The Development of the Promise of the Offspring in the Old and New Testaments

The New Testament understanding of the offspring of Abraham gives a dimension to that element of the promise that is far beyond

---

29. See also D. E. Gowan, "Losing the Promised Land—The Old Testament Considers the Inconceivable," in *From Faith to Faith: Essays in Honor of Donald G. Miller on His Seventieth Birthday*, ed. Dikran Y. Hadidian, Pittsburgh Theological Monograph Series, no. 4 (Pittsburgh: Pickwick, 1979), pp. 247 – 68.

what Abraham may have imagined. The promise that his progeny would be "as numerous as the stars in the sky and as the sand on the seashore" was fulfilled not only in the many physical descendants of Abraham, but also in thousands upon thousands of redeemed people, who, by faith, have been blessed with faithful Abraham.

As the promise of the offspring unfolds throughout both testaments, its complexity becomes apparent. Two patterns emerge. First, there is an expansion observable in the concept, for the ancient promise says that Abraham's immediate descendants are to become as numerous as the stars. The New Testament continues this expansion by including in that multitude all the people of faith. One man becomes the father of uncounted multitudes who follow his example of faithful obedience. The other pattern is a narrowing of the concept. Within this dramatic expansion of the offspring one figure begins to emerge. He is the offspring of David, the "seed" par excellence. This twofold pattern is essential for understanding the covenantal expression of the promise.

The Promise of Blessing for Abraham

The second element of the promise to Abraham is the simple statement *and I will bless you* (Gen. 12:2). The paucity of contextual material makes it difficult to determine its exact scope. Is the blessing defined by the remaining elements of the promise? Does it refer to the material blessing that Abraham enjoyed? Is it an isolated clause that relates to the general bestowment of divine favor on Abraham?

The promise of blessing to Abraham was reaffirmed immediately after he demonstrated his obedience by his willingness to offer his son Isaac to the Lord (Gen. 22:15–18). The promise is stated in Genesis 22:17–18, "I will surely bless you and make your descendants as numerous as the stars in the sky and as the sand on the seashore. Your descendants will take possession of the cities of their enemies, and through your offspring all nations on earth will be blessed, because you have obeyed me." The promise that Abraham would be blessed is accompanied in these verses by three elements: the promise of the offspring, security for Abraham's posterity, and the role of the offspring as the mediator of blessing to Gentiles.

The promise of blessing relates to Abraham, whereas the remaining elements extend to his posterity. Yet it would be impossible to divorce these elements from Abraham's blessing. It would be a blessing for him to know that Isaac would live to father children, that the Lord would give security to his descendants, and that his posterity would be a benign influence in the world. The blessing here seems to relate directly to God's promise of offspring to Abraham.

In Genesis 24, Abraham's servant defined his master's blessing. The aspect of the promised offspring is prominent, but there is an emphasis on material blessing as well. It says in verses 35 — 36, "The LORD has blessed my master abundantly, and he has become wealthy. . . . My master's wife Sarah has borne him a son in her old age. . . ."

The promise of personal blessing was reaffirmed to Isaac in subsequent years (Gen. 26:3). He was told to remain for a while in Philistine territory and the Lord would bless him. The blessing in this case appears to include material wealth, for the reference to his possessions in 26:12 — 14 is accompanied by the words *because the Lord blessed him* (v. 12). Yet the spiritual blessings of that promise are stated as well and cannot be divorced from the blessing. In verse 24, the Lord reaffirmed an aspect of the Abrahamic promise to him: "Do not be afraid, for I am with you; I will bless you and will increase the number of your descendants for the sake of my servant Abraham." Since Isaac had already achieved great wealth (vv. 13 — 14), it seems that the promise of blessing in verse 24 relates to the bestowment of God's favor on him in affirmation of the spiritual blessing of the promise.

When the promise was reiterated to Jacob (Gen. 35:9 — 12), the element of blessing was not stated specifically. However, the statement of the promise is preceded by the words "God appeared to him again and blessed him" (v. 9). The blessing is evidently the promise that Jacob, like Abraham, would be the father of a great nation and that his descendants would occupy the land of Canaan (vv. 11 — 12). Jacob apparently understood the blessing to refer only to the promise and not to material blessing, for shortly before his death he recalled that moment when God reaffirmed the promise to him and said of that time, "God Almighty appeared to me at

Luz in the land of Canaan, and there he blessed me and said to me, 'I am going to . . . increase your numbers' " (Gen. 48:3 – 4).

The blessing of the Abrahamic promise then connotes every aspect of God's favor, both temporal and spiritual, bestowed on the patriarchs. The emphasis seems to be primarily on the spiritual blessing of the promise. This secured a bright future for the progeny of the patriarchs in a land in which they could grow to become a great nation and affirmed that, in some yet unforeseen way, the offspring would become a blessing to Gentiles. It includes all of the redemptive benefits that result from faithful obedience to God.

The apostle Paul emphasized the spiritual aspect of the blessing of Abraham in Galatians 3:9, 14, where he said that the people of faith share that blessing (v. 9). He equated the blessing with "the promise of the Spirit" (v. 14).

The Promise That Abraham's Name Would Be Great

This element of the promise, like the preceding one, relates specifically to Abraham. It is the promise of an enhanced reputation.[30]

The word for "name" (šēm) in Hebrew may connote reputation or fame. David's fame grew (lit., David made a name for himself) because of his military exploits in Syria (2 Sam. 8:13). Abishai, as did David's three chiefs, won a name for himself (lô šēm, lit., a name for him) because of a stunning military success (2 Sam. 23:18). The Korahite rebellion included well-known men (lit., men of a name) who rose up against Moses (Num. 16:2). Even the name or reputation of God himself is enhanced by his mighty acts (Neh. 9:10; Isa. 63:12; Jer. 32:20).

Because of Abraham's faithfulness, his name still lives today. His example of faith and his role as mediator of the promise permeate the teaching of both testaments. He is revered in the major religious systems of the present day. If it were not for his obedience to God, his name probably would have been lost.

---

30. A. K. Jenkins understands this aspect of the promise to occupy "a pivotal position, linking the Primeval History with the patriarchal narratives. . . ." He sees the formula of naming as "a means of providing a theological linkage of the patriarchal traditions. . . ." "A Great Name: Genesis 12:2 and the Editing of the Pentateuch," *JSOT* 10 (1978): 41 – 57.

The Promise of Blessing for Those Who Favor Abraham and Disfavor for Those Who Do Not

This aspect of the promise is set forth in the words "I will bless those who bless you, and whoever curses you I will curse" (Gen. 12:3). The particular nuance inherent in the word *bless* is delineated to a large extent by the word *curse*, which occurs as its antithesis in this statement. The root of the word *curse* is *qll*. It has as its basic idea that of being slight or trifling, and hence, in the piel, to treat contemptuously.[31] The efficacy attributed to the spoken word in ancient times could have led to the frequent connotation of "curse" for this root.

The word *curse* in the statement of the promise clearly denotes the expression of an unfavorable attitude toward Abraham. Its emphasis on treating contemptuously or regarding as unimportant defines an attitude. It is an attitude toward Abraham that deems him unworthy of attention. It regards his example of faith as not important enough to emulate. One who disregards the fact that through Abraham God is urging everyone to faith in the promise is treating Abraham contemptuously, and may expect that God will treat him or her the same way.

One may thus assume that "bless" connotes the concept of honor and respect. This range of meaning is clearly inherent in the word, in both its theological and secular uses.[32] In the theological sense it is God who blesses or who is blessed. In the secular sense the transaction of blessing takes place between individuals. When God is blessed there is always the connotation of a positive attitude toward him expressed in deep gratitude (Josh. 22:33; 2 Chron. 31:8) or praise (1 Chron. 29:20; Neh. 8:6; 9:5; Ps. 34:1 [2]; 145:1). When the word is used of individuals it connotes a positive response of gratitude (2 Sam. 14:22) or honor (Gen. 47:7 – 10).

31. Josef Scharbert defines the root *qll* " 'to make small of,' 'to deal with contemptuously' and therefore also 'to mock,' 'to make ridiculous.' " He cites several examples in which the word means "to slight" (Judg. 9:27; 2 Sam. 16:5, 7, 9 – 13; 1 Kings 2:8) and "to make light of" (1 Sam. 3:13). "Curse," *Sacramentum Verbi: An Encyclopedia of Biblical Theology*, ed. Johannes B. Bauer (New York: Herder and Herder, 1970), vol. 1, p. 175.

32. Scharbert defines *bārak* in the piel as meaning "the opposite of *qillēl*, therefore 'to praise someone as great, successful, mighty, happy.' " "Curse," p. 69. Umberto Cassuto understands the word *bless* in this context similarly: "those who will show you sympathy and friendship and will seek your welfare. . . ." *A Commentary on the Book of Genesis*, trans. Israel Abrahams, 2 vols. (Jerusalem: Magnes Press, Hebrew University, 1961 – 64), vol. 2, p. 314.

This element of the Abrahamic promise affirms that those who respond positively to Abraham, acknowledging with gratitude his example of faith, will in turn be blessed by God. The blessing of God on the individual always involves the bestowal of divine favor. Although the blessing is not clearly defined at this point, it is possible to say that it involves divine acceptance and favor. God will not treat with contempt those who bless Abraham.

The Promise That Abraham's Descendants Would Occupy the Land of Canaan

The promise of occupying the land of Canaan must have seemed an empty hope to the Israelites when they were in bondage in Egypt. Yet, when the Lord revealed the full essence of his character as Yahweh, hurling his plagues on the land governed by the recalcitrant Pharaoh, the people began the first leg of a journey that would lead to the conquest of Canaan.

The conquest was more than a historical event. It was also a theological event, for it served to confirm the promise and assure the pious in Israel that the Lord was continuing to act on their behalf. Since this aspect of the promise will be considered later in its covenantal expression, only its salient features will be noted here.

The Promise of the Land in the Book of Genesis

In the first expression of this aspect of the promise, the land is delineated specifically as the territory of Canaan (Gen. 12:5 − 7). In Genesis 15:18, the boundaries of the promised territory are described as extending from "the river of Egypt to the great river, the Euphrates."[33] The northern reaches of this more extensive territory came under the control of the Israelites in the Aramean campaigns of David (1 Chron. 18:3 − 8).

If the "river of Egypt" is not identified as the Nile, but as one of

33. Buchanan understands "the great river" (Gen. 15:18) to refer not to the Euphrates, but to the Great River north of Mount Akkar in Lebanon. He regards the identification of the Great River with the Euphrates as an interpretive gloss. *The Consequences of the Covenant*, pp. 94 − 101.

the streams at the southern extremity of Canaan,[34] it can be said that the broad extent of territory cited in Genesis 15:18 had come under Israelite dominion during the reigns of David and Solomon. Several of the Canaanite tribes mentioned in the promise of Genesis 15:18−21 are specifically cited as having been conquered by Solomon (2 Chron. 8:7−8).

There is a sense, then, in which it can be said that the promise of the land was fulfilled in the time of David and Solomon. This vast extension of the empire was an earnest of the fact that God was continuing to be faithful to his promise.

The Promise of the Land in the Book of Deuteronomy

The Book of Deuteronomy has a great deal to say about the land, particularly the continuing security of the people in it. This security is guaranteed not only by right of conquest, but also by continuing obedience to the law of God (Deut. 5:32−33; 6:3; 8:19−20; 11:8−9, 13−15).

Even the initial conquest of the land of Canaan is set against the background of spiritual obligation, for the failure of the people to conquer Canaan is attributed to their disobedience and rebellion (Deut. 1:26−36, 43−46). Also, the people were urged by Moses to obey his decrees and laws so that they might "take possession of the land" (Deut. 4:1; 6:17−18; 8:1; 11:8, 22−25).

It is at 12:8−32 that the unique contribution of the Book of Deuteronomy to the concept of the land is found. In verse 9, the land is called a "resting place" (měnûhâ) and an "inheritance" (nahălâ).[35] It is the place where God will choose a site as a "dwelling for his Name" (v. 11).

34. The "river of Egypt" is understood here not to designate the Nile, but either the Wady el-Arish or Nahal Besor. The author prefers the latter in view of the thorough investigation of N. Na'aman, "The Brook of Egypt and Assyrian Policy on the Border of Egypt," *Tel Aviv* 6 (1979): 68−90. It may also be observed that in Isa. 27:12 the river (nāhār), a reference to the Euphrates, is paralleled with nahal miṣrāyim (not nāhār, river). This seems to be a reference to the fulfillment of the promise. Apparently nāhār and nahal are more nearly synonymous than was previously recognized.

35. For a discussion of the implications to Israel of the land as Yahweh's inheritance see H. E. von Waldow, "Israel and Her Land: Some Theological Considerations," in *A Light Unto My Path: Old Testament Studies in Honor of Jacob M. Myers*, ed. Howard N. Bream, Ralph D. Heim, and Carey A. Moore, Gettysburg Theological Studies, no. 4 (Philadelphia: Temple University Press, 1974), pp. 493−508.

The concept of rest in Deuteronomy involves several aspects. One of these is national security.[36] Verse 10 states, "But you will cross the Jordan and settle in the land the LORD your God is giving you as an inheritance, and he will give you rest from all your enemies around you so that you will live in safety."

Another Deuteronomic concept expressed in this passage is of a more spiritual nature, for when that national security is achieved, the people are to bring their offerings to the place the Lord will choose "as a dwelling for his Name" (v. 11). There they are to rejoice before the Lord their God (v. 12) and obey his precepts (vv. 13 – 32). This is the distinct contribution of the Book of Deuteronomy concerning the promise of the land.

The "rest" envisioned in the Book of Deuteronomy provides the context in which the community may worship God and rejoice in him in peace and safety. When that peace is achieved, the Lord will choose a place for his name to dwell. That place is the sanctuary (v. 11). This central sanctuary is the focal point for the worshiping community (v. 11) and is the manifestation of the fact that the Lord has fulfilled his promise to be their God (v. 12; cf. Gen. 17:7 – 8). The concept of rest is both national and spiritual. The ideal picture presented in the Book of Deuteronomy is that of an obedient people worshiping and serving God in a context of national peace and security.

The concept of rest is taken up in the New Testament by the writer of the Epistle to the Hebrews. Once again the New Testament expounds on a theme related to the promise and seems to give it a scope far broader than that intended by the original author. The Book of Hebrews has two chapters devoted to the theme of rest (3 – 4). The writer referred to the faithless generation that failed to enter Canaan (3:7 – 11). Because of their rebellion God declared, "They shall never enter my rest" (v. 11). The writer then warned his readers to heed the example of that disobedient generation and not turn away from God as they did (vv. 12 – 14). It was unbelief, he declared, that kept them from that rest (vv. 16 – 18). He then observed, "Therefore, since the promise of entering his

_____

36. Gerhard von Rad notes, "This 'rest' . . . is not peace of mind, but the altogether tangible peace granted to a nation plagued by enemies and weary of wandering." "There Remains Still a Rest for the People of God: An Investigation of a Biblical Conception," in *The Problem of the Hexateuch, and Other Essays,* trans. E. W. Truman Dicken (New York: McGraw-Hill, 1966), p. 95.

rest still stands ..." (4:1). The promise of rest is still operative, according to the writer of Hebrews.[37] He gave three arguments to support this. First, the promise of rest is the gospel: "We also have had the gospel preached to us, just as they did" (4:2). The promise in the Old Testament was the expression of God's redeeming grace, just as the gospel is today, and the gospel has not ceased. Second, there is an eternal rest that began when God rested from his creative work on the seventh day (4:3–4). God wishes man to rest with him, for it was in God's wrath (4:3) that he kept the unbelieving generation from entering their rest. The fact that God shut them out in anger indicates that it was God's original intention that mankind should share his rest. Third, when David, in Psalm 95:7–11, referred to the unbelieving generation in the wilderness, he warned against unbelief, just as the writer of Hebrews did (4:6–10). But, in verses 7b–8a, David is quoted as saying, "Today, if you hear his voice, do not harden your hearts. . . ." In David's time the offer was still open. The promise was still in effect long after the wilderness experience. The writer of Hebrews concluded that the promise of rest is the promise of the gospel. Just as God rested on the seventh day and found peace and satisfaction in his work, so the believer rests in God and finds his satisfaction in faithful obedience (4:9–11).

This concept of rest is not out of keeping with that found in the Book of Deuteronomy. The promise of the land in Deuteronomy involves a spiritual ideal—the ideal of a believing people worship-

---

37. Bruce says, "The promise of entering the 'rest' of God remains open. The meaning of that 'rest' was not exhausted by the earthly Canaan which was entered by the Israelites of the generation that had grown up to manhood in the wilderness; the spiritual counterpart of the earthly Canaan is the goal of the people of God today." F. F. Bruce, *The Epistle to the Hebrews*, New International Commentary on the New Testament series (Grand Rapids: Eerdmans, 1964), p. 72.

Several commentators have understood the "rest" of which the writer of Hebrews speaks as exclusively future. The view taken here is that the "rest" is the present experience of believers, as well as their future hope. The writer of Hebrews used the present tense of the verb *eiserchomai*. The present tense of Greek verbs may be used to refer to the future, but there is a significant change in the writer's use of this verb that we must observe. The verb is future in Ps. 95:11 in the Septuagint, but the writer of Hebrews changed it to the present tense (*eiserchometha*). David Rancier Darnell observes, "With regard to that promise of 'entrance into rest,' the readers are in serious danger that some of them will be 'lacking' (4:1), and this implies that the promise of entering into God's 'rest' is something that the readers should *now* possess, something they should have already entered into or 'have.' " *Rebellion, Rest, and the Word of God (An Exegetical Study of Hebrews 3:1–4:13)* (Ann Arbor, University Microfilms, 1973), p. 286.

ing God in obedience. That principle still obtains in the Book of Hebrews. The promise of a physical land is not clearly present there, but the rest of which that land is the symbol is still available to those who appropriate it by faith.

Another Deuteronomic aspect of the promise of the land is that of the land as a gift. The fact that God is the owner of the land is not exclusively Deuteronomic, for this concept is found in Leviticus 25:23, but the peculiar emphasis of the book on the land as a gift certainly makes this a distinctive. P. Miller notes that out of eighteen references to the land in the Book of Deuteronomy all but three state that God gave the land to the people.[38] Since the land was a gift, Israel had only to possess it (Deut. 5:31).[39]

The Promise of the Land in the Book of Joshua

A significant reference to the promise of the land occurs in the Book of Joshua in 21:44–45. It states, "The LORD gave them rest on every side, just as he had sworn to their forefathers. Not one of their enemies withstood them; the LORD handed all their enemies over to them. Not one of all the LORD's good promises to the house of Israel failed; every one was fulfilled."

A number of problems arise from these verses. One of them is the fact that when these words were spoken, a number of Canaanite enclaves still existed in the land. Indeed, the Canaanites were not completely conquered until much later. This seems incompatible with the affirmation that "the Lord handed all their enemies over to them." But the words of Joshua accurately represent the course of events to that time and are true to the tradition recorded in the Book of Exodus regarding the expulsion of the Canaanites. Exodus 23:29–30 says of the people of Canaan, "I will drive them out before you, until you have increased enough to take possession of the land." Even though the limits of the new Israelite territories did not yet extend to the distant boundaries cited in Genesis 15:18, the people knew that this extension would not happen immediately. As they trusted God they would continue to extend their borders until the land would reach the promised limits.

38. P. Miller, "The Gift of God: The Deuteronomic Theology of the Land," *Interp* 23 (1969): 454.

39. Ibid., p. 455.

Joshua himself, many years later, realized that there was still much land to possess. He said in Joshua 23:5, "The LORD your God himself will drive them out of your way. He will push them out before you, and you will take possession of their land, as the LORD your God promised you."

Another problem exists relative to the rest spoken of in Joshua 21:44. In each instance where the word *rest* (*nûaḥ*) is used in the Book of Joshua (1:13, 15; 21:44; 22:4; 23:1), it refers primarily to cessation of hostilities, not the spiritual rest of Deuteronomy. This does not deny the spiritual dimension of the promised rest of Deuteronomy; it simply affirms one aspect of it.

Yet, the concept of rest is not entirely divorced from the spiritual dimension in the Book of Joshua. In chapter 23, the experience of rest in the land means not only to live in security because Yahweh had promised absolute victory over their enemies (v. 1; cf. vv. 4−5), but also to be free from the polluting influences of the nations that Yahweh gave into their hands (vv. 9−13).

The major problem in the concept of rest in the Book of Joshua is that the book seems to speak of the promise as though it had been completely fulfilled. Joshua 21:45 says of the Lord's promises to Israel, "every one was fulfilled." Again, this is true, insofar as the words go. To all intents and purposes, the land was theirs. They had only to go on conquering in dependence on God. Any failure that they met would be due to their own unbelief. But this passage is not to be understood as teaching the cessation of the promise of the land. That promise is eternally operative, and, as has been noted, was still valid in David's time (2 Sam. 7:10). Even in the Prophets one finds that expectation (Amos 9:15; Mic. 5:5−6). The promise had been fulfilled in Joshua's time, but not ultimately so. It was to continue in effect, finding a measure of fulfillment in generation after generation until it was invested with even greater scope and glory in the New Testament. W. D. Davies observes, "One thing seems clear: concern with the land and hope for the land emerges at many places in the Old Testament outside the Hexateuch. While the promise was regarded as fulfilled in the settlement, that settlement was not regarded as a complete fulfillment ... the land had to achieve rest and peace."[40]

---

40. W. D. Davies, *The Gospel and the Land: Early Christianity and Jewish Territorial Doctrine* (Berkeley: University of California Press, 1974), p. 36.

In Deuteronomy 10:22 the promise that the offspring would be great in number is also cited in such a way as to imply its fulfillment: "Your forefathers who went down into Egypt were seventy in all, and now the LORD your God has made you as numerous as the stars in the sky." But this does not speak of ultimate fulfillment. It reflects the stage of fulfillment at that point in the progress of revelation. Continued appropriation of that promise was conditioned on obedience. Their disobedience led to its interruption (Neh. 9:23 – 27; Isa. 48:18 – 19), but the eternal promise will yet be realized (Jer. 33:22; Hos. 1:10).

Even the writer of Hebrews said, "Abraham received what was promised" (6:15). But in verse 12, he affirmed the continuing effectiveness of the promise, for he spoke of those "who through faith and patience inherit what has been promised." The writer of Hebrews did not understand the promise of the offspring to have been fulfilled ultimately in Isaac, for he said in 11:12, "And so from this one man [Abraham] ... came descendants as numerous as the stars in the sky and as countless as the sand on the seashore."

The Promise of the Land in the Poetic Material

The promise of the land figures prominently in the Psalms. One aspect of the promise is emphasized there. That is the necessity of obedience for continued appropriation of the promise of the land (Ps. 37:27 – 29, 34; 85:1 [2], cf. vv. 8 – 9 [9 – 10]).

This concept is found in the Book of Proverbs as well. Proverbs 2:21 states, "For the upright will live in the land, and the blameless will remain in it."

This aspect of the promise theme demonstrates the vital principle that although the promise is irrevocable in nature, its benefits are enjoyed only by those who maintain a proper relationship to God through the obedience of faith.

The Promise of the Land in the Prophets

In many ways the promise of the land in the Prophets is similar to what has been noted in Israel's earlier traditions. Obedience is necessary for continued enjoyment of the land. Isaiah said, "If you are willing and obedient, you will eat the best from the land ..." (1:19). But the people proved to be disobedient (Jer. 2:7; 3:2; 23:10;

Ezek. 7:23; 8:17; 33:26), and as a result, the prophets began to predict dire punishment for them—the land was to be wrested from them. Isaiah said that the land would become desolate (7:24). Jeremiah predicted that an enemy would destroy the land (4:7, 20, 27). He pictured the people lamenting,

> "How ruined we are!
> How great is our shame!
> We must leave our land
> because our houses are in ruins." [9:19]

High and low would die (Jer. 16:6) and the king of Babylon would take the people into exile (Jer. 25:8−11).

The prophets envisioned a future restoration to the land, but they made clear that only a righteous people would inherit it (Isa. 60:21; 62:4, cf. v. 1; Jer. 3:16−18). Obedience would bring about the restoration of the blessings of the promise. Jeremiah reflected the ancient promise when he affirmed that in their return to the land the Lord would be their God (24:6−7; 32:38−41). The Davidic promise is recalled in Ezekiel 37:24−25, "My servant David will be king over them. ... They will live in the land I gave to my servant Jacob. . . ." The Deuteronomic concept of the land as an inheritance was taken up by Isaiah, who said that in the restoration "they will rejoice in their inheritance ..." (61:7). Thus, the necessity of obedience for continued appropriation of the land is maintained throughout the Old Testament.

It has already been noted that the promise of the offspring expands in scope as it is reiterated throughout the progress of revelation. A similar expansion occurs with regard to the land. The prophets are in agreement about the basic aspects of the promise of the land, but their emphasis on Gentile inclusion in the plan of redemption and their vision of a world conquered by the people of God lend a cosmic scope to this aspect of the promise—God's people will inherit the world.

This universal dominion of the people of God is cited in Micah 4:11−13: they "will break to pieces many nations" and "devote their ill-gotten gains to the LORD. . . ." Micah pictured the inexorable progress of the remnant as a lion stalking its prey (5:8).[41] The

41. It is not necessary to see a redactive intrusion in this verse or a conflict of ideology with Mic. 5:7, as does the *Interpreter's Bible* when it notes, "Vs. 8 is a direct refutation

remnant will ultimately triumph over the nations, according to verse 9. This triumph is to be accomplished under the aegis of the Messiah (5:2 – 4), not in the remnant's own power (5:10 – 15).

Amos envisioned the remnant as possessing all the nations that bear the Lord's name (9:12).[42] And Isaiah held out the hope that one day the descendants of the Israelites will "possess the nations and will people the desolate cities" (54:3, RSV).

This concept is not distinctly militaristic or nationalistic in the Prophets, for several important passages reflect the Deuteronomic ideal of a worshiping community and apply that ideal to the destiny of the nations. Both Israel and the nations are envisioned in the Prophets as worshiping the Lord, not only in a land that has been conquered by Yahweh, but also in the world over which he reigns. In Isaiah 2:1 – 4, the nations are described as coming willingly to Jerusalem to learn of the ways of the Lord (v. 3). Zechariah said that "the LORD ... will again choose Jerusalem" (2:12), but the great expansion of the people of God by the addition of Gentiles extends God's reign to the entire world. The Gentiles will become the people of God, and the Deuteronomic ideal is seen in the fact that God will live among them (v. 11; cf. Deut. 12:11). Jews and Gentiles will form a community of believing people who will enjoy the blessings of God's presence (cf. Deut. 12:11 – 12).

The Deuteronomic concept of peace and security in the land is also applied universally in the Prophets. Isaiah spoke of a time when the reign of Yahweh will bring universal peace (2:4) and Micah said that the protection the Lord will give to his people (5:4) will extend to the nations, represented in this context by Assyria (vv. 5 – 6).[43]

---

of v. 7. Throughout chs. 4 – 5 there is a fundamental conflict between the pacifist and militarist concepts. This opposition comes to its most pointed focus in the antithesis between these two verses." R. E. Wolfe and H. A. Bosley, *The Book of Micah*, vol. 6, the *Interpretor's Bible*, p. 934. Both verses present the inexorable progress of the remnant; just as the rain and dew do not come at the behest of man (v. 7), so the remnant will not "wait for man." The metaphor of a lion also represents the inexorability of the remnant's progress toward its ultimate goal.

42. This view of Amos 9:12 understands the "they" of verse 12 to find its referent in the remnant (the metaphor of a sieve in v. 9). Some commentators deny that the sieving process of verse 9 involves the preservation of a remnant. See, for example, James Luther Mays, *Amos: A Commentary* (Philadelphia: Westminster, 1969), pp. 161 – 62.

43. Assyria is a symbol for the nations in the Prophets; note Isa. 11:11 where Assyria stands for the nations. Also note Zech. 10:10 where Assyria, long after its demise as a national entity, is still used as a metaphor to denote oppressing nations.

Thus, the prophets expanded the promised inheritance of God's people beyond the definable boundaries of Canaan to include the world. Yet, alongside this expanded concept of the land there are numerous promises of a return to the land of Palestine. We cannot conclude that the prophets considered that promise to have been abrogated.

The Promise of the Land in the New Testament

The New Testament perspective of the promise of the land, like the prophetic perspective, is broad in its scope. Typically, it views the promise as a whole, observing it from the vantage point of the total Old Testament revelation. The New Testament envisions a world conquered by Christ (Rev. 19:11 – 16) and a creation in which monumental changes will take place (Rom. 8:20 – 21).

This discussion of the expansion of the promise of the land in the New Testament must include Romans 4:13, where Paul said, "It was not through law that Abraham and his offspring received the promise that he would be heir of the world (*kosmos*). . . ." If Paul used the word *kosmos* here to include the concept of the inhabited earth, then we have another example of the expansion of the promise of land beyond its scope in the patriarchal narratives. The promise of a land has become the promise of the world.

Most modern commentators understand the word *kosmos* in that sense. C. E. B. Cranfield says, "It is the promise of the ultimate restoration to Abraham and his spiritual seed of man's inheritance (cf. Gen 1:27f.) which was lost through sin."[44] John Murray says, "In the light of Pauline teaching as a whole, however, we cannot exclude from the scope of this promise, as defined by the apostle, the most inclusive messianic purport . . . it is also a promise to his seed and, therefore, can hardly involve anything less than the worldwide dominion promised to Christ and to the spiritual seed of Abraham in him. It is a promise that receives its ultimate fulfillment in the consummated order of the new heavens and the new earth."[45]

44. C. E. B. Cranfield, *A Critical and Exegetical Commentary on the Epistle to the Romans*, 2 vols., International Critical Commentary series (Edinburgh: T. and T. Clark, 1975), vol. 1, p. 240.

45. John Murray, *The Epistle to the Romans*, The New International Commentary on the New Testament series (Grand Rapids: Eerdmans, 1960), p. 142.

However, some commentators understand the word in a non-territorial sense. That is, they apply it not to the physical world, but to those who follow Abraham's example of faith. Everett F. Harrison argues that the word refers to "the multitude of those who will follow Abraham in future generations in terms of his faith. These he can claim as his own."[46] He supports this view with three observations: the concept of world dominion is intrusive in Paul's discussion, for Paul argued that "Abraham's justification came in connection with the promise of offspring . . ."; the word *kosmos* lacks the article and is thus "not likely intended to denote the physical world . . ."; Paul said that Abraham will be heir, not his descendants. This fits best with the promise that Abraham would be the father of many nations.[47] If this view is adopted, Romans 4:13 must be viewed as reflecting the promise of offspring, not the promise of the land.

With regard to the first observation it may be noted that the main thrust of Paul's argument is the means of Abraham's justification; the content of the promise is incidental to that thrust. Paul demonstrated that the promise became valid for Abraham because of his faith, not his adherence to legal stipulations. Since Paul's concern was to demonstrate the means of Abraham's justification, the content of the inheritance is not germane to his argument. It is true that he referred to the promise of the offspring in the subsequent discussion (vv. 17 – 18), but these citations lend support to another facet of Paul's argument, that is, that those who are of faith are the offspring of Abraham. Paul said, "The promise comes by faith . . . to those who are of the faith of Abraham. He is the father of us all. As it is written: 'I have made you the father of many nations' " (vv. 16 – 17).

The absence of the article before *kosmos* does not preclude the possibility that it connotes the physical world. The article is lacking in such clear references to the physical world as Matthew 24:21; 25:34; and Romans 1:20.

The fact that Paul focused on Abraham's role in the inheritance is significant. Paul wrote *to klēronomon auton einai kosmou* (that he would be heir of the world). The statement seems to exclude Abraham's descendants. Since they were clearly promised the land

---

46. Everett F. Harrison, *Romans*, vol. 10, the *Expositor's Bible Commentary* (Grand Rapids: Zondervan, 1976), p. 51.

47. Ibid.

(Gen. 15:18), it appears that we must not see in these words a reference to the promise of the land but to the promise of the offspring, for that aspect of the inheritance was Abraham's alone.

Any effort to resolve this problem must involve an examination of the Old Testament passages to which Paul may have alluded. C. K. Barrett proposes that the allusion to the *kosmos* reflects Genesis 22:17 – 18.[48] He notes that the word *wĕyiraš* (will take possession of) is translated in the Septuagint by *klēronomēsei* (will inherit).[49] The inheritance is described in territorial terminology in the Septuagint. The people inherit the "cities" (*poleis*) of their enemies. The Masoretic Text states that they will possess the "gates" (*ša'ar*) of their enemies.

The possession of the gates in Genesis 22:17 is equated with the promise of the land in Genesis 26:2 – 5. The oath made by God to Abraham after he willingly placed his son on the altar (Gen. 22:17 – 18) is reaffirmed to Isaac in Genesis 26:1 – 5. In the restatement of the elements of the oath (v. 4) the reference to the "gates" is replaced by the words "and will give them all these lands" (v. 4).[50] Thus, the inheritance is represented in strong territorial language in the passage mostly likely to have been in Paul's mind when he wrote Romans 4:13.

There is no reason why Abraham could not stand alone in a reference to the promise of the land. Paul attributed to him the role of principal heir in Galatians 3:16. He is described there as heir to the "promises," not just one aspect of them. It may be that Paul reflected this relationship of Abraham to the promise in the grammatical structure of Romans 4:13. Also, in Psalm 105:7 – 11, the psalmist referred to the covenant made with Abraham. It is given to Abraham alone, according to the first clause of verse 11, where the address is in the singular (*lĕḵā*, you). The covenant is specifically defined as the land (v. 11), with no reference to Abraham's role as the father of nations.

Even if Paul had only the promise of the offspring in mind when writing Romans 4, it is difficult to understand how that concept

---

48. C. K. Barrett, *A Commentary on the Epistle to the Romans* (New York: Harper, 1958), p. 94. See also Ernst Käsemann, *The Epistle to the Romans*, trans. and ed. Geoffrey W. Bromiley (Grand Rapids: Eerdmans, 1980), pp. 119 – 20.

49. Barrett, *Epistle to the Romans*, p. 94.

50. I am indebted to a former graduate assistant, Roger W. Handyside, for his research on the issues discussed in this section.

could have been divorced in his mind from a territorial inheritance. In the Old Testament, the promise of offspring takes on a pronounced territorial connotation as it develops within the prophetic corpus. A key passage for this concept is Isaiah 51—55. The passage begins with a reference to the promise of the offspring (51:2). As God gave to one man a great posterity so he will give great increase to Zion (v. 3). After depicting the role of the servant in this restoration (52:13—53:12), Isaiah pictured the great expansion Zion will experience (54:1—3). This expansion is expressed in territorial terminology. It says, "Your descendants will dispossess nations and settle in their desolate cities" (54:3).[51] This is reminiscent of the territorial connotations noted earlier in Genesis 22:17, where it says Abraham's offspring will possess the gates of their enemies.

Jewish tradition is rich in its references to Abraham's inheritance of the world. Ecclesiasticus 44:20—21 states, "And when he was tested, he was found faithful. Therefore the Lord assured him on oath, that the nations would be blessed through his posterity, that he would multiply him like the dust of the earth and exalt his posterity like the stars, and cause them to inherit from sea to sea, and from the river unto the ends of the earth" (RSV). Mekilta Exodus says, "And so also you find that our father Abraham inherited both this world and the world beyond only as a reward for the faith with which he believed. . . ."[52] Jubilees 32:19 states, "I will give thy seed the whole earth which is under heaven ... and they shall then inherit the whole earth and possess it forever."[53] On the basis of this tradition Paul's inclusion of the whole earth in the inheritance is most natural.[54]

It must not be overlooked that Paul attributed an important role to Abraham's offspring in the inheritance. They too stand to inherit. Abraham may be the principal heir, but the promise was made to his offspring that they would inherit the world. If the "offspring" and the *kosmos* are identical in Paul's argument, then both are the people of faith. This means that they function as the

---

51. The apostle Paul applied the promise of Isa. 54:1 to the church (Gal. 4:24—31).

52. *Mekilta de-Rabbi Ishmael*, trans. Jacob Z. Lauterbach, 3 vols. (1933—35; Philadelphia: Jewish Publication Society of America, 1976), vol. 1, p. 253.

53. *The Apocrypha and Pseudepigrapha of the Old Testament in English*, ed. R. H. Charles, 2 vols. (New York: Oxford University Press, 1963), vol. 2, p. 62.

54. For further references to this concept in Jewish thought see H. Strack and P. Billerbeck, *Kommentar zum Neuen Testament aus Talmud und Midrasch*, 6 vols. (München: Beck, 1961—65), vol. 3, p. 209.

recipients of the inheritance (*tōi spermati autou*) as well as the object of the inheritance. Although this may be possible, it seems to inject an unnecessary complexity into the question. It is clear from the plural *klēronomoi* in verse 14 that the offspring are inheritors along with Abraham.

Paul's discussion of the inheritance in Galatians 3:15 – 29 also supports a territorial connotation for this concept. It is clear that Paul had a definite Old Testament context in mind when he referred to Christ and Abraham as heirs in 3:16; the words *ou legei* (it does not say) substantiate that. The only contexts to which Paul could have alluded are Genesis 12:7; 13:15; 15:18; and 17:8. Each of these passages cites the promise of the land. Since Christ is specified by Paul as one of the offspring, it is difficult to hold that Paul had only justification in mind as the heritage of the offspring. The inheritance includes the promise of land. This promise functions differently for the people of God today than it did for the people under the old covenant, but it has not lost its territorial connotations. Just as Abraham's earliest descendants were promised a land and received it, so the future descendants of Abraham will one day share Abraham's inheritance of a world that has been conquered by the Prince of Peace.

The Promise of Divine Blessing for Gentiles as Well as Jews

This aspect of the promise is expressed in the words "all peoples on earth will be blessed through you." It is a vital element of the promise.

This element of the promise has been the subject of much scholarly debate. There are two possible translations for the statement regarding Gentile blessing. One is the passive "will be blessed," the other the reflexive "shall bless themselves." The latter translation may be found in the text of the Revised Standard Version.

The difficulty arises from the fact that in the five statements expressing this aspect of the promise, the hithpael, which is usually reflexive, is used twice, and the niphal, which is generally passive but sometimes reflexive, is used three times. The occurrences in which the niphal forms are found are sometimes interpreted by the hithpael usages, and the reflexive sense is understood to dominate in all cases. This yields the translation of the Revised Standard Version.

J. Skinner understands the reflexive *bless themselves* to mean that "in invoking blessings on themselves or others they use such words as 'God make thee like Abram. . . .' "[55] S. R. Driver explains the phrase as "in blessing themselves will use thy name as a type of happiness . . . wish for themselves the blessings . . . recognized as the special possession of Abraham. . . ."[56] E. A. Speiser understands it to mean that "the nations of the world will point to Abraham as their ideal, either in blessing themselves . . . or one another. . . ."[57]

O. T. Allis argues masterfully for the meaning *be blessed* in an article that deserves more consideration that it has been given.[58] He demonstrates that the hithpael has a passive sense in Hebrew and points to the strong support for the passive translation of this element of the promise in the ancient versions.

However, it is possible to posit a reflexive connotation for the hithpael usages and still retain the promissory nature of the statement. The hithpael may connote not only a wish for blessing but the actual appropriation of it as well. In Deuteronomy 29:19 [18] it states, "One who, when he hears the words of this sworn covenant, blesses himself (*hitbārēk*) in his heart, saying, 'I shall be safe, though I walk in the stubbornness of my heart' " (RSV). This usage of the hithpael of *bārak* (bless) connotes that the person acknowledges he has received a blessing, albeit the notion is falsely conceived. He believes, as did his later countrymen of the eighth century B.C., that his relationship to the covenant alone was sufficient ground for the blessing of security in spite of his disobedience.

Josef Scharbert concludes that the meaning of the hithpael in Deuteronomy 29:19 [18] is "to consider oneself lucky, to believe oneself to be blessed, to pride oneself in being blessed. . . ."[59] He understands the similar construction in Isaiah 65:16 in the same way.[60] Sharbert suggests the translation "then all the nations of the earth shall confer on themselves blessing under your name with reference to you."[61]

---

55. J. Skinner, *A Critical and Exegetical Commentary on Genesis*, International Critical Commentary series, 2d ed. (Edinburgh: T. and T. Clark, 1930), p. 244.

56. S. R. Driver, *The Book of Genesis* (London: Methuen, 1906), p. 145.

57. E. A. Speiser, *Genesis*, the Anchor Bible (Garden City, N. Y.: Doubleday, 1964), p. 86.

58. O. T. Allis, "The Blessing of Abraham," *PTR* 25 (1927): 263–98.

59. Josef Scharbert, *TDOT*, vol. 2, p. 296.

60. Ibid.

61. Ibid., p. 297.

H. W. Wolff regards the niphal as similar to the Greek middle voice. He translates the word "acquire a blessing (for) himself, procure himself a blessing."[62]

The problem is a difficult one, but the construction need not be understood to deny the promissory character of blessing in the Abrahamic promise.

It is interesting to note that the niphal is used in the passages in Genesis where Abraham is cited and the hithpael where the offspring are cited. It is possible that the niphal functions as a true passive in those passages. This would then reflect Abraham's role as the direct mediator of the blessing from God. The hithpael, which is used with reference to the offspring, may denote that the Gentiles appropriate their blessing in and with the offspring of Abraham.

The Promise That the Lord Would Be God to His People

Another significant aspect of the promise of the offspring appears throughout the Old Testament. It is the promise that the Lord would be God to the offspring (Gen. 17:7 – 8; Exod. 29:45). In other occurrences of this promise the element *you will be my people* is added (Exod. 6:7; Lev. 26:12; Jer. 24:7; 30:22; 31:33; 32:38; Ezek. 36:28; Hos. 2:23; cf. Deut. 26:17 – 18). This element of the promise sets forth the fact that the offspring would experience the blessings of an intimate relationship with God. The Lord would be their God, providing them with the protection and benefits expected in such a loving relationship. This great statement is the heart and soul of the promise because all the gracious benefits of the promise derive from the loving power and volition of God expressed in the intimate and mysterious relationship with him that the people of faith enjoy.

The Promise That Kings Would Be Descended from Abraham

The promise that Abraham would be the progenitor of kings occurs for the first time in the patriarchal narratives at Genesis 17:6. Perhaps this promise remained an enigma for Abraham and his immediate descendants, but as the history of the ancient He-

---

62. H. W. Wolff, "The Kerygma of the Yahwist," *Interp* 20 (1966): 137, n. 31.

brews unfolded, and they became a nation in their own land, they felt the need for a king and the Israelite monarchy was born. It was then that this promise to Abraham began to be realized.

The Davidic covenant (2 Sam. 7) affirmed that the dynasty of David was an important link in the continuum of redemptive events. The Davidic house was not the ultimate fulfillment of the promise of a royal progeny. David's house was the royal line from which would spring the king par excellence—the Messiah—who would take the government upon his shoulder (Isa. 9:6 [5]). When Christ was born of David's lineage, the ancient promise to Abraham received its climactic fulfillment.

This promise will be given further consideration in the subsequent discussion.

Conclusion

The promise to the patriarchs reflects God's gracious intent to form a people for himself. He promises this people numerical growth and a place of security. God also affirms that they will be a medium of blessing and the instrument by which divine favor will extend beyond the Jewish people to include Gentiles as well. Because the promise is eternal, it is in force today, defining God's work in the world relative to the formation of a people for his name.

The promise comprises the heart of the biblical teaching regarding the people of God, for, besides affirming God's intent to form such a people, it serves to define the nature of that people in broad categories. The promise thus provides a theological continuum that spans all of time. The New Testament apostle appealed to that promise just as easily as did the Old Testament prophet. It forms the heart, the very life, of the biblical teaching regarding the people of God.

The New Testament writers did not distort the promise when they applied it messianically, for the Old Testament prophets portrayed the Messiah as both mediator and recipient of the terms of the promise.

The promise was placed in the form of a covenant in Genesis 15 and continues in that form today. It cannot be understood adequately apart from its covenantal expression.

2

The Promise
and the Covenants

From the dramatic moment when Abraham witnessed the Theophany pass between the severed carcasses, the promise has found expression in the form of covenant. This chapter will explore the relationship between promise and covenant.

Promise and Covenant in the Patriarchal Accounts

The Relationship Between Promise and Covenant

To this point the promise has been discussed in isolation from the covenant form in which it came to be placed. This may seem unwarranted in view of the close association that promise and covenant are given in Scripture. Yet, if we base our conclusions on Genesis 12—15 alone, we may conclude that the promise existed apart from the covenant form for some time. It was not until Genesis 15 that the promise given in chapter 12 was placed in the formal structure of a covenant.

It is possible to argue that the giving of the promise in chapter 12 established a covenantal relationship and that such a relationship thus existed before Genesis 15. There is validity to this;[1]

---

1. The giving of the promise to David in 2 Sam. 7 is not called a *bĕrît* in the immediate context, but it is given this designation in 2 Sam. 23:5 and Ps. 89:3 [4]. See O. Palmer Robertson, *The Christ of the Covenants* (Grand Rapids: Baker, 1980), p. 18.

the semantic range of *bĕrît* (covenant) is broad enough to include the relationship of promise established in Genesis 12. But there is a deeper question here: why did not the writer apply the term to the relationship described in chapter 12, and why is the initiation of the covenant in Genesis 15 given such dramatic emphasis in the narrative?[2] We must not allow the broad meaning of *bĕrît* to blur distinctions that the writer may have intended.

The literary shaping of Genesis 12 — 15 warrants the conclusion that the writer intended us to understand that at chapter 15 a new stage is being introduced in the unfolding narrative of Abraham's relationship to the promise.[3] We are awed as we observe the events that took place in the moment when the presence of God passed between the carcasses. It is an event that witnesses to a new and deeper significance to the promise relationship. A covenant has been established in response to Abraham's feverish question, "How can I know . . . ?" (15:8).

The awesome act of self-malediction on the part of God witnessed to a formal ratification of the earlier promise.[4] We may not understand the giving of the promise in chapter 12 in exactly the same way we understand the covenantal relationship established in chapter 15.

On the basis of the narration of events in Genesis 12 — 15 we must conclude that there is no clear evidence that the writer intended us to understand that a covenantal relationship existed before Genesis 15. We must proceed on this assumption unless other evidence presents itself.

We may observe then that the narrative structure of these early chapters of Genesis, and the usages of the word *bĕrît* in them, warrant the conclusion that for a brief period the promise existed apart from the distinct covenantal formulation it was given in Genesis 15. When the promise was given the status of a covenant

2. The word *bĕrît* occurs before Gen. 15 to connote a covenant in Gen. 6:18; 9:9, 11, 12, 13, 15, 16, 17. But it does not refer to the specific content of the Abrahamic covenant. It is the covenant of Elohim with his creation; it does not have the primarily redemptive content of the Abrahamic covenant.

3. For a full discussion of the significance of the shaping of segments of a biblical book from a canonical perspective, see Brevard S. Childs, *Introduction to the Old Testament as Scripture* (Philadelphia: Fortress, 1979).

4. Examples of this type of covenant in ancient Near Eastern materials are given by Meredith G. Kline, *By Oath Consigned: A Reinterpretation of the Covenant Signs of Circumcision and Baptism* (Grand Rapids: Eerdmans, 1968), p. 17.

it took on the force of a sworn oath.[5] The awesome self-
maledictory nature of the covenant invested the promise with the
sovereign affirmation of God himself. Abraham asked for assurance
that the promise would come to fruition, and God responded with
an oath. God swore to uphold the promise eternally. John Murray
says, "It was just because the promise to Abraham had the bonded
and oath-bound character of a covenant that its realization in the
fullness of time was inviolably certain."[6]

The conclusion that the promise was given covenantal status
in Genesis 15 may seem to be an overstatement in view of the fact
that only the promise of land appears to have received covenantal
confirmation in that passage. When the divine presence passed
between the severed carcasses the Lord said, "To your descendants I give this land" (15:18). However, the promise of offspring
is included in that affirmation. The words of the Lord include the
descendants of Abraham. The promise of offspring, as well as the
promise of land, were given covenantal confirmation in that dramatic moment.

When the covenant with Abraham was reaffirmed in Genesis
17:1−8 other elements of the promise were included along with
the promise of land (17:8). The promise that kings would descend
from Abraham (17:6) and the promise that the Lord would be God
to his people (17:7) also are included in the *běrît*, for this restatement of the promise is given the status of a *běrît* in 17:2, 4, and 7.

The promise that the nations of the earth would be blessed
through Abraham's offspring was stated in the context of the oath
sworn by the Lord in Genesis 22:18 (cf. 22:16). Thus, the major
elements of the promise gain the status of covenantal affirmations
in Genesis 15 and 17. The promise became a covenant at Genesis
15:17.

The relationship between promise and covenant in the patriarchal narratives seems to be relatively simple. But as it develops it
takes on a complexity that is not readily apparent in the account
given in chapters 12−15, for at chapter 17 there is introduced a
new function for *běrît*; it is the covenant of circumcision.

---

5. G. M. Tucker argues for a close relationship between covenant and oath. He concludes that "the covenant formula was based on the oath pattern and the contract was
not." "Covenant Forms and Contract Forms," *VT* 15 (1965): 487−503.

6. John Murray, *The Covenant of Grace: A Biblico-Theological Study* (London: Tyndale,
1953), p. 27.

The rite of circumcision is introduced by the words "This is my covenant . . . the covenant you are to keep . . ." (v. 10). It is called a *bĕrît*. The question of the distinction between the *bĕrît* of circumcision and the promise *bĕrît* will be considered fully in the next chapter. It is sufficient to note at this point that in the time of Abraham, the disposition of the inheritance was administered by a complex structure in which we observe the interplay of promise and covenant. The promise was given the form of a *bĕrît* when God swore to uphold his word. The *bĕrît* of circumcision functioned to administer an aspect of obedience necessary for the maintenance of one's relationship to the promise. A male who failed to submit to that rite would be severed from the inheritance, for "he has broken my covenant" (v. 14). Thus, promise covenant and administrative covenant were inextricably bound together in the disposition of the inheritance.

The application of the term *bĕrît* to an eternally valid oath as well as to a covenant that could be broken reflects the broad conceptual range of the word. It is wrong to limit the meaning of the term too narrowly. Walther Eichrodt observes, "The idea that in ancient Israel the *bĕrît* was always and only thought of as Yahweh's pledging of himself, to which human effort was required to make no kind of response . . . can therefore be proven to be erroneous."[7]

The use of the term *bĕrît* with reference to the rite of circumcision may seem to be anomalous. We are used to thinking of covenants as formal verbal or written instruments of intent or agreement. Yet, when the concept of covenant is studied and its various facets are observed it becomes apparent that the application of the term *bĕrît* to the rite of circumcision is quite appropriate. In order to see this it is necessary to examine the broad range of function ascribed to the *bĕrît* in the Old Testament.

One function of *bĕrît* that may be observed is the use of the term to connote an oath apart from any condition. In Genesis 9:9, the *bĕrît* is the sovereign declaration of God that he will never destroy mankind with a flood. Its validity is in no way dependent on human response. Similar to this is the use of *bĕrît* in such contexts as Jeremiah 33:20 and Hosea 2:18, where a *bĕrît* is estab-

---

7. Walther Eichrodt, *Theology of the Old Testament*, trans. J. A. Baker, 2 vols. (Philadelphia: Westminster, 1961), vol. 1, p. 37.

lished by God with such unresponsive entities as the heavens and the animal world. The statement of the promise to David in 2 Samuel 7 falls into this category. It is called a *bĕrît* in 2 Samuel 23:5 and Psalm 89:3 [4], but it is not established on the basis of mutual agreement.[8]

A second function of *bĕrît* is the formal crystallization of terms of mutual agreement (Gen. 21:27, 32; 26:28 – 29; 1 Kings 5:12). This is the more usual type of covenant.

The third function to be noted here is the use of *bĕrît* to denote a statement of unilateral intent which involves the stipulations of obedience by which that intent is formalized and facilitated. For example, in Joshua 24 the people promised to serve the Lord (v. 24). The *bĕrît* that functioned as the formalization of the promise contained stipulations by which the people could carry out their stated intent (vv. 25 – 27).[9]

The basic idea underlying the concept of *bĕrît* is that of a relationship involving obligation. When that obligation is expressed in the form of intent, the intent may be effected unilaterally or bilaterally. Parties must be involved in the *bĕrît*, but there need not always be a mutual response.[10] Other elements, such as confirmation and explication, may be found in covenants in Scripture, but this definition represents an effort to capture the common element of all the functions of *bĕrît* in the Old Testament.

It is apparent that circumcision falls within the conceptual range of *bĕrît*. It involved a relationship between God on the one hand and Abraham and his descendants on the other. It crystallized an aspect of obedience on which the integrity of that relationship depended. Thus, in Abraham's time the promise was governed by two instruments designated *bĕrît*. The promissory covenant con-

8. M. Weinfeld states, "The covenant with Abraham, and so the covenant with David, indeed belong to the grant type and not to the vassal type. Like the royal grants in the Ancient Near East so also the covenants with Abraham and David are gifts bestowed upon individuals who excelled in loyally serving their masters." "The Covenant of Grant in the Old Testament and in the Ancient Near East," *JAOS* 90 (1970): 185.

9. For a full discussion of covenant forms in ancient Israel see George E. Mendenhall, "Covenant Forms in Israelite Tradition," in *Biblical Archaeologist Reader*, ed. David Noel Freedman and G. Ernest Wright (Garden City, N. Y.: Anchor, 1961 – 70), vol. 3, pp. 25 – 53.

10. Weinfeld draws a distinction between promissory and obligatory types of covenants and discusses them against the background of treaty forms of the ancient Near East, particularly the covenant of grant. "The Covenant of Grant," pp. 184 – 203.

firmed the promise, and the covenant of circumcision administered an aspect of obedience.

The Question of Conditionality in the Abrahamic Covenant

The promise is eternal. It does not depend on human obedience, but on the sovereign intent of God. The disobedience of
individuals cannot frustrate the purpose of God to bring salvation
to the Gentiles.

Yet, several statements seem to indicate that obedience on the
part of Abraham was a necessary corollary to the promise. In
Genesis 12:1 God said to Abraham, "Leave your country, your people and your father's household and go to the land I will show
you." Abraham's obedience was assumed by God, as it is throughout the patriarchal narratives. The promise is followed by the
matter-of-fact statement "So Abram left, as the LORD had told him"
(v. 4).

In Genesis 17:1 – 2, when the covenant was confirmed, God said,
"I am God Almighty; walk before me, and be blameless. And I will
make my covenant between me and you . . ." (RSV). The conjunction
and (Heb. waw) that begins verse 2 is significant, for it connects the
command of verse 1 to the statement of verse 2, implying either
"and I will make" or "that I may make." The obedience of Abraham
was thus a necessary corollary to the "making" of the covenant.

The word translated "make" in this passage is the word nātan.
It is the common word for "give" in Hebrew. It need not be understood to connote the initiation of the covenant; that is expressed
in Genesis 15:18 by the word kārat (cut). The word nātan means
to "set up" or "establish."[11] This is confirmed by the use of the
hiphil of qûm (cause to stand) in 17:7 (see also Gen. 9:9, 11).

In Genesis 26:1 – 5 the covenant with Abraham was confirmed
to Isaac. In verse 5 God reaffirms his intent to carry out the stipulations of the promise, "because Abraham obeyed me. . . ." And,
in Genesis 22, when Abraham's faith was proven by his willingness

---

11. It is most likely that the word nātan means "establish" here rather than "initiate."
The covenant was initiated in Gen. 15:18. The word nātan means "establish" (with reference to statutes and ordinances) in Lev. 26:46. It also utilizes bēn (between) in the
construction, as is the case in Gen. 17:2. H. C. Leupold defines the term nātan in relation
to covenants: "to put into force, or to make operative, the one that is in force." Exposition
of Genesis, 2 vols. (1942; Grand Rapids: Baker, 1949), vol. 1, p. 514.

to sacrifice Isaac, God said, "Because you have done this ... I will surely bless you and make your descendants as numerous as the stars..." (vv. 16 – 17).

With regard to Abraham's response to God's command to leave Ur of the Chaldees (Gen. 12:1), it may be noted that this is simply the response of faith. God's promise elicited trust. If Abraham had not believed God, he would not have obeyed. This is an example of the kind of faith set forth in the Old Testament. It is more than abstract belief, it is commitment to God. Murray says, "The conditions in view are not really conditions of bestowal. They are simply the reciprocal responses of faith, love and obedience, apart from which the enjoyment of the covenant blessing and of the covenant relation is inconceivable. In a word, keeping the covenant presupposes the covenant relation as established rather than the condition upon which its establishment is contingent."[12]

Abraham's faith set the promise in operation for him, and his continued obedience attested to the continuing validity of his faith. Because the promise was so ratified it became valid for his descendants who were beneficiaries of the promise. That is why God could say to Isaac that he was an inheritor of the promise. It was because "Abraham believed [God] and kept [his] requirements ..." (Gen. 26:5). The seeming disparity between the eternality of the promise and the role of human faith and obedience can be resolved when one recognizes the promise to be unconditional insofar as it relates to God's purposes, but conditioned on a living faith when it relates to the nation or the individual.

The sovereign will of God to keep his promises is illustrated in Leviticus 26, where the punishment for national disobedience was exile in the land of their enemies (vv. 38 – 39); yet God could say, "In spite of this, when they are in the land of their enemies, I will not reject them or abhor them so as to destroy them completely, breaking my covenant with them. I am the LORD their God" (v. 44). It was God's solemn purpose to maintain Israel as a nation until the scion of David should come, bringing salvation to the Gentiles. Yet, the disobedience of a specific generation would result in their failure to enjoy the promise of the land. The promise covenant

---

12. John Murray, *The Covenant of Grace* (London: Tyndale, 1953), p. 19. For a discussion of Murray's views regarding human responsibility in the covenant relationship and those of Kline, see O. Palmer Robertson, "Current Reformed Thinking on the Nature of the Divine Covenants," *WTJ* 40 (1977 – 78): 63 – 76.

itself would never be vitiated, but individual participation in the promise was conditioned on a continuing faith that manifested itself in obedience.

The unbelief and disobedience of the nation in the wilderness kept them from seeing the land that the Lord had promised to their forefathers (Num. 14:22 − 23). Most of the people of that generation never attained the promise of the land because of their lack of faith and resultant disobedience, but the purpose of God was maintained in the families of Caleb and Joshua who entered the land because of their faith. This illustrates the relationship of individuals to the promise as well as the obligation of God to maintain his promise.

Thus, the covenant was initiated and established by God with Abraham on the basis of Abraham's faith. However, his faith was not simply an affirmative cognition of God's word; it was true biblical faith, which is trust in God manifested in ethical response. This is living faith, and this faith established Abraham's relationship with God through covenant.

Promise and Covenant in the Mosaic Legislation

The Promise in the Mosaic Covenant

When Moses climbed the crags of Mount Sinai and received the law amid the lightning and the crashing thunder, a new era was born in the history of Israel.[13] The period of Israelite history governed by the Mosaic covenant was a period in which it may seem to the casual reader that the promise had receded into the background. This period was dominated by the tables of stone and the great Levitical institutions. The blood of the sacrifices, the stern legal code, the dire punishments that befell the people, all present an aspect of God that was not so apparent in the period of history governed by the Abrahamic covenant. Yet all these elements of the Mosaic covenant relate to the promise in a remarkably direct way.

It is necessary to establish at the outset that the promise is an

13. Since this work is primarily a theology of the covenants, attention will not be given to the structure of the Mosaic covenant. For a cogent discussion of that topic see Mendenhall, "Covenant Forms in Israelite Tradition."

essential part of the Mosaic covenant. This fact may be seen not only in direct statements in the Pentateuch, but also in the elements of the promise that figure prominently in the content of the Mosaic covenant.

The great events of the exodus from Egypt have as their background the promise to the patriarchs (Exod. 6:2–4). Indeed the entry into the land of Canaan is a direct fulfillment of that promise (Exod. 6:8). The relationship between the Abrahamic promise and the Mosaic covenant is reflected in the phrase *the God of Abraham, Isaac and Jacob* in the account of the exodus (Exod. 2:24; 3:15–16). If one should object that these statements were made before the formal ratification of the covenant (Exod. 19), a glance at Exodus 32:13 and 33:1 will show that the promise to Abraham was regarded as still in effect after the giving of the law; it was not nullified by it.[14]

In the Book of Deuteronomy, when Moses summoned the people to obedience to the stipulations of the covenant, he said, "You are standing here in order to enter into a covenant with the LORD your God ... that he may be your God as he promised you and as he swore to your fathers, Abraham, Isaac and Jacob" (Deut. 29:12–13). In Deuteronomy 6:3 the Lord said, "Hear, O Israel, and be careful to obey so that it may go well with you and that you may increase greatly in a land flowing with milk and honey, just as the LORD, the God of your fathers, promised you."

The promise is inherent in the law, not only in the statements noted above, but also in the terms of the promise that find expression there. The Mosaic covenant does not express all these terms; however, the promise is unmistakably present within it.

The promise of the offspring

The first occurrence of the concept of the offspring in the Mosaic covenant is found in Exodus 19:5–6, "Now if you obey me fully and keep my covenant, then out of all nations you will be my treasured possession. Although the whole earth is mine, you will be for me a kingdom of priests and a holy nation."

This promise that Israel would become a national entity, sustaining a unique relationship to God, is not without historical antecedent. It has been observed that the Abrahamic promise en-

---

14. Note the argument of Paul in Gal. 3:17.

visioned a people who would become a great nation and who would have the Lord as their God. But is the promise of Exodus 19:5 – 6 really a reaffirmation of the promise of the offspring? Is there a conscious effort to tie this promise together with the Abrahamic promise?

These questions may be answered unequivocally in the affirmative. In Deuteronomy 7:6, the promise of Exodus 19:5 – 6 is restated, "For you are a people holy to the LORD your God. The LORD your God has chosen you out of all the peoples on the face of the earth to be his people, his treasured possession." The reason for this loving choice is given in verses 7 – 8, "The LORD did not ... choose you because you were more numerous than other peoples, ... it was because the LORD loved you and kept the oath he swore to your forefathers that he brought you out. ..." The choice of Israel to be the Lord's people was based not on Israel's might, but on the Lord's loving faithfulness to his promise to the patriarchs.

The terminology used to express Israel's relationship to God under the Mosaic covenant has great significance. In Exodus 19:5 – 6 Israel is called to be a "treasured possession" (sĕgullâ), a "kingdom of priests" (mamleket kōhănîm) and a "holy nation" (gôy qādôš).

The word sĕgullâ is used infrequently in the Old Testament, but there are a few occurrences that shed light on its meaning.[15] In 1 Chronicles 29:3 it denotes David's personal treasure of gold and silver. In Ecclesiastes 2:8 it refers to the treasure of kings; in Malachi 3:17, those who fear the Lord are described as belonging to God and being his special possession. The use of this word denotes that Israel was called to a position of special worth in the eyes of God. As the sĕgullâ of God they could expect to be protected by him and cared for in a way unique among the nations of the world.

As a royal body of priests, the nation was called to high privilege. They were to sustain a unique relationship to God as well as to the nations for whom they mediated divine redemption. Charles A. Briggs observes, "The essential thing became the relation which they were to assume on the one side to God their king,

---

15. The word sĕgullā is discussed against its Near Eastern background by Moshe Greenberg, "Hebrew segullā: Akkadian sikiltu," JAOS 71 (1951): 172ff.; and Weinfeld, "The Covenant of Grant," p. 195.

and on the other to the nations. . . . As the redeemed of God, they are His priests, and are to mediate the redemption of the world."[16]

This ideal was not entirely realized under the old covenant, but it is realized under the new covenant. Peter affirmed this privilege of the people of God in 1 Peter 2:5, 9, where the dual role of the priesthood is emphasized. In verse 5, he spoke of the godward aspect of the priestly role of God's people. He said they are "offering spiritual sacrifices acceptable to God through Jesus Christ." In verse 9, he emphasized the manward aspect of their priestly function: "But you are . . . a royal priesthood . . . that you may declare the praises of him who called you. . . ." As a holy people, the nation would be separate from that which defiled, set apart to a holy God who sovereignly called his people to holiness.[17]

The promise that the Lord will be God to his people

The promise that the Lord would be their God and they his people is not given great prominence in the Abrahamic covenant. It appears only in Genesis 17:7−8, but it takes on greater significance in the Mosaic covenant.

The first occurrence of this element in the Mosaic era is in Exodus 6:7, where the Lord says, "I will take you as my own people, and I will be your God." This element, like the previous one, is integrally related to the Abrahamic covenant, for it is one of several promises contained in verses 6−8 that are joined by the word *therefore* (*lākēn*) to the statement *I have remembered my covenant* (v. 5). The covenant referred to here is, of course, the Abrahamic covenant (vv. 3−4).

This affirmation of the divine-human relationship in Exodus 6:7 is not within the confines of the formal Mosaic covenant. The covenant was not ratified until the events recorded in Exodus 19 took place. However, it is clearly expressed in covenant terminology later. It can be said to continue intact in the Mosaic covenant, for it is stated in Exodus 29:45−46 in the context of the covenantal institutions of the tabernacle and the priesthood. It is found also

---

16. Charles A. Briggs, *Messianic Prophecy: The Prediction of the Fulfilment of Redemption Through the Messiah* (New York: Scribner's, 1886), p. 102.

17. The basic connotation of the root *qds* (holy) in Hebrew is the "state of that which belongs to the sacred" and is thus "distinct from the common or profane." Thomas E. McComiskey, "*qādaš*," in *Theological Wordbook of the Old Testament*, ed. R. Laird Harris, Gleason L. Archer, Jr., and Bruce K. Waltke (Chicago: Moody, 1980), vol. 2, pp. 1989−91.

in the Book of Deuteronomy, which is a covenantal formulation of the divine revelation, where numerous references to this aspect of the promise occur (4:20; 7:6; 14:2; 27:9).[18]

The promise of the land

The third aspect of the Abrahamic covenant to find expression in the Mosaic covenant is the promise of the land. This element of the promise is prominent there because the prospect of a homeland loomed on the horizon throughout the period of Israel's infancy as a nation. This promise, like the others, is tied to the Abrahamic promise. In Exodus 6:3 the Lord refers to the patriarchs and then affirms in verse 8, "And I will bring you to the land I swore with uplifted hand to give to Abraham, to Isaac and to Jacob."

In Deuteronomy 4:1 the promise of the land is given formal covenantal status. It says with reference to the commandments, "Follow them so that you may live and go in and take possession of the land that the LORD, the God of your fathers, is giving you."

The promise of divine blessing for Gentiles

The only major aspect of the promise not given prominence in the Mosaic covenant is the extension of divine favor to Gentiles. Does this indicate that this element of the promise has been abrogated, or that concern for the inclusion of Gentiles in the divine program was suspended during the Mosaic era? The lack of emphasis on this aspect of the promise is significant because it has implications for the nature of the function of covenant. The question as to whether an element of the promise has been abrogated because it is not given formal covenantal expression must be considered.

A number of scholars have affirmed the presence of this element in the Mosaic covenant. Willis J. Beecher argues that the concept may be found in Deuteronomy 28:9 – 10, where Israel's obedience will cause the nations to see that she is "called by the name of the LORD," and the nations will fear Israel. He concludes, "To this ex-

18. The covenantal formulation of the Book of Deuteronomy is generally acknowledged. See further Meredith G. Kline, *Treaty of the Great King: The Covenant Structure of Deuteronomy* (Grand Rapids: Eerdmans, 1963); Mendenhall, "Covenant Forms in Israelite Tradition"; D. J. McCarthy, *Treaty and Covenant,* new ed. (Rome: Biblical Institute Press, 1978).

tent, at least, Israel is to transmit to the nations the monotheism of the religion of Yahweh."[19]

However, this verse falls far short of affirming Gentile inclusion within the benefits of the promise. It is best to place this verse within the bank of material in Deuteronomy that speaks of Israel's exaltation over the nations which results from her obedience to the Lord's commands (7:22; 9:1; 11:23; 15:6; 18:14; 26:19; 28:1, 12). The Book of Deuteronomy teaches that if Israel is disobedient she will become subject to these nations (28:49, 65). These verses deal with Israel's destiny among the nations as determined by her relationship to God. They do not relate primarily to the question of Gentile inclusion.

Yet, we have noted that Israel's function as royal priests must bear some relation to the nations. Jeremiah reflected this function in 4:2, which says an obedient Israel effects a fundamental change in the attitude of the nations to God. However, it must be admitted that this aspect of the promise is not strongly represented in the Mosaic covenant.

The paucity of emphasis on Gentile blessing in the Mosaic covenant does not imply the abrogation of that element of the promise. The prophets who ministered under that covenant clearly affirmed that God's grace would extend to Gentiles. Rather, it serves to place in clearer light the relationship between the promise and the Mosaic covenant. The covenant expressed the promise in terms that were appropriate for its recipients and for the circumstances in which it was given. The focus of the Mosaic legislation is on the formation of Israel as a nation. It sought to delineate the glorious future that Israel could have if the people lived in obedience to God. The Mosaic covenant served to affirm the promise and to emphasize those aspects of the promise which applied directly to the Israelite tribes soon to be welded into a nation. The terms of the promise were never annulled, but since the promise covenant maintains its own integrity throughout salvation history it could continue in force while the Mosaic covenant served to extract those elements of the promise that were of particular importance for that time. The immediate concern of the Mosaic covenant was to forge and protect a nation through which the promise would be mediated. If the perspective of the law was not oriented in the

19. Willis J. Beecher, *The Prophets and the Promise* (Grand Rapids: Baker, 1963), p. 222.

direction of Gentiles it does not imply the abrogation of that element of the promise; it implies only that that aspect was not of primary concern for the function of the law.

The Relationship of Law and Promise in the Mosaic Covenant

The Mosaic covenant is thus not opposed to the promise. It is, in a sense, a vehicle of the promise. It defines and amplifies that promise for a new generation. The statement of the promise to Abraham was quite suitable for the nomadic family-clans of the patriarchs, but when Israel became a nation, a new era dawned. Israel was given a covenant that would govern her as a nation for centuries to come.

It has been noted that when the law covenant was ratified in Exodus 19:5–8 it was intended to secure the promise of the offspring for the burgeoning nation (vv. 5–6). But that promise has clearly undergone change since its earlier expression in the Abrahamic covenant. The offspring, according to the Abrahamic promise, were to become a great nation with Yahweh as their God; they were to occupy the land of Canaan and become the medium of blessing to Gentiles. In the Mosaic covenant the significance of the reign of Yahweh over the nation is given greater emphasis. If the people are obedient, they will become God's treasured possession, enjoying the status of a holy nation in which all have the access to God that was the distinct prerogative of the priesthood. The promise has been amplified and adapted to the new situation. The motley assemblage in the wilderness was to become a proud nation. The changing historical situation led to a restatement of the promise more appropriate to the national structure of the people. This did not change its essential nature, but revealed greater depths than were evident in its first statement to Abraham.

Not only did the law covenant define and amplify the promise, but it served to protect and secure the promise as well. This is particularly evident in the Deuteronomic expression of the law. According to Deuteronomy 4:1, obedience to the law would insure the successful conquest of the land of promise, and Deuteronomy 7:12 states that obedience to the law would guarantee continued participation in the promise covenant. This is the central concept of chapters 28–32 as well (see also 8:1; 11:8; 18–25).

The protective function of the law is also apparent in the various legal stipulations. The health laws and the prohibitions against Canaanite practices served to preserve the nation and to maintain its solidarity. The law guaranteed Israel's integrity as a nation by preventing the dissolution that would come through inter-marriage and the adoption of Canaanite religious practices. The law protected the offspring through whom God was working to bring his promised blessing to Gentiles.

The law also sought to define the terms of obedience for those whose faith was in the promise it perpetuated. It pointed out what sin is. It delineated holiness and defined transgression for those who would seek true holiness. But the nation whose forefathers affirmed, "We will do everything the LORD has said" (Exod. 19:8) violated the covenant and were led away at swordpoint to the land of their enemies, seemingly rejected by their God.

The law is not the promise; it is a covenant distinct from the promise covenant. It establishes the conditions under which the terms of the promise could be maintained. The promise is the eternal expression of God's will. The law is the temporary frame-work that prescribed the terms of obedience for the people of God in the Mosaic era.

Like circumcision, the law is a *běrît* that functions in conjunc-tion with the promise covenant. Just as circumcision specified an aspect of obedience which had an important function for the people of God, so the law set forth a complex of stipulations to which the people were to be obedient. These stipulations served the benign functions we have noted in the previous discussion.

The law did not give the inheritance; it served to provide the framework necessary for the people to maintain their relationship to it. However, several passages in Scripture seem to give the law a greater role in the disposition of the inheritance. For example, Deuteronomy 7:12 says, "If you pay attention to these laws and are careful to follow them, then the LORD your God will keep his covenant of love with you, as he swore to your forefathers." This verse seems to give a primacy to the law that renders the Abra-hamic covenant ineffectual apart from it. It appears to place the blessings of the promise squarely on the basis of obedience to the commandments of Moses and thus to make them the primary source of life.

However, this is not consonant with the description of the relation between faith and law set forth in the introductory chapters of Deuteronomy. We find there Moses' own explanation of the law, for in Deuteronomy 1:5 we are told he undertook to explain (bē'ēr) it.[20]

The explanation involves a recital of historical events, the central theme of which is the failure of the people to believe that God would fulfill his promises. The sovereign promise is very much in view here. The people have only to take all the territory promised in the Abrahamic covenant (1:7–8). The promise has been fulfilled in a measure (1:10), but Moses prays for even greater realization of the promise (1:11). At Kadesh Barnea the people were on the threshold of the fulfillment of the promise of the land (1:19–21), but they proved to lack faith in the promise of God (1:26–28). Moses reminded the people of the sovereignty of the God who promised (1:30–31), but Moses' words failed, and the section ends with the dismal observation, "Yet in spite of this word you did not believe the LORD your God" (1:32, RSV).

Because of their lack of faith the Israelites were shut out of the land (1:35). But Caleb and Joshua received that promise (1:34–38). It was theirs through faith, not law. From Moses' explanation of the function of the law thus far we cannot conclude that the terms of the promise were realized through legal obedience.

There follows a long recital of the conquests effected by Israel (2:1–3:20). One nation after another is given into the Israelites' hand as the Lord marches triumphantly before them. They had only to exercise faith in what the Lord said he would do.

It is at 4:1 that Moses comes to the matter of the law. He explains it against the background of the events that occurred at Baal Peor (4:3–4). It was there that the people broke the law by falling into idolatry (Num. 25:1–5). He says in Deuteronomy 4:4 that those who "held fast" (dābaq) to the Lord were "still alive" (ḥayyîm). He concludes, "See, I have taught you decrees and laws as the LORD my God commanded me, so that you may follow them in the land you are entering to take possession of it. Observe them carefully, for this will show your wisdom and understanding to the nations" (vv. 5–6).

This lengthy passage presents the interplay of law and grace.

---

20. The root b'r can mean "to explain" or "to expound." The latter meaning can hardly apply here, for what follows in the immediate context is not exposition of the law but an explanation of its function.

It is the promise which is the repository of grace. It had only to be believed and the inheritance would be granted. The function of the law was not to grant the inheritance but to preserve and protect the people for the inheritance. This is the point of Moses' reference to the failure of the people at Baal Peor. Obedience to the law prevented the dissolution of the entire nation at the hand of an angry God. It thereby insured the continuation of the nation and thus perpetuated the promise. It did this by providing the "wisdom and understanding" (v. 6) necessary for them to remain a strong and viable community that would continue to enjoy the prospect of the inheritance.

Throughout this section there is the consciousness that faith in the sworn promise is the key to the inheritance. The law was given to protect the people for the promise, to aid them in the pursuit of their destiny, and to provide the legal standards so necessary to an orderly society. The law did not usurp the role of faith. The people at Baal Peor who "held fast" to the Lord were already people of faith. Their faith was manifested by their obedience, and that obedience to the law had a salutary effect on their relationship to the promise.

It is thus difficult to understand Deuteronomy 7:12 as teaching equal functions for faith and law or the usurpation of the role of faith by law. The Book of Deuteronomy pictures too clearly a sovereign God acting on behalf of a believing people for that conclusion to be warranted. Neither does the verse teach that the Abrahamic covenant has been nullified by law; both are understood to be in effect. Rather, the law is to be seen as a vehicle for the manifestation of faith, as it was at Baal Peor. The covenant sworn to the fathers could never become effectual for a disobedient people, for their disobedience meant they did not sincerely believe that God would do what he said; they did not have faith. Those who were obedient to the Lord at Baal Peor contributed to the preservation of the nation and they continued to enjoy the promises given to them by the sovereign disposition of God.

This concept of the relationship of law and promise is evident also in Deuteronomy 4:25–31. There Moses affirmed that if the people disobey the law they will be disinherited (vv. 25–26), but when God acts to restore them as a result of their obedience (v. 30), it is on the basis of the promise covenant that he acts (v. 31). The promise was not invalidated by law. It guaranteed that God would always act on behalf of a faithful people.

The sovereign promise is the guarantee of Israel's destiny. The law, according to Deuteronomy, was a benign institution given to facilitate the perpetuation of the promise for the individual and the nation.

The New Testament and the Mosaic Covenant

Although the new covenant has yet to be studied, it is important to bring the discussion of the relationship between law and promise to the New Testament at this point, because the benign function of the law set forth in the preceding section appears to be belied by a number of statements in the New Testament. These are found particularly in the writings of Paul, where the law seems to be regarded as a source of misery and death.

The question of the relationship between law and promise, or to express it in more familiar terms, law and grace, is of vital importance to the Christian and is one of the most misunderstood facets of the Christian experience. There is no question that Paul understood the gospel to be related to the ancient promise given to Abraham. He could say, "The words 'it was credited to him' were written not for him alone, but also for us, to whom God will credit righteousness ..." (Rom. 4:23–24). The promise is in force today as it was in the Old Testament (see Rom. 4:1–8, 16–17; Gal. 3:6–9).

But what about the law? Does it relate to the gospel promise as it related to promise in the Old Testament? This question is important because it will introduce us to one of the most important aspects of our study, the question of continuity and discontinuity as determined by covenant. The New Testament authors wrote under the aegis of a new covenant. To what extent, if at all, did they carry over elements of the old covenant?

The exegetical problems involved in this study are numerous and difficult, and much has been written on the topic. The following conclusions concerning the law in the New Testament are based on an exegetical study of the major New Testament passages that relate to the law. The evidence for these conclusions is given in the two appendixes that follow this chapter. They are an important part of the discussion and should be read in connection with it. The material in the appendixes does not give an exhaustive exposition of each passage; the purpose is to seek to determine how the New Testament attitude toward the law relates to the function of covenant.

The law in the teaching of Jesus

The question of the place of the law in the Christian ethic is an important one. Many views have been presented with regard to Jesus' attitude to the law. These range from the assertion that the Gospels represent Jesus as replacing the old law with his higher teaching[21] to the view that he functioned as an expositor of the Mosaic law, which he upheld and humbly obeyed.[22]

The law figured prominently in the teaching of Jesus. One reason for this is that he was often forced to express his views on it in theological disputation. This becomes apparent in Jesus' major statements on the law: the incident in the grainfield (Matt. 12:1 – 8; Mark 2:23 – 28; Luke 6:1 – 5), the healing of the man in the synagogue (Matt. 12:9 – 14; Mark 3:1 – 6; Luke 6:6 – 11), the more important matters of the law (Matt. 23:23 – 24; Luke 11:42 – 44), and the Sermon on the Mount (Matt. 5:17 – 48).

Jesus established himself as the sole authority over the law; thus man does not have the right to abrogate any aspect of the law. The central concept of the law is love; its statutes urge us to deeds of love and kindness.

When Jesus appeared, a new era dawned in the history of redemption, for law, history, and prophetic prediction found their ultimate fulfillment in him. In his loving yet authoritative way he called his followers to live according to the law; not the oppressive legal structure of Pharisaism, but the joyful expression of love for one's fellow man that characterizes the teaching of the Sermon on the Mount.

There is a sense of eschatological fulfillment in the Sermon on

21. B. Bacon concludes, "It would appear to be one of the main objects of Matthew to counteract what he designates 'lawlessness' . . . by presenting the whole message of Jesus as a new and higher Torah with apocalyptic sanctions." "Jesus and the Law: A Study of the First 'Book' of Matthew (Mt. 3 – 7)," *JBL* 47 (1928): 204.

22. Herman N. Ridderbos, *The Coming of the Kingdom*, ed. Raymond O. Zorn, trans. H. de Jongste (Philadelphia: Presbyterian and Reformed, 1962), pp. 292 – 321. Ridderbos says, "So Jesus' most radical commandments . . . do not represent a new kind of righteousness . . . but only give expression to what Jesus proclaims as the demands of the law and the prophets" (p. 293).

the Mount that heralds a new age; an age when the law can be kept as God intended it; an age when righteousness can be attained not through oppressive attention to minute detail, but through the example of Christ.

Jesus announced certain modifications in the law which were appropriate for the new age. Aspects of the old law were abrogated by him. In the teaching of Jesus we find that the Mosaic covenant was not a rigid legal code that was intended to stand unchanging for eternity. We are thus prepared for the subsequent statements in the New Testament concerning the new covenant.

This consideration of Jesus and the law relates to the study of the Old Testament covenants in that it prepares us for a certain measure of discontinuity in the transition from the old covenant to the new covenant. But it also demonstrates a pronounced continuity in the function of law in the two eras. Jesus did not forsake the ethic of the law: he sought to explicate it and implement it in the lives of his followers.

The law in the teaching of Paul

A cursory reading of the passages in which Paul speaks of the law may create the impression that he despised it and affirmed its abolition for the believer. But such a conclusion is difficult in the light of Paul's comment to the Romans: "Do we, then, nullify the law by this faith? Not at all! Rather, we uphold the law" (3:31). The law could not impart the righteousness essential for salvation. This righteousness is granted only through faith.

The law continues as a viable entity in the Pauline theology. Paul called believers to obey it (Eph. 6:2), and he honored it by pronouncing it "holy," "righteous," and "good" (Rom. 7:12). The difference between the relationships to the law sustained by the New Testament Christian and the Old Testament believer is in the motivation for obedience to its statutes. Paul exulted that the motivation for obedience is now the Spirit whose operation in human hearts is administered by the new covenant (Rom. 8:3–4; 2 Cor. 3:6).

Any failure that Paul saw in connection with the operation of the law he attributed directly to the sinful human heart. He affirmed no intrinsic evil in God's righteous requirements as expressed in the law. It is the sinful human nature that weakened the law and rendered it powerless to effect its true purpose (Rom. 8:2 – 4).

The covenant righteousness of the law is obedience, and the covenant righteousness of the promise covenant is faith. This concept enables us to understand Paul's words, "The law is not based on faith . . ." (Gal. 3:12), in their most basic sense. The law did not grant the inheritance in the Old Testament. The inheritance was granted by the promise covenant which had faith as its covenant righteousness. So, in the present era of the new covenant, adherence to the principle of law alone cannot grant the great spiritual inheritance that God has for his people. The inheritance is granted by faith in Christ. Now that Christ has entered the sphere of human history he has become the embodiment of the faith principle (Rom. 3:21 – 22). He is the object of faith. The inheritance is granted to all whose faith is in Christ alone.

Obedience is not nullified by faith. Paul affirmed that "we have an obligation . . ." (Rom. 8:12). It is an obligation to the Spirit (v. 13). But this obligation to live according to the Holy Spirit's promptings in the heart is not radically divorced from the ethic of the law in Pauline theology. Paul made enough positive statements about the law to render such a conclusion questionable. The relationship of faith to the law is vividly illustrated by Paul in his use of Deuteronomy 30:11 – 14 in Romans 10:6 – 8. Obedience does not grant the inheritance, according to Pauline theology (faith has that function), but Paul nonetheless urges obedience to the great spiritual ethic of the law.

The dark statements that one finds in Paul's discussion of the law should not be understood as a total rejection of the law on Paul's part. Such a suggestion goes too far, for it does not take into account the positive statements we have noted. The freedom from the law in which Paul exulted is not freedom from the delightful privilege of obedience to God, but from the condemnation of the law (see the discussion of Romans 8:2 – 4 in Appendix 2). If one seeks to be righteous in God's eyes on the basis of legal obedience alone, one is condemned, for the law is powerless to grant that status with God. This is the point of Paul's appeal to the experience of Abraham (Gen. 15:6) in Romans 4 and Galatians 3:6 – 9. It is only in the principle of faith that one finds glorious freedom in Christ and release from the law's condemning function. It is sin that makes the law a cruel and tyrannical master (Rom. 7:9 – 11), for

the law reveals sin in all its heinousness (v. 9). The law intensifies
the struggle between the two natures that lie deep within the
consciousness of the believer. But, because Christ condemned sin,
doing what the law could not do (Rom. 8:3), the believer can cry
out with Paul, "Thanks be to God—through Jesus Christ our Lord!"
This is a cry that reflects the exultation of one who has escaped
the law's condemnation through Jesus Christ (Rom. 8:1).

Paul affirmed that the era of the new covenant had dawned.
The era governed by this covenant surpasses the glory of the old
covenant because of the new work of the Spirit (2 Cor. 3:6—11).

In the span of redemptive history from Abraham to the present
one may observe the uninterrupted reign of the promise covenant.
Paul observed that this reign was unbroken by the ratification of
the Mosaic covenant (Gal. 3:17). The two covenantal instruments
existed side by side, fulfilling functions that were not in conflict.
Paul said, "Is the law, therefore, opposed to the promises of God?
Absolutely not!" (Gal. 3:21). The conclusion of this work is that the
law "was added" (v. 19) because of the transgressions of the ancient
Hebrews—their penchant to rebel against God. Therefore, the law
was a means of protection; it prescribed the general outlines of
obedience by which the nation would be preserved from social
decay and would fulfill the will of God. Because of the benign
influence of the law they would continue to enjoy a viable relationship to the promise, enjoying their status as God's treasured
possession and living in the land of promise.

It is not the law that Paul condemns; it is legalism. In the Pauline
theology legalism is dependence on works for the attainment of
righteousness. Legalism is a deadly error, for it gives no place to
the principle of faith which alone grants the inheritance (Gal. 3:18).

The New Covenant and the Promise

The New Covenant in Jeremiah

The days in which Jeremiah the prophet carried on his ministry
were filled with uncertainty and foreboding. The citizens of Judah,
like drowning men, grasped at every straw of hope, until at last
all failed and Judah succumbed to the might of Babylon.

Jeremiah laid the fault for Judah's demise not primarily with weak leaders or unwise international policies, but with the people, whom he regarded as having forsaken the Lord (2:1 – 3:5).

Jeremiah was to flee the Babylonian onslaught to live out his days in Egypt. But toward the close of his prophetic ministry he foresaw the ratification of a new covenant (Jer. 31:31 – 34). It was a prophecy that would bring a ray of hope to those unsettled times. It would find its ultimate realization in Christianity.

The promise and the new covenant of Jeremiah

The new covenant that Jeremiah envisioned, like the previous administrative covenants, serves to explicate the terms of the promise for those who are governed by it and to determine the nature of obedience essential to the maintenance of their relationship to the promise.

This covenant is rooted in hope. It emerges from a context in which Israel's glorious future is affirmed.

"The days are coming," declares the LORD, "when I will plant the house of Israel and the house of Judah with the offspring of men and of animals. Just as I watched over them to uproot and tear down, and to overthrow, destroy and bring disaster, so I will watch over them to build and to plant," declares the LORD. [Jer. 31:27 – 28]

These words serve to introduce the passage that announces the new covenant. In this passage Jeremiah depicts a time quite unlike the period in which he was living. Many of the people were about to be taken from their land and transported to Babylon, but the prophet envisioned a time of great repopulation. The long siege had brought economic ruin, but he affirmed a time of prosperity when there would be an abundance of livestock. The Lord had brought Israel to disaster, but he would eventually reverse his dealings with her and restore her fortunes.

This message of hope, indeed the greatest statement of hope in Jeremiah, answers to the theological emergency of the time.[23] The demise of the nation, the fall of the Davidic monarchy, and the capture of Jerusalem would undoubtedly raise questions in

23. Yehezkel Kaufmann refers to Jeremiah's prediction of the new covenant as "the jewel of his prophecy of consolation. . . ." *The Religion of Israel, From Its Beginnings to the Babylonian Exile*, trans. and abridged by Moshe Greenberg (Chicago: University of Chicago Press, 1960), p. 425.

the minds of the people relative to the promise. Has God forsaken
his promise because of the disobedience of the people? Is their
disobedience so acute that even God must turn from his promise
in disgust?

The prophet Jeremiah would hear no such thing. The promise
was still in effect.[24] God would still deal with Israel in love. Although this affirmation seemed to have little relevance to the citizens of Jerusalem, most of whom would die in a foreign land, it
nevertheless affirmed that God had not forsaken his people. Prophetic statements such as this served to maintain a remnant of
faithful people throughout the ages.

The new covenant of Jeremiah contains a number of terms common to both the Abrahamic and Davidic covenants. There is first
the element of the offspring. It has been noted that the earlier
statements of the promise in the Old Testament anticipate an offspring, a people of God to whom the blessings of the promise are
mediated. The concept of offspring is also inherent in the new
covenant:

> "The time is coming," declares the LORD,
> "when I will make a new covenant
> with the house of Israel
> and with the house of Judah." [31:31]

There is also a definite link with earlier statements concerning the
offspring in the words "I will be their God, and they will be my
people" (31:33; cf. Gen. 17:7 – 8; Exod. 6:7; 29:45; Lev. 26:12; Deut.
26:17 – 18).

Yet a number of important elements of the promise are con-
spicuously absent in Jeremiah 31:33 – 34. There is no reference to
the land, no reference to a spiritual relationship to God initiated
and sustained by faith, no reference to the individual offspring,
and no reference to Gentile inclusion in the blessing of the promise.
This need not militate against the contention that the new cove-

---

24. Claus Westermann states that "the real significance of the oracle concerning the
new covenant . . . lies in the fact that here the covenant is included in the promise." Since
a covenant can only be concluded, not promised, he writes, "With the inclusion of the
covenant in the promise the nature of the covenant was radically changed; it now means
the end of the previous history of God with his people." "The Way of the Promise through
the Old Testament," in *The Old Testament and Christian Faith*, ed. Bernard W. Anderson
(New York: Harper and Row, 1963), pp. 218 – 19.

nant is an expression of the promise, for Jeremiah's description of the benefits of the new covenant is not limited to this passage. In Jeremiah 32:36–41, the covenant is again referred to by the prophet. In verse 40 it is called an "everlasting covenant." This covenant is without doubt the new covenant of Jeremiah 31. The references to the fact that Yahweh would be their God (32:38) and to the renewed heart (32:39) are found in Jeremiah 31:33 as well. It is quite unlikely that Jeremiah envisioned two vaguely defined eschatological covenants with similar terms governing God's people and accomplishing the same redemptive acts. The emphasis on the eternality of the covenant in Jeremiah 32 is consonant with the eternality of the covenant in Jeremiah 31, for in 31:34, 36 the prophet declares that only when the heavens vanish will God forsake his promise. This emphasis on the everlasting nature of the covenant in Jeremiah 32:40 simply reveals a different dimension of the new covenant. It confirms to the faithful in Israel that the devastating results of the fall of Jerusalem (32:36) were not final.

The covenant of Jeremiah 32:36–41 affirms several aspects of the promise not cited in Jeremiah 31:33–34. One of these is the promise of the land, "I will rejoice in doing them good and will assuredly plant them in this land with all my heart and·soul" (32:41; cf. v. 37).

This statement of the covenant also affirms the necessity of a spiritual relationship to God that is unquestionably based on the obedience of his people, for God says, "They will always fear me" (v. 39).

The individual offspring, the Messiah, called "the Branch" by Jeremiah, is cited in 33:15. He is not specifically identified with the benefits of the new covenant, but his gracious work is clearly tied to the promise (33:14–15, 17). The prophet states that Israel and Judah are to dwell securely (lābeṭaḥ) in the days of the Branch (Jer. 33:16; cf. 23:6). This promise of security is also one of the blessings of the everlasting covenant of Jeremiah 32 (v. 37) where the same word (lābeṭaḥ) is used to describe the security of the people. Since this security is achieved by the regnal activity of the Branch, there is warrant for seeing the promise of the individual offspring reflected in the new covenant as well.

It appears from this study that Jeremiah understood the new covenant to be an expression of the eternal promise. Only the reference to Gentile inclusion is lacking covenantal expression. Yet

Jeremiah seems to imply that Gentiles would come to recognize the truth of Yahweh (16:19 – 20).

The terms of the new covenant in Jeremiah 31:31 – 34

The new covenant differs from the old covenant in several significant aspects. These differences are enunciated by Jeremiah in the terms of the new covenant cited in verses 33 and 34.

Obedience will be facilitated by a change in the nature of those who are included in the covenant. The description of the new covenant begins with a glance in two directions. Jeremiah looked ahead to the new covenant with its promise of better things, and back to the old covenant and the abject failure of the people under its administration. He said in 31:31 – 32:

> "The time is coming," declares the LORD,
> "when I will make a new covenant
> with the house of Israel
> and with the house of Judah.
> It will not be like the covenant
> I made with their forefathers
> when I took them by the hand
> to lead them out of Egypt,
> because they broke my covenant,
> though I was a husband to them,"
>
> declares the LORD.

A new covenant is to be made with Israel and Judah because they broke God's covenant. It is significant that Jeremiah attributed no fault to the old covenant. He did not speak of it in negative terms. It was the people who broke that covenant and rendered it void. This is consonant with the Pauline attitude toward the law.

Jeremiah was so far from attributing an inherent inadequacy to the regulations of the law that he affirmed the perpetuity of the law. He stated that the law (*tôrāh*) will be placed within the hearts of the people. Although it is possible that the prophet used the word *tôrāh* in the more general sense of the will of God, without reference to the Mosaic law, it is highly unlikely. He spoke not of a change in the nature of *tôrāh*, but of its localization. The covenant context of the passage would certainly lead Jeremiah's hearers to think in terms of the Mosaic legislation, and Jeremiah used the term *tôrāh* to refer to the statutes of the Mosaic covenant in every one of its occurrences in his prophecy.

The *tôrāh* was the revelation of God's will for his people. Conceived in this way, it could never be abrogated. The heart of the law was the expression of God's longing for holiness on the part of his people, his concern for their welfare, his desire to see their expression of love for him and their fellow man, and his affirmation of their election. These concepts have never been abrogated. The New Testament affirms that the forms and rituals of the law have faded into the realities they represented, but it does not claim that the monumental spiritual imperatives of the law have been set aside.

The first element of the new covenant guarantees obedience on the part of the people and thereby negates the possibility of invalidation of the covenant. Jeremiah said, " 'This is the covenant I will make with the house of Israel after that time,' declares the LORD. 'I will put my law in their minds and write it on their hearts' " (31:33).

It is inadequate to see Jeremiah's contrast between the two covenants solely as expressing the externality of the old covenant as opposed to the internality of the new covenant. The old covenant also had as its ideal an inward orientation of the law. Deuteronomy 6:6 states, "These commandments that I give you today are to be upon your hearts," and circumcision was ethical as well as physical under the old covenant (Deut. 10:16; 30:6). The primary reason for the abrogation of the old covenant was the failure of the people to receive the law into their hearts.

It is precisely this weakness that the new covenant overcomes because it promises a new heart, a responsive attitude to God's law. The prophet said, "I will give them singleness of heart and action, so that they will always fear me ..." (Jer. 32:39). Gerhard von Rad states the matter well: "What is here outlined is the picture of a new man, a man who is able to obey perfectly because of a miraculous change of his nature."[25]

The old covenant was external in the sense that God set it before the people so that they might receive it into their hearts and obey it. Under the new covenant the law is placed directly within the

---

25. Gerhard von Rad, *Old Testament Theology,* trans. D. M. G. Stalker, 2 vols. (New York: Harper, 1962 – 65), vol. 2, pp. 213 – 14.

heart. It thus becomes a motivating factor, the standard by which all actions are governed, the animating principle that produces genuine obedience.[26]

A divine-human relationship will be established.   The second term of the new covenant is expressed in the words "I will be their God, and they will be my people" (Jer. 31:33). We have found this element to be an important constituent of the Abrahamic, Davidic, and Mosaic covenants. It is the heart of the promise.

This element of the promise was reaffirmed to the Israelites when they were slaves in Egypt (Exod. 6:6 – 8). It guaranteed for them the manifestation of the divine might in leading them into the land of promise. It is like a golden thread woven into the tapestry of the law, glistening with hope even when hope seemed gone. The apostle Paul appealed to this great truth when he discussed the union that exists between God and the Christian (2 Cor. 6:16). And in the Book of Revelation a great voice proclaims the ancient covenant promise again, announcing its final fulfillment for the people of God (Rev. 21:3).

This element of the new covenant was also an integral part of the old covenant. The Lord wished to establish a relationship with his people, but their disobedience to the covenant stipulations nullified the promises contained in the covenant. The new covenant, however, is eternal (Jer. 32:40) and guarantees the obedience of its participants. It thus secures the promises for the covenant community.

The participants in the covenant will have a new relationship with God.   Jeremiah went on to say, "No longer will a man teach his neighbor, or a man his brother, saying, 'Know the LORD,' because they will all know me, from the least of them to the greatest" (31:34).

This does not mean that instruction in the knowledge of God will be abolished under the new covenant. The prophet is not speaking of theoretical knowledge but of the inward, personal re-

26. R. Nixon notes, "Yet the highest form of ethical conduct comes not so much from obeying what comes from outside as from responding in a spirit of love, inspired by gratitude to God and a sense of relationship to him, to the inward impulses which he implants in us (Je 31:31 – 34; Ho 6:6). This is the fruit of the new covenant." "Fulfilling the Law: The Gospels and Acts," in *Law, Morality and the Bible: A Symposium,* ed. Bruce Kaye and Gordon Wenham (Downers Grove, Ill.: Inter-Varsity, 1978), p. 57.

lationship with God inherent in the word *know*. Under the old covenant the knowledge of God was communicated by priests and prophets, and his grace was received by the people only through these mediators. Under the new covenant the believer's relationship with God is immediate and therefore different from the believer's relationship with God under the old covenant.

The emphasis on the abolition of a mediatorial function under the new covenant is heightened by the words "they will all know me, from the least of them to the greatest." All who are under the administration of this covenant enjoy the same inward experience of grace, regardless of their station in life or their position in the service of God.

This promise calls to mind the prophecy of Joel 2:28 – 29:

> "And afterward,
>   I will pour out my Spirit on all people.
> Your sons and daughters will prophesy,
>   your old men will dream dreams,
>   your young men will see visions.
> Even on my servants, both men and women,
>   I will pour out my Spirit in those days."

Here, as in Jeremiah 31:34, a prophet envisions a universal relationship of the people of God with the Holy Spirit. The Spirit will no longer be poured out only on select individuals but on all, no matter their age, sex, or station.

The prophet Jeremiah pictured the same great era as Joel, when even the most lowly believer will have the same rights of access to God as did the prophets who ministered under the old covenant.

God will no longer remember the sins of his people.

> "For I will forgive their wickedness
>   and will remember their sins no more." [Jer. 31:34]

This gracious promise is connected to the foregoing material by the particle *kî* (for) and establishes the basis on which God will effect the inward change of heart by which they become God's people.

Jeremiah did not deny that sin was forgiven under the old covenant. The word used here for "forgive" (*sālaḥ*) is used throughout the Old Testament. The great difference is in the fact that God will not remember their sin. It is this blotting out of sin that is a characteristic of the new covenant.

The act of remembering in the Old Testament involves much more than simply recalling something. It often connotes appropriate and obligatory action. God will remember his covenant and never again use a flood as judgment (Gen. 9:15). The people are to remember God's commands and obey them (Num. 15:39). Abigail's discreet request that David remember her (1 Sam. 25:31) was in actuality a request for his favor when he became king. When God remembers sin he is obligated to punish it. Hosea declared that God remembered the sin of Israel and would bring destruction (7:2; see also vv. 12 – 16; 8:13). And Jeremiah said, "He will now remember their wickedness and punish them for their sins" (14:10).

Because God will no longer remember sin under the new covenant, the threat of punishment is eliminated and the covenant will never be broken. It was Israel's sin that separated her from the realization of the promise under the old covenant and which rendered the old covenant ineffectual. But under the new covenant the grace of God will abound in justification for the sinner. F. F. Bruce observes, "If men's sins are remembered by God, His holiness must take action against them; if they are not remembered, it is because His grace has determined to forgive them— not in spite of His holiness, but in harmony with it."[27]

The promise of the new covenant is one of the high points of redemptive history. Its importance cannot be minimized. It stands above the abject failure of God's ancient people and points to a time when God will transform the rebellious heart by his sovereign grace. Its words were spoken when Judah was crumbling and the people were about to be led captive. The national blessing promised by the old covenant seemed now a hollow mockery, but the words of Jeremiah would continue to ring in the ears of the humble believers in Judah and they knew that a new and different era would dawn one day.

The new covenant affirms God's faithfulness to his promise and provides the theological ground for the blessings of justification by faith. It envisions that great day when in the dusk of an upper

---

27. F. F. Bruce, *The Epistle to the Hebrews*, New International Commentary on the New Testament series (Grand Rapids: Eerdmans, 1964), p. 175.

room the words were spoken, "This cup is the new covenant in my blood."

The New Covenant in Ezekiel

Ezekiel's vision of the restoration of Israel also involved a covenant between God and his people (16:60 − 63; 34:25 − 31; 37:26 − 28). Ezekiel calls this covenant an everlasting covenant (16:60; 37:26).

The elements of the promise are clearly set forth in Ezekiel's new covenant. The promise of security in the land is affirmed by the prophet in 34:27; it is set in the context of covenant in verse 25. The corporate concept of the offspring is found in the reference to the people in 34:22 − 24. The individualistic aspect of the promise of the offspring is found in the ascription of the name *David* to the Messiah (v. 23). This ascription also calls to mind the promises given to David in 2 Samuel 7. The promise that the Lord would be their God and they his people occurs in verses 30 − 31.

In chapter 37 Ezekiel again refers to this covenant. It is placed in a Davidic context (v. 24), as was the previous description of the covenant. It includes security in the land (v. 25), the concept of the offspring being fulfilled in the Davidic Messiah (v. 25), the concept of numerous offspring (v. 26), and the unique relationship of God to his people (v. 27).

The promise of Gentile inclusion is not clearly set forth in the everlasting covenant of Ezekiel, but it may be present in 36:23 where Ezekiel refers to the vindication of the name of the Lord among the house of Israel and says, "Then the nations will know that I am the LORD. . . ." It is not certain that this refers to a future conversion of Gentiles, but it certainly reflects a change in their attitude toward Yahweh. This is not set in a context where the covenant is specifically cited, but the covenant promises of the offspring (36:9 − 11) and the land (36:24) are clearly present.

The everlasting covenant of Ezekiel, like the new covenant of Jeremiah 31:31 − 34, also promises forgiveness of sin (16:63). And, as the law was to be placed in the heart, according to Jeremiah, so in Ezekiel's covenant a new heart and a new spirit were promised (36:27). Obedience would be facilitated not by a new code of laws, but by the Holy Spirit. The words of Ezekiel in 36:27 are unsurpassed in the Prophets, "And I will put my Spirit in you and move you to follow my decrees and be careful to keep my laws."

This is the promise of the new covenant of Jeremiah and the precursor of the blessings of the Spirit that play such an important role in the exposition of the gospel in the Pauline theology. Just as the new covenant of Jeremiah promised the facilitation of obedience by the internalization of the law, so the new covenant of Ezekiel would secure obedience through the presence of God's Spirit in the heart.

The New Covenant in Isaiah

Isaiah spoke of the new covenant in 61:8. It is called an everlasting covenant, as it is in Ezekiel. It too includes elements of the promise. The offspring are cited in verse 9 and that verse foresees their great blessing.

The prophet emphasized another aspect of the covenant in 42:6 and 49:8. In both passages the servant himself is called a covenant. The latter verse appears to refer to the servant as an individual, not as the nation.[28] The elements of the promise apparent in this context are the restoration to the land (49:8), the people as the offspring (49:8, 12), and Gentile salvation (49:6).

The reference to the servant as a covenant is a unique concept in the Old Testament.[29] It evidently means that the servant would function as does a covenant. The covenant in view here is best understood as the promise-oath, which is called a covenant in Genesis 15:18. It is the terms of that promise that are mentioned. The promise-oath secured the terms inherent in it and promised a bright future for the offspring.

If the servant is to function as a covenant, then he will secure those promises that effect the realization of the inheritance of God's people. The promise is to be fulfilled in him. He realizes the promise of the land and he is the instrument that assures the inclusion of Gentiles in the promised inheritance.

This very personal concept of covenant may be reflected in the theology of Paul, where he spoke of the blessings of the new covenant in terms of "Spirit." In 2 Corinthians 3:5 — 18 Paul contrasted the new covenant with the old covenant and in the course of his

---

28. Compare the earlier discussion of the servant songs in Isaiah.

29. For a discussion of the function of Christ as a covenant, see Robertson, *The Christ of the Covenants*, pp. 271 — 300.

exposition said, "Now the Lord is the Spirit, and where the Spirit of the Lord is, there is freedom" (v. 17). The blessings of the new covenant, which are blessings of the "Spirit," are effected by Christ. This personal concept of covenant is thus similar to that of the function of the servant in the everlasting covenant of Isaiah.

Conclusion

The covenantal formulation of the promise in the time of Abraham marked a monumental event in the biblical record of divine activity. From that moment on, the promise became a *běrît* that the Lord swore to uphold eternally. The promise covenant found expression not only in its patriarchal formulation, but in the Mosaic and new covenants as well. The promise is expressed in administrative covenants that define its terms and govern obedience.

The law is viewed in the Old Testament not as a burdensome institution, but as the structure that gave protection to the promise. It thus had an integral relationship with the continuing welfare of the nation.

The preceding discussion has led to the conclusion that the view of the law in the New Testament is not different from that of the Old Testament. The apparently negative statements of Paul are directed against a legalistic use of law that made it an end in itself. The law is to be honored and obeyed as it finds expression in the new covenant. Gone are the trappings of an older age, but the great ethical requirements of the law found expression in the teaching of Jesus and Paul. It thus has a continuing role. It no longer condemns the believer. Now that the era of the new covenant has dawned, God's righteous demands are met by the believer as he walks in the freedom of the Spirit.

This establishes an element of continuity between the Mosaic covenant and the new covenant. But a strong element of discontinuity exists in Jesus' attitude toward certain aspects of the law. He could utilize his authority over the law to abrogate the dietary regulations. When the believer looks to Christ he finds him upholding the great ethical demands of the law, but the believer learns that certain aspects of the law do not apply now that Christ has explained the law for the new age of the Spirit.

In the Pauline theology of law a continuity exists between the

Mosaic and new covenants as well. Paul honored the law. He stated that the law is good (Rom. 7:7 – 13; 1 Tim. 1:8). He called Christians to observe the law expressed in Leviticus 19:18 (Gal. 5:13 – 15) and to honor their parents (Exod. 20:12; Eph. 6:2).

Yet there is discontinuity as well. In Paul, the major difference between the two covenantal eras dominated by Moses and Christ is the mode of obedience. In the new covenant the heart of the individual has been revolutionized by the new work of the Holy Spirit, and thus valid obedience is facilitated. In this way Paul stood in the mainstream of the prophets Isaiah, Jeremiah, Ezekiel, and Joel, who foresaw the new age in which the Spirit would be manifested in a new way.

Paul saw faith as an operating principle in the old covenant; he even saw Christ present in the law. If Christ was not seen there by Paul's compatriots it was not the fault of the law; it was because a veil was over their faces.

Believers may look to the law in the Old Testament and find the bold outlines by which they may continue to find satisfaction in the joyous obedience to the expression of the divine will found there. Jesus' explanation of the law did not abrogate all of the law; it exposed the law's heart and purpose. The application of the commandments to life will not bring salvation, but it continues to impart wisdom and happiness. There is deep satisfaction in life when the principles of the law are applied to marriage, inter-personal relationships, rearing children—indeed, to all the areas to which the law speaks. If our understanding of the Pauline view of the law is correct, Paul honored the law and said that he was a slave to it.

It is also evident from this study that the new covenant is not absolutely different from the Mosaic covenant. There is an integral relationship to the promise in each of those covenants. Although certain aspects of the law are not carried over into the new cove-nant, the spirit of obedience that the law sought to foster is nur-tured in the teaching of Christ. He adapted the law to the new era in redemptive history. The major difference between the two cove-nants is in the new relationship of God to his people expressed in the new covenant. This relationship facilitates obedience by the gracious work of God which it expresses and guarantees.

We must not think of the adminstrative covenants as distinct components lacking any relationship one to the other. They administer aspects of God's redemptive activity, but they are not administrative categories that are completely isolated one from the other.

Their function is to provide a covenantal context for the promise and to administer obedience to God. It is difficult to conclude that the new covenant represents an absolute break with the preceding covenantal eras, but it does represent an era of gracious divine activity that causes the old covenant to pale before it.

APPENDIX 1

The Law
in the Teaching
of Jesus

The Incident in the Grainfield: Matthew 12:1–8; Mark 2:23–28; Luke 6:1–5

These passages record the criticism of the Pharisees when Jesus' disciples picked grain on the Sabbath. Jesus responded first by referring to the time when David and his companions ate the consecrated bread because they were hungry (1 Sam. 21:1–6). There is a broad spectrum of views on Jesus' allusion to David's act. One approach is to conclude that Jesus was teaching that humanitarian principles take precedence over the ceremonial law.[30] Another is that David functions as a type of Jesus. If David could reinterpret the law as he did when he provisioned his men with the consecrated bread, then Jesus, the antitype, must have greater authority over the law because he is greater than David.[31]

Humanitarian concerns cannot be eliminated from this account. Even though a reference to the hunger of the disciples may be found only in Matthew,[32] there is a strong possibility that this concept underlies the recounting of the event in Mark and Luke

30. See, for example, H. Anderson, *The Gospel of Mark*, New Century Bible (London: Oliphants, 1976), p. 110.

31. R. T. France, *Jesus and the Old Testament* (Downer's Grove, Ill.: Inter-Varsity, 1971), pp. 46–47.

32. Willy Rordorff argues that the use of the word *hungry* by Matthew is an effort on his part to "assimilate the story . . . to the quotation from Scripture." *Sunday*, trans. A. A. K. Graham (Philadelphia: Westminster, 1968), p. 6. But see the comments in D. A. Carson, ed., *From Sabbath to Lord's Day: A Biblical, Historical, and Theological Investigation* (Grand Rapids: Zondervan, 1982), p. 62.

as well. The reference to the hunger of David and his men in all three accounts may be sufficient to establish an analogical relationship between the two events. The words, "Have you never read what David did when he and his companions were hungry and in need?" (Mark 2:25) may imply that Jesus' disciples were also hungry.[33]

The eating of the consecrated bread is pronounced unlawful in all three Synoptics, yet it was used by Jesus in support of the disciples' actions. This does not permit the conclusion that Jesus' reference to David meant that David's act would have been in violation only of the rigid oral interpretation of the Pharisees. David violated a ceremonial law.

The second allusion to the Old Testament in the Matthean pericope is to the profaning of the Sabbath by priests who perform temple duties on that day (12:5). The reference is to passages such as Numbers 28:9–10, where the law provided for such observances on the Sabbath. The conclusion of Jesus, as presented by Matthew, must be understood against the background of these two allusions and the three sayings that follow.[34]

The common element in the two allusions is that the law was not regarded in the Old Testament as being so rigid that it would tolerate absolutely no deviation from its standards. It was not a cruel taskmaster that punished those who violated its demands, no matter how slightly. In the case of David, Ahimelech the priest did not raise a serious objection (1 Sam. 21:4), and the allusion to the temple service on the Sabbath shows that the law was not absolutely rigid in its regulations relating to the Sabbath.

It seems best to interpret the pericope on the basis of this common element. Several approaches to this passage take into account mainly the allusion to David. Typical of this approach is the

33. It is not necessary to hold that Mark presupposes a different infraction of the law from Matthew because he says the disciples *ērxanto hodon poiein* (began to make a way). The phrase may connote walking along. C. E. B. Cranfield draws attention to a similar phrase in classical Greek which means "to journey." *The Gospel According to Mark* (Cambridge: At the University Press, 1959), p. 114. Anderson points out that as "the episode develops, it is 'reaping' and eating corn on the sabbath that constitutes the disciples' offence. . . ." *The Gospel of Mark*, p. 109.

34. The authenticity of these sayings has been questioned by a number of scholars on various grounds. For a summary of their views and a cogent discussion of the relationship of these sayings to their contexts, see Carson, *From Sabbath to Lord's Day*, pp. 60–69.

view that David functions as a type of Christ, and Jesus' conclusion is that one has come who has greater authority over the law.[35] This certainly is inherent in Jesus' argument, but it centers on only one Old Testament allusion, and one may wonder whether the typological relationship intended is not really between Jesus and the temple (v. 6), rather than Jesus and David.[36] The two allusions have one thrust in common; the ceremonial laws were not so inflexible that they stood in the way of service to God and the exercise of human compassion.

This is amplified by one of the sayings reported by Matthew. It is the quotation from Hosea 6:6, " 'I desire mercy, not sacrifice.' " This quotation (v. 7) places the teaching of Jesus squarely in the mainstream of Old Testament prophetic proclamation. Jesus' view of the law may be understood by the prophetic view. The prophets honored the law and called for obedience to it. They denounced a strict adherence to the ceremonial aspects of the law which did not issue from true heartfelt obedience. The law called for love to God and one's fellow man. The prophets observed that sacrifice was rigidly practiced by the people, but societal wrongs were prevalent. This was not an expression of the covenantal religion desired by Yahweh.

It is difficult to assert that the prophets advocated the abolition of sacrifice as an institution in the worship of Yahweh.[37] They were concerned with a proper balance between the two, just as Jesus was. Jesus did not urge the abolition of ceremonial observance, but he did urge that it not be at the expense of love and concern. He said of the Pharisaical administration of the tithe that they "should have practiced the latter, without neglecting the for-

35. France, *Jesus and the Old Testament*, pp. 46–47.

36. R. Banks counters the typological approach by noting that "nowhere else in the gospels does Jesus portray himself as David's successor, and here the emphasis is upon the authority exercised rather than status possessed." *Jesus and the Law in the Synoptic Tradition* (Cambridge: At the University Press, 1975), p. 115.

37. Samuel said, "To obey is better than sacrifice ..." (1 Sam. 15:22), yet he officiated at the sacrifice (1 Sam. 9:13). The comment of H. H. Rowley is significant: "It has been maintained that the sacrificial ritual of Israel was essentially of Canaanite origin ... I have more than once offered my reasons for dissenting from the common view. In passages of greater antiquity than the time of Amos we find references to sacrifices in the time of Moses, and if Amos and Jeremiah had wished to challenge this tradition they would have done so more directly than by a rhetorical question and a passing allusion." *The Faith of Israel: Aspects of Old Testament Thought* (Philadelphia: Westminster, 1957), pp. 92–93.

mer," that is, "the more important matters of the law—justice, mercy and faithfulness" (Matt. 23:23).

There is a hierarchy in the values of the law, according to Jesus, and that hierarchy is evident in the two allusions to the Old Testament made by him. The Pharisees had distorted this hierarchy. By their structured observances, the light of love that shines at the heart of the law was ever being dimmed, threatening the supreme purpose of God for his people. Yahweh wanted worship, not legalistic, unmeaning ritual, but a loving response of the human heart over which he reigns and in which his character finds expression in deeds of compassion.

The allusion to Hosea 6:6 is preceded in this pericope by the saying "one greater than the temple is here" (v. 6). Jesus does not say that one greater than David is here. He affirms his superiority to the temple regulations, and hence to the ceremonial law. It is a matter of authority that is central here. R. T. France observes that the allusion to David "is not simply an appeal to precedent. . . . It is a question of authority."[38]

Is Jesus thus teaching that the ceremonial law could be broken by anyone where humanitarian concerns are in question? It seems not. He gives that authority only to himself. He advocated the ceremonial law. We have seen that he said the tithe should have been observed, but not at the expense of love. If Jesus were asserting that the ceremonial law could be broken by individuals whenever a judgment was made that human need predominated, all sorts of subjective judgments could lead to the dissolution of law.

Jesus did not delegate the authority for interpreting the law to mankind. He kept it for himself. He demonstrated that the law fostered mercy and justice, but he said he was "Lord of the Sabbath" (v. 8).

This saying that Jesus is Lord of the Sabbath must be examined in the fuller context of the Markan pericope where it is connected to the words "The Sabbath was made for man, not man for the Sabbath."[39] These words are followed by "So (hōste) the Son of Man is Lord even of the Sabbath."

38. France, *Jesus and the Old Testament*, p. 46.

39. See the similar saying attributed to Rabbi Simon ben Menasiah, "The Sabbath is given to you but you are not surrendered to the Sabbath." *Mekilta de-Rabbi Ishmael*, Tractate Shabbata, I; 27, 28, 43, 44.

This saying asserts that man was not made for the Sabbath, that is, the Sabbath did not exist as an inviolable entity at creation solely for which man was made. Man was not created to be subservient to the Sabbath. The Sabbath is not to be regarded as lord over mankind, punishing when one fails to meet its demands. The Sabbath was made for man. It is to be his delight. It is to be used for his benefit and honored by him because it was given to man by God. But it is not to be a taskmaster that exacts such unswerving obedience that it loses its purpose as a beneficial observance given from a loving God.

Isaiah affirmed this:

> If you keep your feet from breaking the Sabbath
>   and from doing as you please on my holy day,
> if you call the Sabbath a delight
>   and the LORD's holy day honorable,
> and if you honor it by not going your own way
>   and not doing as you please or speaking idle words,
> then you will find your joy in the LORD,
>   and I will cause you to ride on the heights of the land
>   and to feast on the inheritance of your father Jacob. [58:13 – 14]

If the Sabbath is not lord of man, is man then lord of the Sabbath? If the Sabbath was made for man, has man the right to set himself up as an authority over the Sabbath, and, by extension, over the whole law? Do love and humanitarian concerns, all vital aspects of the law, negate other written commands? The syllogism suggested by Jesus' statement may seem to call for affirmative answers to these questions; the Sabbath is not lord of man, man is lord of the Sabbath. But Jesus affirms that man's lordship of the Sabbath is not his by inherent right, but by right of representation. It is not man who is lord of the Sabbath, but "the Son of Man." Man has this right only in his supreme representative, the Lord Jesus Christ, who became the Son of Man by sharing our humanity.[40] By virtue of the title *Son of Man,* Jesus established not only

---

40. The understanding of the title *Son of man* to refer to Jesus' identification with mankind may appear to be at variance with the usage of this title in Daniel. I. Howard Marshall notes that the application of the term *Son of man* to mankind "conflicts to some extent with the usual significance of the Son of Man as a heavenly figure." *Luke: Historian and Theologian,* Contemporary Evangelical Perspectives series (Grand Rapids: Zondervan, 1971), p. 232. However, our understanding of the term should be based pri-

his role as representative of mankind, but his authority over the law as well. In the teaching of Jesus that emerged from this encounter with the Pharisees, he affirmed, both in historical allusion and reference to the law itself, that the ceremonial regulations were not to stifle the law's concern for the expression of human compassion.

The primary thrust of the account, as it is expressed in all three Synoptics, is the authority of Jesus over the law. He is its authoritative exponent. He did not abrogate the Sabbath, but placed the current Sabbath observance against the background of the practice of the law in the Old Testament itself and demonstrated the lack of consonance of that observance with the spirit of the law; in that way he countered the Pharisees. Jesus' expression of the law represents its true spirit and original intent. The Pharisees represent an aberration in the long history of the reign of law. They destroyed its purpose and rendered the law ineffectual by their attention to minute detail. They occupied themselves with its details so much that they lost sight of its meaning. Jesus, in his two allusions to the Old Testament, presented a panorama that extended from the Pentateuch to Samuel and showed that the Pharisaical attitude toward the disciples eating grain on the Sabbath was not in keeping with the heart of the law.

A number of principles emerge from this study of the incident in the grainfield. They relate to the law as a whole. Even though the Sabbath is the only aspect of the law to figure in this incident, it reflects Jesus' attitude to the law in general. Jesus' understanding of the Sabbath law must color his attitude to the whole law.

The first principle is that the Sabbath was meant to be a delight to mankind. The rigid oral interpretation of the Pharisees may well have made the Sabbath a burden. It was a violation of the spirit of the law which legislated the Sabbath for man's joy. The oral traditions had gone beyond the original intent of the law. The law which was meant to benefit Israel and promote the type of obe-

marily on Jesus' use of it. In Mark 10:42−45 the term is applied by Jesus to his role as servant. See also Mark 8:31; 9:31. Richard N. Longenecker observes, "What Jesus was evidently telling his disciples ... was that his person and ministry are not to be defined according to popular Jewish expectations of Messiahship ... but rather that he should be understood first of all in terms of his redemptive identification with men and his sufferings for men." " 'Son of Man' Imagery: Some Implications for Theology and Discipleship," *JETS* 18 (1975): 13.

dience that would guarantee the realization of the promise had become a maze of minute stipulations. Jesus denounced this; the Sabbath was made for man.

Second, Jesus established his authority over the law. We are thus led to expect an authoritative interpretation of the law on the part of Jesus. But, if he is lord of the law, he has the authority to make changes within that law. To be sure, Jesus was countering oral tradition in the discourse with the Pharisees, but he included the Mosaic law in his discussion when he said he is lord of the Sabbath. As lord of the Sabbath and hence the law, it is his prerogative to interpret and even modify the law so as to make it applicable to the new era in redemptive history instituted by him.

We are not surprised then to learn of the abrogation of the food laws in the early Christian church (Acts 10:9–16; 11:1–18; cf. Mark 7:18–19); nor are we surprised to observe certain modifications in the law as interpreted by Jesus. These will be discussed subsequently.

We cannot conclude that Jesus abrogated the Sabbath principle; he opposed the prevalent oral tradition concerning the regulation of the Sabbath.

It is not humanitarian interests that relate to abrogation or modification of a commandment. The law of love does not supersede written commandment. The sole authority over the law is Christ, the lord of the Sabbath.

The Healing of the Man in the Synagogue: Matthew 12:9–14; Mark 3:1–6; Luke 6:6–11

A prevalent interpretation of Jesus' teaching in this incident is that "doing good" is a fundamental requirement of God, and the law may be broken in cases where the paramount virtue of human good will be achieved.[41]

Another view is that Jesus is interpreting the law of the Sabbath and delineating what the Old Testament Sabbath law actually entailed.[42]

---

41. B. H. Branscomb, *Jesus and the Law of Moses* (New York: R. R. Smith, 1930), p. 148; Anderson, *The Gospel of Mark*, pp. 113–14.

42. Marshall comments, "Jesus relates the institution of the Sabbath to the good purpose of God for men which lay behind it and hence to the principle of love for each other which ought to characterise their use of it." *Luke*, p. 235.

The latter interpretation is better supported by the context. The question of lawful Sabbath observance is underscored by Jesus' question, "Which is lawful on the Sabbath . . . ?" This concept is common to all three accounts (Mark 3:4; Luke 6:9; cf. Matt. 12:12).

Rather than allowing that the law may be breached for humanitarian purposes, Jesus is asserting that "doing good" is lawful on the Sabbath. It is an integral part of the fabric of the law.

The Pharisees allowed certain situations to override the law,[43] but Jesus' action affirmed that general deeds of love and kindness are not unlawful. Once again Jesus demonstrated that the law has as its chief concern the good of mankind.

The More Important Matters of the Law: Matthew 23:23 – 24; Luke 11:42 – 44

When Jesus accused the Pharisees of neglecting "the more important matters of the law—justice, mercy and faithfulness," he did not assert that these ethical demands of the law superseded or abrogated all others. He referred to the detailed administration of the law of the tithe on the part of the Pharisees (Matt. 23:23; Luke 11:42) and said they should have practiced the tithe, but not to the neglect of the law of love.

There are several important observations to be made here. First, Jesus did not regard all the commandments to be of equal weight or value. Clearly, the ethical requirements of the law are of greater importance in his teaching. Second, Jesus taught that the practice of no single commandment should jeopardize the law of love which is at the heart of the law. He said, "You should have practiced the latter, without neglecting the former" (Matt. 23:23; Luke 11:42). The ceremonial aspects of the law should have been carried on in the law of love which shines at the center of the law and which radiates out through all the legal regulations, no matter how minute or mundane.

The Sermon on the Mount: Matthew 5:17 – 48

The saying in Matthew 5:17 – 18 evinces a very high regard for the Old Testament on the part of Jesus. He said he came not to

43. Sabbath 18:3 allows midwives to deliver and permits performance of the rite of circumcision on the Sabbath. Yoma 8:6 states that the Sabbath law is superseded in instances where life is endangered.

abolish (*katalusai*) the Law and the Prophets but to fulfill (*plērōsai*) them (v. 17). The so-called "antitheses" that follow in the discourse seem to be in sharp contrast to this statement. There, Jesus seems to expand, deepen, or even modify certain aspects of the Mosaic law.

It is clear that much of the sermon is a reaction against Pharisaical misinterpretation,[44] but, in the section of the discourse in which Jesus deals with divorce, there appears to be a break with Moses. Jesus allowed for divorce only on the basis of unfaithfulness (vv. 31 – 32). In the section of the law to which Jesus referred (Deut. 24:1 – 4) divorce is not prohibited. Jesus' teaching on divorce is more rigid than that of the law.

The Pharisees recognized the difference between Jesus and Moses on this issue and used it in a dispute with Jesus (Mark 10:2 – 9). They said, "Moses permitted a man to write a certificate of divorce and send her away" (v. 4). Jesus responded by saying, "It was because your hearts were hard that Moses wrote you this law" (v. 5). He then referred to God's original intent as evidenced in the creation (vv. 6 – 9).

Jesus regarded the Mosaic tradition on divorce as a concession. He departed from a statute of Moses, but it was not a departure from divine law; it was a recognition of the divine law. He used his authority to modify the ancient law to more accurately express the divine will.

Another statement of Jesus must be considered here. Even though it does not occur in the Sermon on the Mount, it is of a similar type. In Mark 7:18, Jesus affirmed that it is not what goes into a person that defiles the person. This was later understood to refer to the abolition of the dietary regulations: "In saying this, Jesus declared all foods 'clean' " (v. 19).

Even if one regards the latter statement as a redactive intrusion that applies Jesus' saying to the practice of the early Christian community,[45] it cannot be denied that his words have a direct bearing on the dietary regulations of the law and the concept of defilement inherent in them. I. Howard Marshall says, "By this

---

44. R. Laird Harris, *Inspiration and Canonicity of the Bible: An Historical and Exegetical Study* (Grand Rapids: Zondervan, 1957), pp. 46 – 57.

45. There is no cogent reason why this cannot be Mark's own comment. William L. Lane says, "It represents Mark's interpretation of the word and explanation of Jesus." *The Gospel According to Mark*, New International Commentary on the New Testament series (Grand Rapids: Eerdmans, 1974), p. 256.

declaration Jesus rendered obsolete all distinctions between clean and unclean foods, vessels and people. A whole section of Old Testament legislation, which had served a purpose in its time was thus 'fulfilled' and finished by Jesus."[46]

Yet, in spite of this, Jesus did not terminate the law. It would be wrong to assert that he made an absolute break with the law or that his teaching bore no relationship to it. He affirmed that he did not come to abolish it (v. 17). An examination of the Sermon on the Mount shows that the great ethical demands of the law are a vital part of Jesus' teaching. For example, he condemned murder and adultery as the law did, but he exposed the heart of the law and showed that its true intent was to promote love. He instilled the law with life and rescued it from the hands of the Pharisees whose caricature of the law had robbed it of its original glory as the guarantor of blessing in the promise.

Once again Jesus is pictured as the absolute authority over the law. He could pronounce one segment a concession and could abrogate another. Jesus' teaching, when compared with the law, evinces both continuity and discontinuity with that law.

The apparent abrogation of aspects of the ceremonial law, such as the dietary regulations and the Levitical sacrifices, raises the problem of how this may be understood in view of Jesus' statement that "not the smallest letter" would pass from the law until everything is accomplished (Matt. 5:18). This is a difficult problem that permits no easy answers. Complex questions of redaction criticism as well as exegesis are involved that cannot be explored here.

It seems best to attempt a resolution of the problem on the basis of the concept of "fulfillment," a concept that figures prominently in Jesus' discourse. Basic to the understanding of history in the Old Testament was the consciousness that history was a theological record of divine activity. But there is a prophetic perspective to history as well. F. Foulkes has demonstrated how both law and history point to the future, giving us the immutable principles on which God acts.[47] The Law can be fulfilled as well as the Prophets. This is confirmed by Matthew himself in 11:13, where he speaks of the law prophesying until John.

The use of "fulfill" on the part of Jesus in Matthew 5:17 heralds,

46. I. Howard Marshall, *St. Mark* (London: Scripture Union, 1968), p. 27.
47. F. Foulkes, *The Acts of God* (London: Tyndale, 1955), pp. 9–22.

in a sense, the dawn of eschatological fulfillment. The goal of the law, the righteousness it reflected, is now available in Christ.

The passing ceremonies have not been abrogated in Christ; they have been fulfilled, in that they have found their eschatological realization. Old Testament history moved forward to a goal. Foulkes shows how historical events in the Old Testament pointed forward to greater and more glorious divine acts, many of which are realized in Christ.[48] R. Banks observes, "The prophetic teachings point forward (principally) to the actions of Christ and have been realised in them in an incomparably greater way. The Mosaic laws pointed forward (principally) to the teachings of Christ and have also been realised in them in a more profound manner. The word 'fulfill' in 5:17, then, includes not only an element of discontinuity (that which has now been realised transcends the Law) but an element of continuity as well (that which transcends the Law is nevertheless something to which the Law itself pointed forward)."[49]

It may be said that the law finds its realization in Christ and is thus fulfilled. It is not difficult to understand how the Levitical sacrifices found their goal in Christ and were fulfilled in his sacrifice. It is more difficult to understand how the dietary regulations are continued principally in the new covenant. Perhaps they find their fulfillment in the exhortations to moral purity and discrimination in ethical and moral decisions. The dietary laws as practiced in the Old Testament, if not severely modified, would have created a chasm between Jew and Gentile that would belie the spirit of that covenant in which Gentiles have found participation in the promise. Gentiles were urged by Paul to avoid the immoral practices that characterized the lifestyles of non-Jews in his time. They were to discriminate between what was clean and unclean, but the potentially divisive dietary regulations were not to be observed in the same way as they were in the Old Testament.

The word *fulfill* thus does not connote the concept of absolute termination.[50] Jesus did not sever his relationship to the law. He fulfilled the law. That is, the law found its goal in Christ and his

---

48. Ibid., pp. 23 – 33.

49. Banks, *Jesus and the Law*, p. 210.

50. F. V. Filson explains "fulfill" in this context to mean that Jesus' teaching "gives the fullest expression to the divine intent in the ancient utterances. The changes he makes are conservative, true to the aim of Scripture; they more clearly express the full purpose and will of God." *A Commentary on the Gospel According to St. Matthew*, 2d ed. (London: A. and C. Black, 1971), p. 83.

teaching is the consummate expression of the meaning of the law and its outworking in the life.

If Jesus pronounced an aspect of the law a concession for the time, he was by no means abrogating the whole law, nor was he affirming that his teaching concerning divorce is a new standard that replaces the old. The very point of his statement is that his teaching is not new; it has always been the divine plan.

Jesus was illuminating and explicating the law. As the supreme teacher of the law he asserted that the peculiar circumstances of Moses' day warranted somewhat different regulations concerning divorce. These were not the perfect expression of God's will. Jesus' teaching on divorce reflected the will of God in this respect and thus the divine will was upheld.

This view does not render the Old Testament invalid for the Christian. The heart of the law—the great ethical concern of the law—still calls the Christian to obedience. Jesus and the New Testament writers constantly appealed to the Old Testament as God's authoritative word. The interpreter of the Old Testament will proclaim its ethical imperatives with the same zeal with which he proclaims the imperatives of the New Testament. They have not been abrogated. The aspects of the law that were distinctly for the Mosaic era will be seen as vessels filled with spiritual truth that foresee their eschatological realization in Christ. Thus, an apologetic element is added to Christian proclamation.

However one approaches the question of the continuing validity of the law, it is difficult to affirm an absolute break between Jesus and the law. The continuing validity of the law is established in the words *until heaven and earth disappear* (v. 18).[51] Jesus upheld the law, but it was the law freed from circumstances and conditions that had relevance only to the Mosaic period and which would not be appropriate to the age of the new covenant with its once-for-all sacrifice and its righteousness in Christ.[52]

51. For a discussion of the continuing validity of the law see Gerhard Barth, "Matthew's Understanding of the Law," in *Tradition and Interpretation in Matthew*, trans. Percy Scott (Philadelphia: Westminster, 1963), pp. 62–75; William Barclay, "New Wine in Old Wineskins," *ET* 86 (1974–75): 100–103.

52. The writer acknowledges his indebtedness in this section to an unpublished paper on Jesus and the law by Douglas J. Moo which provided assistance with current bibliography and delineated the major issues involved in Jesus' attitude toward the law.

The Law
in the Teaching
of Paul

Romans 3:20–21

> Therefore no one will be declared righteous in his sight by observing the law. . . . But now a righteousness from God, apart from law, has been made known, to which the Law and the Prophets testify.

The phrase *apart from law* seems to teach that the law has been nullified as a principle of obedience because the righteousness of God is now obtainable through faith (v. 22). This view of Paul's words is rendered difficult by the statement in verse 31: "Do we, then, nullify the law by this faith? Not at all! Rather, we uphold the law." The solution to this exegetical problem must balance on the one hand a continuing validity of the law and on the other an apparent dichotomy between law and the righteousness obtained by faith.

This can be done when the law is understood to be honored by the righteousness of faith, to be fulfilled by that faith, and thus silenced in its condemning function because of the righteousness obtained through faith. The principle of law cannot give such righteousness; it is the standard of righteousness. When the standard is broken it condemns because it is law. But the law does not change human hearts. If hearts are to be conformed to the law, the change will be accomplished not by law, but by the revolutionary act of faith in Christ which imparts new motivation and radical obedience.

In 3:20 Paul affirmed that the principle of law cannot effect righteousness. It functions as a means of revealing how far one is from God's righteous requirements. Faith effects justification apart from the observance of law (3:28).

The words *apart from law* in 3:21 need not thus be understood to deny the continuation of the law, for Paul attributed several important functions to the law and called believers to obedience to it (Eph. 6:2).[53] Nor does the passage unequivocally teach that righteousness was only by law in the Mosaic era. The words "now a righteousness from God, apart from law, has been made known ..." (v. 21) may seem to imply that. But the argument of Paul in the subsequent passage is that Abraham found that righteousness (4:1 – 8) and found it apart from law (4:13). The righteousness that has now appeared is not different from Abraham's, except that it is now associated directly with Christ (4:23 – 25).

The reign of promise with its righteousness of faith was not interrupted by law in the Pauline theology. The period of the law was not an interregnum in the dominion of the promise covenant. Paul countered that idea in Galatians 3:17, "The law ... does not set aside the covenant previously established by God and thus do away with the promise." And he said in Romans 9:31 – 32 that the righteousness of the law should have been pursued by faith. The law did not supersede or vitiate the need to pursue righteousness on the basis of faith.

How is it, then, that this righteousness "has been manifested" (RSV)? We must observe that Paul defined this righteousness "apart from law" as righteousness that comes through faith in Christ (3:22); it is the righteousness foreseen by the prophets (3:21). The latter statement gives an eschatological perspective to this righteousness. It has found its realization in the present age. Just as Jesus' use of "fulfill" in Matthew 5:17 heralded the dawn of a new age in which the righteousness of the law found its fulfillment in him, so Paul heralded that age. It is a new era in divine history, characterized by events of such magnitude as the death and resurrection of Christ (4:24 – 25).

The righteousness apart from law is essentially the same as

---

53. C. E. B. Cranfield, "St. Paul and the Law," *SJT* 17 (1964): 45 – 48.

Abraham's, but Paul can say of this righteousness that it "has been made known" (3:21) because it has come to its full manifestation in Christ.[54] The prophets looked forward to a new era in which the achievement of righteousness would be facilitated for the people of God in an unprecedented way. The appearance of Christ in history marked that era. The new covenant has been ratified, the Holy Spirit indwells believers universally, all believers have access to God, and sin is no longer remembered because of the incomparably great sacrifice of Christ.[55]

There is in this context a strong motivation on the part of Paul to honor and uphold the law. The law has a continuing role to play in human obedience, but it does not usurp the role of the promise in Pauline theology. Observance of the law cannot produce righteousness, but Paul was not willing to pronounce the law a dead institution that had no significance for the Christian. He said, "We uphold the law" (3:31).

Romans 6:14

You are not under law, but under grace.

The use of the word *under* denotes dominion. Believers are not under the dominion of law, but under the dominion of "grace." Paul used "grace" in the sense of the new administration of God in Christ, as he did in Ephesians 3:2. Under the dominion of law the people failed miserably. However, this failure was not due to the law, but to their sinful hearts (Rom. 8:3). The dominion of grace is the new era of the Spirit envisioned by Joel (2:28 – 29) and the era of the renewed heart that Jeremiah predicted (31:33). Because of the momentous changes effected in the nature of believers as

54. John Murray argues that the statement of Paul in Rom. 3:21 does not denote discontinuity between the Old and New Testaments. He says, "But consistently with this continuity there can still be distinct emphasis upon the momentous change in the New Testament in respect of manifestation. The temporal force of the 'now' can therefore be recognized without impairing either the contrast of relations or the continuity of the two periods contrasted." *The Epistle to the Romans*, New International Commentary on the New Testament series, 2 vols. (Grand Rapids: Eerdmans, 1960), vol. 1, p. 109.

55. For a discussion of the way in which the concept of "Spirit" in Paul fulfills the law see Cranfield, "St. Paul and the Law," pp. 65 – 67.

a result of the work of the Holy Spirit and the pliancy of the changed heart, "sin shall not be your master" (Rom. 6:14).[56]

The assertion of Paul in Romans 6:14 does not mean the end of law any more than Jeremiah 31:33 does when it speaks of the law that is placed in the hearts. The law is not abrogated, according to this passage. Since we have seen that Paul honored the law and even fostered obedience to it, it is difficult to assert that Paul's words herald an absolute end to the ethical content of the law as a model of obedience. The ethic of the ancient law is a revelation from God in which the bold outline of human obedience has been sketched. Under "grace" man has the capability of fulfilling the ideal of the law (Rom. 3:31).

Romans 7:4 – 6

So, my brothers, you also died to the law through the body of Christ. ... We have been released from the law so that we serve in the new way of the Spirit, and not in the old way of the written code.

Paul appears to deny the continuing validity of law in this passage. He said, "We have been released from the law. ..." There are two important questions that must be considered in the study of Paul's view of the law in this passage: how are we released from the law and whether Paul is describing the experience of the unregenerate or regenerate person in verses 9 – 25.

The latter question is the more basic of the two, because Paul said in verse 25b, "So then, I myself in my mind am a slave to God's law. ..." If Paul was speaking as a regenerate person, he was affirming the continuing validity of law and the responsibility of the Christian to honor it. We must therefore understand the words "we have been released from the law" in a sense other than the complete abolition of the law. If he was describing the bondage to the law of an unregenerate person, he thus reflected a negative view of the law in the passage.

If Paul was speaking of the servitude of an unsaved person under the law in verses 21 – 25 it is difficult to understand the

---

56. Everett F. Harrison understands the word *under* to depict grace as "a disciplinary power in line with the apostle's effort to show that grace is not license. ..." *Romans*, the *Expositor's Bible Commentary*, vol. 10 (Grand Rapids: Zondervan, 1976), p. 72.

words of verse 25a, "Thanks be to God—through Jesus Christ our
Lord!" Why does this cry of thanksgiving appear between two
statements that characterize the hopelessness of the state of the
unregenerate person?

Ernst Käsemann understands the passage in a salvation-
historical fashion and concludes that the experience cited by Paul
describes the person who "lives in the illusion that he can and
should help himself and thereby repeats the story of Adam even
when he is acting piously and ethically."[57] Käsemann suggests that
verse 25a is a gloss, "admitting that this suggestion goes . . . against
the whole textual tradition. . . ."[58]

Matthew Black adopts the view that the "I" in this passage is
"the unredeemed man"[59] and entertains the suggestion that 8:2
should be taken after 7:25. He says, "It is possible that there has
been some dislocation in these verses."[60]

C. H. Dodd follows James Moffatt in placing verse 25b before
verse 24, "for it is scarcely conceivable that, after giving thanks to
God for deliverance, Paul should describe himself as being in exactly the same position as before."[61]

Not all who hold that Paul is describing the pre-Christian experience suggest rearranging the verses. Everett F. Harrison, following William Manson, holds that "the experience pictured here
. . . is deliberately presented in such a way as to demonstrate what
would indeed be the situation if one who is faced with the demands of the law and the power of sin in his life were to attempt
to solve his problem independently of the power of Christ and the
enablement of the Spirit."[62]

The scholars who hold that Paul is depicting the state of the
regenerate person point to various statements in the narrative of
7:14 – 25 that they believe could be uttered only by a Christian.[63]

57. Ernst Käsemann, The Epistle to the Romans, trans. and ed. Geoffrey W. Bromiley
(Grand Rapids: Eerdmans, 1980), p. 210.

58. Ibid., p. 211.

59. Matthew Black, Romans, New Century Bible Commentary (1973; Grand Rapids:
Eerdmans, 1981), p. 101.

60. Ibid., p. 108.

61. C. H. Dodd, The Epistle of Paul to the Romans (London: Hodder and Stoughton,
1932), pp. 114 – 15.

62. Harrison, Romans, p. 84. William Manson describes the passage as "the hypo-
thetical condition of a Christian under law. . . ." Jesus and the Christian (Grand Rapids:
Eerdmans, 1967), p. 159.

63. Murray, The Epistle to the Romans, pp. 257 – 58.

The difficulties faced by interpreters in this important passage are obvious.

It is clear that verse 25a is a problem for those who hold that Paul is describing the unregenerate state in verses 14 – 25. It is difficult to understand the words as the cry of thanksgiving of anyone other than one who is assured of the deliverance that there is in Christ.

In view of the complete lack of textual support for a rearrangement of the verses, it is best to attempt first to understand the passage on the basis of its existing structure. Only if this fails should one consider the possibility of textual corruption or intrusion.

The argument of Paul in this chapter began with the affirmation that believers have died to the law. Paul enlarged on that affirmation with an illustration of a woman whose legal responsibilities to her husband cease when he has died (vv. 1 – 6). On the basis of this analogy he went on to assert that death to the law has a positive side: "that we might bear fruit to God" (v. 4). There is an aspect of dedicated service involved.

This release from the law allows the believer to "serve in the new way of the Spirit, and not in the old way of the written code" (v. 6). The "newness" (*kainotēs*) of the Spirit in Paul is the new age of the Spirit, the era of the new covenant, when the believer's obedience to God springs from a heart that has been made new, and from motives changed by the Holy Spirit.

Paul identified the new age of the Spirit with the new covenant in 2 Corinthians 3:6. He said, "He has made us competent as ministers of a new covenant—not of the letter but of the Spirit...." The new motivation for keeping the law, about which Jeremiah spoke, is also present in the Pauline theology of law, for Paul said that God condemned sin in us "in order that the righteous requirements of the law might be fully met in us, who do not live according to the sinful nature but according to the Spirit" (Rom. 8:4).

We should not be quick to claim that Paul taught that the law has absolutely no relevance to the Christian. This would put him at odds with the prophet Jeremiah who taught that the law would be changed only with regard to its localization, not its ethical precepts (Jer. 31:33).

The freedom from the law about which Paul spoke is amplified in verses 4 – 6. He said the believer has died to what once bound him ("dead to that which held us captive," RSV). The way in which the law bound its adherents is described in verse 5. Apart from the Spirit the law aroused the sinful passions. The sinful nature, with its false pride, rebels when it is shown by the law to be wanting. The sinful human ego is unwilling to recognize its corruption and seeks to justify itself. When it stands exposed before God's law it recognizes all manner of ways in which it violates the righteous standards of God (vv. 7 – 8), and the result is condemnation and death (vv. 9 – 11).

It is this function of the law about which Paul spoke in the context immediately preceding his statement that believers are released from the law. It is thus reasonable to assume that the release is not from the law's benign ethic, but from its condemning and convicting force. C. E. B. Cranfield says that *ho nomos* (the law) in verse 6 "is here used in a limited sense—'the law (as condemning us)', 'the law('s condemnation)'."[64]

We must not regard "law" in Paul as a static element that always denotes exactly the same thing. Paul spoke of functions of the law, and since he attributed a positive function to the law in this chapter (v. 12), we cannot conclude that he regarded the whole law in a negative light. Cranfield says, "That ... the meaning is not that we have been discharged from the law simpliciter is clear enough from v. 25b (cf. vv. 12 and 14a; also 3.31; 8.4; 13.8 – 10)."[65]

The law enabled Paul to recognize what sin is, and therefore he could say that the law is "holy, righteous and good" (v. 12). Sin has exploited the law. It has taken advantage of the law to promote its own evil purposes (v. 8), but we must not conclude that the law is intrinsically evil because sin has perverted it.

Most commentators agree that Paul was speaking of mankind in general in verses 7 – 13. The use of the pronoun *I* in these verses has been explained in numerous ways: it seems best to understand it as autobiographical, but in the sense that Paul recognized his experiences to be those of all mankind. However, a difficulty in understanding this passage to be autobiographical is Paul's statement in verse 9, "Once I was alive apart from law. . . ." But this

---

64. C. E. B. Cranfield, *A Critical and Exegetical Commentary on the Epistle to the Romans*, International Critical Commentary series, 2 vols. (Edinburgh: T. and T. Clark, 1975), vol. 1, p. 338.

65. Ibid.

may depict a time before the law began to enforce its convicting power on Paul. He spoke of a time when the commandment against coveting exposed the covetous desires that lay in the heart of this proud Pharisee (vv. 7 – 8). It may be that he depicted the stirrings of dissatisfaction with his legalistic religion that led him to recognize how hopeless his sinful state was and to find release in the same faith that his father Abraham had found.

The major problem in this passage as a whole is the identification of "I" in verses 14 – 25. This problem has been given a great deal of consideration in the literature. The view taken here is that Paul was describing the experience of the believer. To be sure, certain statements in this section are difficult to understand on the basis of this view, but, as Murray observes, "Once we admit that sin persists in the believer, the tension of 7:14 – 25 is inevitable and it is not the way of truth to ignore it."[66] We may stumble over the statements *I am carnal* (v. 14, RSV) and *nothing good lives in me* (v. 18), but these may be understood as part of the Christian experience and there is enough in the passage to indicate that this individual serves God.[67]

It is important to note that the grammar supports the observance of a transition at verse 14, for Paul changed from the past tense to the present tense. He described a present state, whereas in verses 7 – 13, his perspective was in the past.

The negative statements about his experience in verses 14 – 18 are qualified by a crucial clause in verse 18, "that is, in my sinful nature." The RSV translates it, "that is, in my flesh" (*en tēi sarki mou*). Paul was not describing the whole man by the negative characterizations that precede this statement; rather, he was describing the sinful nature, that nature that makes itself felt the more one seeks purity and holiness.

The individual of verses 14 – 25 delights in the law of God. He desires to serve God, but he is acutely aware of the sinful nature which is in conflict with his new nature. The inability to please God perfectly leaves him feeling wretched. But it is not the wretchedness of absolute defeat. For while the passage describes the experience of all believers, this is not the ultimate state of the Christian. There is a foregleam in verse 25 of the glorious freedom

66. Murray, *The Epistle to the Romans*, p. 258.
67. Ibid., pp. 257 – 59.

expounded by Paul in chapter 8. Only the believer can sound the note of triumph in that verse, "Thanks be to God—through Jesus Christ our Lord!"

The conflict of two natures in the believer is expressed elsewhere in the Pauline writings. In Romans 13:14 he exhorted Christians not to "think about how to gratify the desires of the sinful nature" (*sarkos*). However, it is in Galatians 5:17 that we find the most important passage. Paul referred to his hearers as "brothers" and said they "were called to be free" (v. 13). He was evidently speaking of Christians. He went on to say that if they live by the Spirit, they "will not gratify the desires of the sinful nature." He affirmed that the two natures are in conflict with one another (v. 17).

Paul pointed the erring believers in Galatia to the freedom there is in the Holy Spirit and to the victory that one may find over the sinful nature in following his direction (v. 25).

The release from the law about which Paul spoke in Romans 7:6, then, is understood to mean release from its captive power, its condemning function which could only magnify sin and produce the consciousness of sin and hopeless despair.

If it is this function of law, and not the ethical aspect of the law, from which the believer has been freed, we may understand the exultant cry of 7:25a as the triumphant thankfulness of the regenerate person who is painfully aware of the tension of the psychological forces that exist within him, but has learned that in the Spirit there is freedom and the power to control the sinful nature. We may also understand the words of 7:25b in a positive sense. There is no need to rearrange the verse.

The believer is a slave to the law of sin (*nomōi hamartias*) only in his sinful nature (v. 25b). That law was depicted earlier by Paul in verse 23. Paul described two laws at work in the believer. One is the law of God (v. 22); the other law principle is that of the sinful nature (v. 23). This sinful nature is the opposite of "mind" (*nous*), according to verse 23. Evidently, it is with the mind, the inner motivating force, that one responds to God in obedience.

It is with the "mind" (*nous*) that Paul was a slave to the law of God (v. 25). If one affirms that we have in this section the depiction of the inner conflict of two natures in the believer, not only can we maintain the integrity of the structure of the passage, but also we may understand Paul to uphold the law as he so clearly does in other passages. Paul delighted in the law of God (v. 22), but not in its function as a force that condemned him.

On the basis of this view, the "written code" (*palaiotēti grammatos*), of which Paul spoke in 7:6, is understood to refer to the mode of one's service to God; that is Paul's concern in that verse. It is the law engraved on stone—the law apart from Spirit; or to put it in other terminology, the law approached only through legalistic motives, not through faith (Rom. 9:31 – 32).[68]

Romans 8:2 – 4

... the law of the Spirit of life set me free from the law of sin and death. For what the law was powerless to do in that it was weakened by the sinful nature, God did by sending his own Son. ... And so he condemned sin in sinful man, in order that the righteous requirements of the law might be fully met in us. ...

Paul saw no weakness inherent in the law. The powerlessness (*adunatos*) of which he spoke is not to be found in the demands or intrinsic nature of the law, but in the weakness of the flesh (*sarkos*). The blame for the failure of the law is placed on man's sinful nature, not the law itself. Once again Paul avoided implying that the law is intrinsically evil.

When the righteous principles of the law come face to face with human rebellion and disobedience, the law can only condemn. It cannot lead to life, for its true spiritual purpose is frustrated in the presence of disobedience to its requirements. But the new relationship of the Holy Spirit restores the spiritual nature of the law by condemning sin (v. 3). Cranfield says, "The law, which God intended to be 'unto life' (Rom. 7:10), which was essentially 'spiritual' (Rom. 7:14), but which encountering sin, pronounced God's condemnation and brought death, and, being misunderstood, misused and perverted by men, actually resulted in their sinning

68. The contention of Paul in this passage and others, that the law could not be kept satisfactorily apart from the Holy Spirit, appears to be at variance with several passages in the Old Testament, notably Deut. 30:11 – 14, where the facility of obedience to the law is clearly set forth. But it should be noted that the Book of Deuteronomy elsewhere holds little hope that it would be obeyed (31:16, 20, 29). The reason for this failure lies within the rebellious hearts of the Israelites (31:21, 27 – 29) and their failure to remain loyal to the Lord. Within Deut. 30 itself there is the consciousness that the fulfillment of the promise is dependent on faith (v. 20).

more and more, God has by the ministry of His Son and the gift of His Spirit re-established in its true character and proper office as 'spiritual' and 'unto life,' as 'the law of the Spirit of life' which sets us free from the tyranny of sin and death (Rom. 8:2)."[69]

Paul spoke of two condemnations in this passage: the condemning function of the law (v. 1) and the condemnation of God on human sin (v. 3). The former is canceled for all who are under the law of the Spirit of life (*pneuma tēs zōēs*); the latter has pronounced judgment on sin itself and has delivered it up to judgment. Because the deadly power of sin has been canceled for all who are "in Christ" (v. 1), the law can fulfill its spiritual function as the expression of the divine will and the pattern of obedience. It is not the law that has been changed, but the human heart.

The age of the Spirit, foreseen by the ancient prophets, has dawned. The law has been placed in the heart. For Paul, the blessings of the Spirit are the blessings of the new age.

The eighth chapter of Romans makes it clear that while the work of the Holy Spirit in human hearts establishes God's law, the law no longer presents itself to the Christian as a taskmaster harshly imposing its painful obligation on those who are yet under its control. The Christian enjoys freedom and life in the Holy Spirit; he has the relationship of a child to its father (v. 15). His obedience is motivated by grace and that obedience upholds the law. It is no longer the obedience of the flesh, for the flesh seeks to justify itself. The flesh loves to boast of the measure of its attainment with regard to the law. But in the Spirit the "I" gives way to Christ.[70] The believer still may fail, but his response to the call of grace, his answer to the impulses of the Holy Spirit comprise an obedience to the divine will that is based not on the self-justifying motives of the sinful nature but on a mind controlled by the Spirit (v. 6).

Does the believer's new relationship to the law eliminate all obligation to God? Paul was not antinomian, for he said, "Therefore, brothers, we have an obligation—but it is not to the sinful nature, to live according to it" (v. 12). The believer's obligation is to put to death the sinful nature and to live according to the Holy Spirit. In this way "the righteous requirements of the law" will be fully met (v. 4).

69. Cranfield, "St. Paul and the Law," p. 65.
70. For a discussion of the terms *flesh* and *spirit* in Rom. 8 see Harrison, *Romans*, pp. 88–89.

Romans 9:31 – 32

> ... but Israel, who pursued a law of righteousness, has not attained
> it. Why not? Because they pursued it not by faith but as if it were
> by works.

In order to facilitate the discussion of the exegetical considerations in this passage a literal interpretation of the Greek text is
given: "But Israel, who pursued a law (*nomos*) of righteousness,
unto law (*nomos*) has not attained. Why? Because [they did not
pursue it] out of faith, but as if it were by works."

A major exegetical problem in this passage is the meaning of
the second use of *nomos* (law) in verse 31. Several commentators
understand it in the principial sense, that is, as connoting the
principle of justification by faith.[71] One can understand the incli-
nation of exegetes to interpret the passage this way, for there are
several statements in the Pauline material that set forth an apparent dichotomy between law and faith (Rom. 10:5; Gal. 3:12).

However, the interpretation of the second use of *nomos* in this
fashion involves an unnatural shift in the flow of thought, for the
first use must refer to the law that was distinctly Israel's, that is,
the Mosaic law. Even though *nomos* is used principially by Paul
in other contexts (Rom. 7:21, 23; 8:2), the application of that connotation to the word here is rendered questionable by the lack of
contextual evidence and particularly by the fact that the second
use of *nomos* is in the same clause with the first. It would be most
unnatural for Paul to move to a different meaning of the word in
such a narrow compass, without qualifying it. The law that Israel
did not attain (*phthanō*) must be the same law that Israel pursued
(*diōkō*). The most natural understanding of the second use of *nomos* is that it refers to the Mosaic law which Israel sought to obey
but failed.

Paul went on to say that the Israelites failed to attain the law
because they pursued it wrongly. They pursued it not from the
motive of faith (*ek pisteōs*) but from the motive of works (*ex ergōn*).

71. Charles Hodge, *Commentary on the Epistle to the Romans* (1835; Grand Rapids:
Eerdmans, 1950); Floyd E. Hamilton, *The Epistle to the Romans: An Exegetical and Devotional Commentary* (Grand Rapids: Baker, 1958), p. 168. Some commentators understand
both uses of *nomos* in the sense of principle. Murray, *The Epistle to the Romans*, vol. 2,
pp. 42 – 43; H. A. W. Meyer, *Critical and Exegetical Hand-book to the Epistle to the Romans*,
trans. John C. Moore and Edwin Johnson, rev. ed. (New York: Funk and Wagnalls, 1884),
pp. 391 – 92.

Daniel P. Fuller correctly draws attention to the importance of the particle *hōs* (as if it were) in verse 32.[72] If it is translated "as if it were," Paul may be understood as making the judgment that the law was pursued by the Israelites "as if it were" based on works, but it is not; it is based on faith. Such a conclusion, if correct, has monumental implications for the Pauline theology and appears to be at variance with other contexts where Paul does not posit faith as the basis of law.

An examination of the earlier context suggests another approach. In verses 30−31 Paul was speaking primarily of righteousness. He said, "What then shall we say? That the Gentiles, who did not pursue righteousness, have attained it, a righteousness that is by faith; but Israel, who pursued a law of righteousness, has not attained it." The context here deals with the pursuit of righteousness. Gentiles have found righteousness. But what irony! Jews, who throughout their history pursued righteousness in the context of law (*nomon dikaiosunēs*), did not attain that goal. Gentiles were not a people of law; the Jews were, but they failed to attain the righteousness of the law that was the very cornerstone of their national and religious heritage.

The Gentiles were not known for their pursuit of righteousness as were the Jews, but they found righteousness through faith (v. 30). Israel was known for its pursuit of righteousness, for it pursued a "law of righteousness." Paul did not say the Israelites pursued righteousness through law, but they pursued a law characterized by righteousness, and in that sense the righteousness of law was their goal. Since the pursuit of righteousness is the main thought at the beginning of the context (v. 30) and a central concept in the subsequent context (10:3−4), we may thus find support for that concept in 9:31−32.

If the passage is understood in this way, Paul was affirming that it is righteousness that is not attained through works but through faith. Israel's pursuit of a law that was intrinsically righteous failed, because they sought to achieve its righteousness in the wrong way. If Israel had sought righteousness on the basis of faith, they would have attained it and would have kept the law satisfactorily. However, Israel pursued righteousness "as though it were" (*hōs*)

---

72. Daniel P. Fuller, *Gospel and Law: Contrast or Continuum?* (Grand Rapids: Eerdmans, 1980), pp. 73−76.

based on works. They should have pursued it on the basis of faith. In this view, the second use of *nomos* would be understood in the same way as the first, that is, to refer to the "law of righteousness" cited earlier; the Mosaic law, which was the crystallization of the righteousness sought by Israel.

This view, then, regards *hōs* as referring to the righteousness that found its expression in the law. It does not regard Paul as stating that the law is based on faith. Rather, the law crystallizes the obedience which flows from faith.

In his discussion Paul drew attention to the fact that in the Old Testament righteousness was obtained by faith in the promise. He demonstrated that Abraham was declared righteous in this way. True righteousness in the Old Testament was achieved by faith, and its validity was manifested by obedience to the legal stipulations given by divine decree. Faith in God's promise gave the inheritance. Obedience alone, whether to the requirement of circumcision or the complex Mosaic legislation, could not grant the inheritance. It came by faith, but faith which manifested itself in obedience. Paul said the Jews of his day sought righteousness on the basis of law alone and "stumbled over the 'stumbling stone.' " The term *stone* is understood, by the vast majority of commentators, to refer to Christ.[73] The Jews omitted the principle of faith, represented in Paul's discussion by the word *stone*. They stumbled over the fact that true righteousness could be attained, and the inheritance granted, only by faith. This is how Abraham was justified. In the Pauline theology, the principle of faith is represented by Christ who is the object of faith for all who are under the new covenant.

Romans 10:4

Christ is the end of the law so that there may be righteousness for everyone who believes.

The major question in this passage is whether "end" (*telos*) connotes cessation or fulfillment. Did Christ end the law, in that he

---

73. However, P. W. Meyer understands the word *stone* to refer to the Torah. "Romans 10:4 and the 'End' of the Law," in *The Divine Helmsman: Studies on God's Control of Human Events, Presented to Lou H. Silberman*, ed. James L. Crenshaw and Samuel Sandmel (New York: Ktav, 1980).

terminated it, or does it find its end, that is, its goal and fulfillment, in him?[74] The question has given rise to much discussion and for the purpose of this work it is unnecessary to examine the question exhaustively.[75]

The view that *telos* means only "termination" has profound implications for our study. It may lead to the conclusion that faith and law are diametrically opposed because Christ ended the law in order that righteousness may be based on faith (v. 4).[76] The most telling argument against this conclusion is that Paul faulted the Jews in the preceding verses (9:31−32) for failing to pursue the righteousness of the law through faith. They sought to achieve that righteousness on the basis of works, not faith. If they had approached the law through faith, they would not have failed to achieve its righteousness. The Pauline theology does not allow for an absolute dichotomy between faith and law.[77] Paul did not say they should not have pursued the law; he said they did not achieve its righteousness because they pursued a legal righteousness rather than a righteousness of faith. They sought righteousness in a way that is beyond the ability of fallen man.

74. Heikki Räisänen concludes that both concepts are present in Paul's thinking due to a dichotomism in his approach to the law. He holds that *telos* means "termination" in Rom. 10:4, but the continuing relevance of the law may be found in Gal. 5:14 and Rom. 13:8−10. "Paul's Theological Difficulties With the Law," in *Studia Biblica 1978, III: Papers on Paul and Other New Testament Authors*, ed. E. A. Livingstone, Sixth International Congress on Biblical Studies (Sheffield: JSOT, 1980), pp. 306−7.

75. A number of the more significant discussions of the subject are given here. They are arranged according to the view taken of the meaning of *telos*. 1) *Telos* meaning "fulfillment" or goal: Cranfield, "St. Paul and the Law," pp. 48−53; C. T. Rhyne, "Romans 10:4 Once More," in *Faith Establishes the Law* (Chico, Calif.: Scholars, 1981), pp. 95−116; W. S. Campbell, "Christ the End of the Law: Romans 10:4," in *Studia Biblica 1978, III: Papers on Paul and Other New Testament Authors*, ed. E. A. Livingstone, Sixth International Congress on Biblical Studies (Sheffield: JSOT, 1980), pp. 73−81; Meyer, "Romans 10:4 and the 'End' of the Law"; G. E. Howard, "Christ the End of the Law: The Meaning of Romans 10:4ff.," *JBL* 88 (1969): pp. 331−37. 2) *Telos* as termination and goal: F. F. Bruce, "Paul and the Law of Moses," *Bulletin of the John Rylands University Library* 57 (1974/1975): 262−64. 3) *Telos* as termination: Käsemann, *The Epistle to the Romans*, pp. 280−83.

76. The word *telos* has the connotation of absolute termination in numerous instances in the New Testament (e.g., Matt. 24:6; Luke 1:33; Heb. 6:14). Käsemann concludes that "the Mosaic Torah comes to an end with Christ because man now renounces his own right in order to grant God his right (3:4)." *The Epistle to the Romans*, p. 283.

77. Räisänen argues that 9:31 is not to be taken into account in the interpretation of Rom. 10:4 because it "only shows the elasticity of Paul's thought; in 10:1 a new start is made, and in this passage Paul speaks of the law in polemical terms." "Paul's Theological Difficulties with the Law," p. 306. But it is difficult to posit an abrupt start at 10:1, especially since Paul is continuing his discussion of the pursuit of righteousness (10:3) which he began in 9:30.

R. Bring observes that "Law" and "righteousness" are "almost synomymous concepts" in Paul's argument in this passage.[78] He goes on to say, "One's own righteousness (righteousness of the law) corresponds to law when it is used as a means by which to make oneself righteous, righteousness from God corresponds to the law of Moses in the Scriptures, which is in itself holy and good (Rom. 7:10, 12)."[79] If this conclusion is correct, it is difficult to assert that Christ terminated the law.

If *telos* is understood to mean "goal," then Paul's view is compatible with Matthew 5, where Jesus demonstrated his goal of fulfilling the law by explicating it, defining it, and enjoining it on his followers. If Paul believed the Old Testament law was absolutely terminated, several statements of his are difficult to comprehend, such as his injunction to keep the law in Ephesians 6:2 and his assertion in Romans 7:25 that he was a slave to God's law.

Romans 10:5 – 13

The exposition of the law by Paul in this section contains two quotations from the Old Testament: Leviticus 18:5 and Deuteronomy 30:12 – 14.

Leviticus 18:5 says, "Keep my decrees and laws, for the man who obeys them will live by them. I am the LORD." In the context of Leviticus this statement does not have a negative connotation, but Paul seems to appeal to it to illustrate the wrong way of pursuing the law. He explains the "righteousness that is by law" (v. 5) by quoting Leviticus 18:5.

In its original context Leviticus 18:5 offers life in return for obedience to the law. The concept of "life" (*ḥay*) in this passage is of the utmost importance to our consideration. Does the law offer eternal life? Is it a valid option for salvation to anyone who can obey its commands?

The term *life*, when used in connection with the law, connotes the continued participation of the nation or the individual in the blessings of the inheritance. This results from obedience. In other words, "life," when used of the nation, denotes national vitality. As long as the people are in the land, enjoying its benefits, they are

78. R. Bring, "Paul and the Old Testament," *ST* 25 (1971): 46.
79. Ibid.

alive. If, through disobedience, they should be expelled from the land, they would perish as a nation. In this sense "life" does not connote the giving of the inheritance but the maintenance of the inheritance.

Both Leviticus 18 and Deuteronomy 30 support this definition. In Leviticus 18, obedience to the commands of the law leads to life (v. 5) but disobedience leads to expulsion from the land (v. 28). In Deuteronomy 30:16 − 18 it says, "If you obey the commandments of the LORD your God . . . you shall live and multiply, and the LORD your God will bless you in the land. . . . But if . . . you will not hear . . . you shall perish; you shall not live long in the land" (RSV). (See also Deut. 4:1; 5:33; 8:1; 16:20; Amos 5:14.) In verses 19 − 20, life is defined in this way: "choose life, that you and your descendants may live, loving the LORD your God, obeying his voice, . . . for that means life . . . and length of days, that you may dwell in the land which the LORD swore to your fathers . . ." (RSV). In neither of these contexts can the word *life* be understood to connote the state of receiving the inheritance. It relates only to continued participation in the inheritance and thus is effected by obedience to the law.[80]

The inheritance is granted only by the Abrahamic covenant. The law covenant does not grant the inheritance but functions to govern the obedience necessary for the maintenance of one's participation in it. Thus, the disposition of the inheritance in the Old Testament is effected by two covenantal instruments, each with a distinct function and each based on a different covenantal righteousness. We have already observed the interplay of these two covenants in the Book of Deuteronomy. More will be said about this later, but it is suggested here that this bicovenantal structure lies at the heart of Paul's use of the two Old Testament passages in Romans 10:5 − 8.

The relationship of the two Old Testament passages in Romans 10 poses serious problems for the exegete. One of the important questions concerns the use of the particle *de* (but, v. 6). Does it function as an adversative particle or does it have a transitional function? If it functions adversatively, Paul is to be under-

---

80. The sequence of the verbal concepts in Deut. 30:15 is significant for the meaning of life. "Life" is not paired with "death" in the structure, but with "good" (*tôb*); "death" is paired with "evil." This demonstrates that the semantic range of the concept of life is broad enough to include the concept of national welfare.

stood as pitting Leviticus 18:5 against Deuteronomy 30. If it is transitional, he is to be understood as using the two passages to support a benign function for the law. In the latter view, both Leviticus 18:5 and Deuteronomy 30:12 – 14 are understood to lend support to Paul's assertion in 10:4 that Christ is the end of the law.

This problem is an important one in modern scholarship. F. Flückiger opposes the antithetical structure because "it is not like Paul to cite the Old Testament with the idea that it has no more validity."[81] Karl Barth says that we do not have the "Jewish and Christian concepts of righteousness here opposed to one another, as if here the voice of the 'righteousness of faith' were polemically played off against the voice of Moses and the latter proved, as it were, to be false...."[82] Fuller objects that if an adversative structure is posited, one must conclude "that Paul, while holding to the intended meaning of Leviticus 18:5 in Romans 10:5, nevertheless ignored the intended meaning of Deuteronomy 30:11 – 14 when he used the wording of those verses to describe the righteousness of faith in Romans 10:6 – 8."[83] In short, a major problem in the adversative structure is that it seems that Paul is pitting Moses against Moses.[84] This is anomalous in the Pauline writings and would not strengthen his case with the Judaizing opponents he faced. However, if we view Paul's argument against the background of the bicovenantal structure, an adversative function for the *de* is necessary and does not meet the objections usually brought against it.

Leviticus 18:5, in Paul's argument, is used to show only that life comes by practicing the righteousness of the law. He said, "The man who does (*ho poiēsas*) these things will live by them." If life is defined (as it is in the two Old Testament contexts) as continued enjoyment of the inheritance, we may not read into Paul's usage of the verse the concept of eternal life. We need to consider seriously the possibility that Paul was observing that the covenant righteousness of the law covenant is obedience and not faith. Faith

81. F. Flückiger, "Christus des Gesetzes *telos*," *TZ* 11 (1955): 155.

82. Karl Barth, *Church Dogmatics*, vol. 2, *The Doctrine of God*, trans. G. T. Thomson (Edinburgh: T. and T. Clark, 1936), p. 245.

83. Fuller, *Gospel and Law*, p. 67.

84. Fuller states, "The first difficulty emerges from the consideration that Paul cites passages from the Pentateuch to support both what he meant by 'the righteousness based on faith' ... and also what he meant by 'the righteousness based on law'." Ibid.

is the covenant righteousness of the Abrahamic covenant. That is
not to say that the law is divorced from faith. Rather, the two
covenants must be seen as working together to effect the disposition of the inheritance. If one covenant is separated from the
other, the promise of the inheritance is vitiated.

We may thus understand Leviticus 18:5 to say only that the
covenant principle of law is obedience. It is an obvious statement,
but viewed against Paul's unique use of Deuteronomy 30, this stark
statement of the function of the law is significant.

Deuteronomy 30:12–14 is given a relevance by Paul that is not
apparent in its original context. In that context Moses spoke about
the law. He affirmed that the law is not too difficult to keep, nor
is it inaccessible to the people (v. 11). He said it is not in heaven,
that they should seek it there (v. 12), nor beyond the sea, that they
should wonder who will bring it to them (v. 13). It is not an esoteric
body of material that they could not obey.

But Paul made the passage say something more by the christological intrusions. The question "Who will ascend into heaven?"
is explained by Paul: "that is, to bring Christ down. . . ." The second
question is explained in the same way, and the "word" of which
Moses spoke in Deuteronomy 30:14 was identified by Paul with
the gospel that he preached (v. 8).

There is no need to think that Paul understood Deuteronomy 30
to have had an original christological intent, although some have
suggested that.[85] That concept is not essential to the understanding of Paul here, and may cloud the issue. The essential question
is that of the relationship of the two passages. The one is a stark
statement of the requirement of law; the other is rich with the
presence of Christ.[86]

In the Old Testament, both passages say essentially the same

85. Martin Luther explained Paul's use of Deut. 30 as an indication of the fact that all
Scripture points to Christ. He said, "Every word in the Bible points to Christ. That this
is really so, he proves by showing that this word here, which seems to have nothing
whatsoever to do with Christ, nevertheless signifies Christ." *Lectures on Romans*, ed. and
trans. Wilhelm Pauck (Philadelphia: Westminster, 1961), p. 288.

86. The statement of Bring concerning Paul's use of Deut. 30 is significant. "Paul
understands these and the following words to refer to Christ. The commandment of the
law . . . has now become incarnate in Christ. Now he is here; he is himself present in the
word about him; one could say that Christ is the commandment, in its fulfilled and
revealed form. Christ is himself the law of God and the command of God. . . ." "Paul and
the Old Testament," pp. 49–50.

thing. Both offer life on condition of obedience and both deal with the inheritance. The major difference is that Deuteronomy 30 emphasizes the accessibility of the law.

By intruding Christ into Deuteronomy 30:12−14, Paul vividly illustrated the argument of 9:30−33, which is that the pursuit of righteousness on the basis of law alone will not succeed. The full-orbed righteousness of the Old Testament is based on faith. It includes obedience, but legal obedience alone cannot lead to justification; that is contradicted by Abraham's experience. Such a concept bifurcates the covenantal disposition of the inheritance. Paul's concept of faith in 9:30−33 is represented by Christ, depicted as the stone of stumbling (v. 33). True righteousness cannot be achieved apart from faith in Christ, according to this argument. Paul did not negate the law or berate the Jews for pursuing its righteousness. He lamented that they pursued it solely on the basis of legal obedience, and thus they stumbled over the "stone."

Paul's distinctive use of Deuteronomy 30, like his reference to the stone, admits Christ into the argument. It is an effective device that unites the two covenant principles of faith and obedience in one. In his usage of Leviticus 18:5, the law stands alone, and its condition of obedience is underscored. One achieves life by obeying the law. That statement cannot be refuted, and is in no way a denegration of the law. Moses himself said that the "man who does these things will live by them." Paul's detractors need not have seen that appeal to Moses as a rejection of the law or even as a lightly veiled slur. It is a true statement of the covenant righteousness of the law. Law demands obedience. But in Paul's use of Deuteronomy 30, law and faith combine to form the full-orbed righteousness that governed the granting and maintaining of the inheritance in the Old Testament.

This view fits with the statement of verse 4 that Christ is the *telos* (goal) of the law. It amplifies the relationship between Christ and the law established in that verse.

Yet an objection to this view may be found in its relationship to verse 4. The structure in which the two verses occur contains the particles *gar* and *de*. Since it begins with *gar* (for), it must have a logical connection with what precedes.[87] If one adopts the view that *telos* means "goal," not "termination," it is likely that Leviticus

---

87. Fuller, *Gospel and Law*, pp. 85−86.

18:5 should have been used by Paul to illustrate the positive relationship Christ sustains to the law. However, the view presented here isolates Leviticus 18:5 from the preceding verse and understands it to refer only to the function of the law.[88]

An examination of the *gar/de* clauses in Romans indicates several important concepts.[89] First, the *gar/de* clause may function as a contrastive structure as it does in Romans 6:23: "For (*gar*) the wages of sin is death, but (*de*) the gift of God is eternal life."[90] Second, *gar* does not always connect a clause to the clause immediately preceding. This is also apparent in the context of Romans 6:23 where the clause "for (*gar*) the wages of sin is death" reflects the concept of 6:21, where the return received for slavery to sin is death. Romans 6:23 combines that concept with that of the preceding verse where the reward for turning from sin to God is eternal life.

If Leviticus 18:5 is understood to function in Paul's argument as a statement of the requirement of the law apart from faith it may then be understood to reflect the concept of verse 3 rather than verse 4. In verse 3 Paul spoke of the efforts of the Jews of his day to establish their own righteousness. Since we have observed from his argument in 9:30−33 that this was done by omitting Christ from their pursuit of righteousness we conclude that the representation of the law without Christ in Leviticus 18:5 relates to verse 3 rather than verse 4. This view establishes a positive unity in the whole context and is not open to the objections generally leveled against the adversative structure.

This interpretation also allows for a consistent usage of Leviticus 18:5 in the Pauline theology. In Galatians 3:12 Paul affirmed that the covenant righteousness of the law is not faith but obedience. He said, "The law is not based on faith; on the contrary,

88. Karl Barth, in his argument against the adversative structure, says, "Even the γαρ with which the quotation from Moses is introduced in v. 5 points in another direction." *The Doctrine of God,* p. 245. Fuller says, "The *gar* that introduces the clausal structure signifies that Leviticus 18:5 was intended by Paul to summarize what was meant by the affirmation of v. 4 that Christ is the continuation (*telos*) of the law." *Gospel and Law,* p. 85.

89. The writer is indebted to a former student, Roger W. Handyside, whose detailed study of the *gar/de* clauses in Romans is reflected here.

90. Fuller follows Liddell and Scott in his argument that when *de* is not accompanied by *men* it is "used merely to pass from one thing to another." *Gospel and Law,* p. 67.

'The man who does these things will live by them.' "[91] Thus, to attribute to Leviticus 18:5 the function of characterizing the law as based on works is not out of keeping with the use of that verse elsewhere in Paul's theology.

Given this conclusion, we may understand Paul's use of the Old Testament passages to set forth a definitive statement regarding law and grace. The basis of the law is obedience (Lev. 18:5). However, dependence on that principle alone is insufficient. That is legalism. The pursuit of righteousness must be based on faith. Faith is represented in Paul's argument by Christ, who is the object of faith today. True righteousness can never be attained if the faith principle is omitted from one's pursuit of it. That is the argument of 9:30−33. It is also the point of Paul's use of Deuteronomy 30 where he deftly combined both principles by intruding Christ into that passage. This is the full-orbed disposition of the inheritance that we observed in the Old Testament.

We need not conclude that Paul's intrusion of Christ and the gospel into Deuteronomy 30 ignores the original intent of that passage. That intent, we have observed, is to set forth the concept of the accessibility of the law. Paul utilized that intent to underscore the accessibility of justification in the gospel that he preached. In this way he established a continuum with the Old Testament.

Paul did not assert that the Old Testament has no more validity. Rather, he affirmed that the gospel he preached is consonant with the mode of reception of the inheritance in the Old Testament. Nor is Moses proved to be false in Paul's argument. He quoted Moses authoritatively to demonstrate that the basis of law is obedience.

We need not feel that Paul understood the Pentateuch to teach opposing concepts. It is Paul's use of the passages that sets up the contrast. Deuteronomy 30:12−14 is different from Leviticus 18:5 in Romans 10 only because Paul read a reference to Christ into Deuteronomy 30. The essential meaning of Deuteronomy 30, which is the accessibility of the law, was retained by Paul. His addition

91. Cranfield sees a positive function for Lev. 18:5. In this context he notes, "But it is probable that in Gal. 3:12 also Paul, in quoting Lev. 18:5 has in mind Christ's perfect obedience; for otherwise a step in the argument is missing." *The Epistle to the Romans*, vol. 2, p. 522, n. 2.

to the passage communicates that only in Christ can the true righteousness of the law be attained.

Other exegetical problems remain,[92] but it is sufficient to note in conclusion that Paul did not teach here the termination of law. He said that if the concept of faith is ignored, and law only is made the basis of one's pursuit of righteousness, it cannot be achieved.

2 Corinthians 3:6 – 11

In this passage Paul spoke of the glory of the old covenant. He contrasted this with the greater glory of the new covenant. In the course of his discussion he referred to the law, "engraved in letters on stone," as the "ministry that brought death" (v. 7). He contrasted the "letter" with the "Spirit" and stated that "the letter kills" (v. 6).

It is not correct to assume that Paul believed the old covenant consisted only of "letter" and was devoid of "spirit." If this were true, there would have been no salvation under Moses. There was promise in that old covenant. Those who sought salvation in the letter alone, and failed to accept in faith the promise that gave life, found that the letter killed.

That Paul had in mind the temporary structure of the law alone, and not the eternal promise, is clear from his reference to the fact that the Law "was fading away" (v. 11). Paul would never have said that of the promise. He was thinking of the "letter" itself. The Law "killed" those who sought life in the letter alone and not in the promise.

92. J. Suggs suggests that Paul's use of the word *abyss* rather than the words *across the sea*, which occur in both MT and LXX, expresses the concept of Christ as "Wisdom." The reason for this is that the term *abyss* signifies the lower extremity in Jewish wisdom literature. Thus, Paul modified Deut. 30:13 to express that concept. "The Word Is Near You: Romans 10:6 – 10 Within the Purpose of the Letter," in *Christian History and Interpretation: Studies Presented to John Knox*, ed. W. R. Farmer, C. F. D. Moule, and R. R. Niebuhr (Cambridge: At the University Press, 1967), pp. 308 – 9. But an examination of the Old Testament passages before and after Rom. 10:5 – 8 indicates that Paul did not quote the Old Testament with precision in those verses. Most of the quotations are paraphrastic. It seems best to regard Paul's quotation of Deut. 30:13 in the same light.

Flückiger applies Paul's reference to ascending to heaven and descending into the abyss to the superhuman attempts of the Jews of Paul's day to achieve justification by law. "Christus des Gesetzes *telos*," p. 155. He is followed by Fuller, *Gospel and Law*, pp. 69 – 71. But this view does not have the clear support of either the Old or the New Testament context. The passage in Deut. 30:12 – 14 rather emphasizes the accessibility of the law.

Paul's reference to the new covenant recalls the classic exposition of that covenant in Jeremiah 31:31 − 34. There, the prophet did not predict the termination of law (tôrāh) but the placing of the law in the heart.

Paul spoke of the greater glory of the Spirit in verse 8, but he did not deny the glory of the old covenant. If that ministry condemned (v. 9), it is not because it was intrinsically evil. One wonders why God would subject the Old Testament people to an administration of law that could only condemn. We have found that Paul blamed the failure of the law on the human heart, not the law itself. In Romans 7:10 he said that the law proved to be death to him. In verse 11 he gave the reason: "For sin, seizing the opportunity afforded by the commandment, deceived me...." Cranfield says, "In the absence of the Spirit the law is misused and comes to be for those who misuse it simply 'letter' ... and this law without the Spirit 'killeth'. ... Not until Christ's resurrection and the gift of the Spirit could law come into its own as the law which is 'unto life' (Rom 7:10)."[93]

In verse 13 Paul referred to the veil that Moses put over his face after speaking the commandments (Exod. 34:29 − 35). Paul said that this was done that the Israelites might not see the telos ("end," RSV) of what was passing away (tou katargoumenou). It is generally agreed that the word katargoumenou (fading away) refers to the glory of the old covenant. Paul used the word twice in this context (vv. 7, 11) and this usage of the word helps us to understand its meaning in verse 13. Perhaps that is why Paul gave us no stated subject for the word; he had already expressed it. That which is passing away in verse 7 is the glory reflected on Moses' face (tēn doxan tou prosōpou autou tēn katargoumenēn) which represents the glory of Moses' ministry of the old covenant. In verse 11 the metaphor refers directly to the old covenant itself, which "came with glory." In verse 13 Paul said that Moses covered his face to keep the Israelites from gazing at the end (telos) of that which was passing away. The word telos is best understood as "goal" here rather than "termination" because of the difficulty of observing the termination of something which is yet in process of passing away and which has not yet come to its end. That which is passing away is the old covenant with its glorious splendor. The telos is

93. Cranfield, "St. Paul and the Law," p. 57.

Christ, for only in Christ is the veil removed (v. 14), and when it is removed Christ is revealed in his glory (v. 18).[94]

The glory of the old covenant gave way to the greater glory of the new covenant. Christ was present in that old covenant, but the veil that Paul pictured over the eyes of his fellow Israelites (v. 15) kept them from beholding him there. When one comes to Christ the veil is removed (v. 16). Now, under the new covenant, the Spirit reigns, giving life (v. 6) and transforming believers into the likeness of Christ (v. 18).

One does not find a suggestion here that the law, as a principle of obedience, has been abrogated. The emphasis is on two ministries (*diakonia*), the ministry of Moses which had glory, albeit a transient glory, and the ministry of those who serve under the new covenant. One aspect of the glory of the new covenant is its emphasis on freedom (v. 17) and the way in which obedience is facilitated. Obedience comes not by servitude to "letter" devoid of Spirit, but by the work of the Spirit who transforms believers into his likeness, effecting an obedience that the "letter" could not produce. We may not conclude that law as such passed away. It was the ministry of law that passed away. That is the way in which it administered obedience. In the new covenant, obedience is administered in the new way of the Spirit.

There is here the contrast of two covenants, the old and the new. Both administer obedience. But under the new covenant the reality of Christ facilitates obedience in a way that the old covenant could not, for when the veil is lifted, "we . . . are being transformed into his likeness with ever-increasing glory" (v. 18).

Galatians 2:16

> . . . know that a man is not justified by observing the law, but by faith in Jesus Christ. . . . By observing the law no one will be justified.

The principle set forth here is clear. The law is not a means of salvation. Paul affirmed that justification is not achieved through

---

94. But see Philip Edgcumbe Hughes, *Paul's Second Epistle to the Corinthians* (Grand Rapids: Eerdmans, 1962), pp. 108–10. Hughes understands *telos* in the sense of "to the end of the glory which was passing away, that is, that they might behold it without interruption or concealment."

the law. Legalism is condemned. Faith in Christ and trust in the works of the law for salvation are incompatible.

The same thought is set forth by the apostle in Romans 3 where he upheld the law (v. 31) but affirmed that the principle of legalism (*ex ergōn nomou*) will not save (v. 20).

Galatians 3:10 – 14

This section appears to be a scathing indictment of the law. We are told that all who "rely on observing the law are under a curse" (v. 10). "Christ redeemed us from the curse of the law" (v. 13). Most condemning of all is the statement that "the law is not based on faith" (v. 12). Paul buttressed this with a quotation from Leviticus 18:5, "The man who does these things will live by them."

Basic to the argument of Paul here is his contrast between two types of people, "those who have faith" and who are thus "blessed along with Abraham . . ." (v. 9), and those who "rely on observing the law" (v. 10).[95] The first group is called *hoi ek pisteōs* (those of faith). The second group is described as *ex ergōn nomou* (of works of law).[96] The latter phrase describes those who adhere to the principle of righteousness through works as opposed to right-eousness through faith. The passage presents a contrast between those who are of faith and those who are of law, a contrast between grace and legalism.

Paul was not condemning the law; he was condemning legal-ism. We have seen that Paul affirmed that the righteousness of the law could be pursued by faith (Rom. 9:32). When the law of right-eousness (*nomon dikaiosunēs*) was pursued on the basis of works and not faith its righteousness was sought in the wrong way (Rom. 9:32).

Paul's quotation of Leviticus 18:5 in Galatians 3:12 need not be understood as an affirmation that the law claimed a solely legal-istic function for itself. That would be out of keeping with Romans 9:32 as well as other passages in which Paul affirmed the spiri-tuality of the law.

95. For a discussion of the exegetical difficulties involved in the interpretation of v. 10, see Fuller, *Gospel and Law*, pp. 88 – 97.

96. This phrase is discussed by Douglas J. Moo in " 'Law,' 'Works of the Law,' and Legalism in Paul," *WTJ* 45 (1983): 73 – 100.

We must seek the answer to Paul's use of Leviticus 18:5 in the context of Galatians 3. Paul affirmed in Galatians 3:6 – 9 that the blessings of justification come by faith (v. 9). The ground of faith is the promise (vv. 6 – 8). The promise establishes the basis of redemption and it is faith that unleashes the blessings of justification. Righteousness is obtained through faith, not legalism.

Those who are *ek nomou* (of law) have not obtained righteousness through faith in the promise, but have sought it through trust in law. They have made the law itself the means of achieving righteousness. They have taken what was meant to be only the means of obedience and have made it the foundation of justification; and that is their error.

We must recall what was said earlier about the function of the covenants, even though it anticipates a fuller discussion later. Central to the thesis of this work is the distinction between the Abrahamic covenant and the covenants that had as their function the administration of obedience. If the righteousness of faith offered by the Abrahamic covenant is rejected, the Mosaic covenant stands alone. Its principal concern was to administer obedience for the people of God who put their faith in the Abrahamic promise covenant. If it is divorced from its cooperative role with the Abrahamic covenant, the law becomes a sterile call to obedience that cannot offer the blessings of the promise. It remains only a law covenant, divorced from promise. It is based on works. Only when it operates in conjunction with the promise covenant does it fill its proper role. Without that promise covenant it is death. Faith can no longer be the chief motivating factor in one's relationship with God.

The separation of the two covenantal principles is evident in Paul's earlier statement concerning those of faith and those of law. Understood in light of the covenantal structure suggested here, Paul's statement that "no one is justified before God by the law ..." refers to law apart from faith, that is, legalism.

We can then understand the quotation from Leviticus 18:5 in its simplest sense. The law is not of faith (*ouk estin ek pisteōs*), because it is a covenant that administers obedience, and its conditions are met by fulfilling its righteous demands. Paul quoted from Leviticus 18:5 to support his contention, "The law is not based on faith; on the contrary, 'The man who does these things will live by them.' " The words are quoted only slightly differently from the Septuagint, but reflect the Masoretic Text most accurately.[97] In each case the words emphasize that the maintenance of life through the law comes by doing the law.

The contribution of Leviticus 18:5 here is to show that the law calls for "doing," not "faith." But is not the law then opposed to faith? Is it not thus inherently evil? No! Its function was to promote obedience and thus to ensure the continued participation of the people in the promise. Their relationship to the promise had already been graciously established when the Lord sovereignly affirmed his will to be the God of Abraham's descendants. That promise was in God's mind as he led them out of Egypt. He had established the relationship; they had only to believe. The promise was the basis on which they entered the land and ultimately conquered it. The law did not establish that relationship. Its function was to maintain the standing of the people in the promise. Their continued "life" as a nation was dependent on obedience to the law. We saw life defined in this way in Leviticus 18. If they did not obey they would lose their right to the land, and hence their relationship to the promise would be forfeited (Lev. 18:24 – 28).

The law is based on obedience; the promise is based on faith. The law sets forth the principles of obedience by which one's relationship to the promise is maintained. The promise establishes the relationship in answer to the response of faith.

By quoting Leviticus 18:5 Paul was affirming that law viewed apart from faith or promise is sterile. It is only the structure of obedience. Legalists put their faith in the structure, not the life-giving promise.

Galatians 3:15 – 25

The introductory verses of this section will be discussed in a subsequent chapter. However, we may observe at this point that Paul made several important statements concerning the relationship between the promise and the law. He said in verse 17 that the promise was not nullified by law. In verse 18 he affirmed that the

---

97. The Septuagint reads *ha poiēsas auta anthrōpos zēsetai en autois*, whereas the Greek text reads *ho poiēsas auta zēsetai en autois*.

inheritance is not granted by law. And in verse 16 he spoke of the mediatorial function that Christ sustains to the promise.

Paul made several statements about the law in this passage that at first glance appear to be quite negative. He said, "We were held prisoners by the law, locked up until faith should be revealed" (v. 23). "Now that faith has come, we are no longer under the supervision of the law" (v. 25).

These statements are part of Paul's exposition of the function of the law that begins in verse 19 with the question "What, then, was the purpose of the law?" He began his answer with the words *it was added because of transgressions (tōn parabaseōn charin prosetethē).*

The word *charin* (because of) may connote either "for the sake of" or "on account of" in this clause. The former would carry the idea of pointing out transgression; to reveal to the human heart what God regarded as sin. This view is in keeping with Paul's statement in Romans 3:20, "through the law we become conscious of sin." The latter understanding of *charin* would connote that the law was added because of the sins of the Israelites; to check their propensity to sin and thus guard the promise.[98]

The former view has the advantage of being consonant with a broad spectrum of Pauline teaching with regard to the function of the law. According to Paul, not only does the law reveal what sin is (Rom. 3:20), but it creates transgression (Rom. 7:7). However, the latter view is the one taken here. The question is a difficult one and is not essential to the main conclusions of this section, but it appears to be the view that best fits with empirical considerations of the function of the law itself and the subsequent context of this passage.

The law claims to be far more than simply a means of defining sin. If it were only this, how could Paul encourage us to obey it? It obviously had a more benign function as well. True, its definition of sin was an important function. After all it is law, and law is intended to define wrongdoing. But it is difficult to conclude that this is the only reason why the law was "added" (v. 19). If it were, then Paul consigned a revered institution that governed Is-

98. For a discussion of the possible translations of *charin* in this context see J. Eadie, *Commentary on the Epistle of Paul to the Galatians* (1884; Grand Rapids: Zondervan, n.d.), pp. 263–65; J. B. Lightfoot, *The Epistle of St. Paul to the Galatians* (1865; Grand Rapids: Zondervan, 1962), pp. 144–45.

rael for centuries solely to the function of revealing the nature of sin. A whole administration of God is given only a condemnatory function.

Yet, viewed in its entirety, the law had a broader purpose. It was related to grace, in that it functioned as a structure that protected the promise. The health laws preserved the people from whom the Messiah would emerge. Even the most obscure proscriptions against Canaanite practices had the effect of preserving the promise. Magnificent institutions of the law have been carried over into the new covenant. It is difficult to say the law was added only to define sin.

The second interpretation of Paul's statement fits best with what we know of the nature of the law. As a covenant it had to do with obedience and disobedience. The law protected the promise. From what? From pagan religion? From dangerous Canaanite social practice? Not primarily. These would not have jeopardized the promise as long as the people of the promise were obedient. The threat to the promise was the disobedience of the people.

Yet their disobedience and their propensity to transgression were already known. It may be seen in the incident of the golden calf.[99] There had to be some instrument that would govern a recalcitrant people amid the new circumstances in Canaan.

The greatly expanded requirements of obedience served not only to define sin, but also to protect the promise from being invalidated due to the tendency of the people to transgress God's commandments. True, they failed under the law, but the promise was preserved. Even as they began the journey from Jerusalem to Babylon they were an intact nation. They were still the descendants of Abraham. They were not a mixture of races. They were the offspring through whom Christ would come. The law had preserved the promise but had not preserved that generation. They had taken themselves off the ground of faithful obedience to the covenant. Thus the view that the "transgressions" are those of the people seems to fit best with the broad function of the law. It would have been difficult for Paul to have convinced his Judaizing opponents that the only function of the law was to point out sin.

A possible objection to the use of "transgressions" (parabaseōn) in this way is that Paul used the word to refer to "violation of

99. Thomas E. McComiskey, "Idolatry," *ISBE*, vol. 2, p. 797.

explicit law."[100] It is difficult to see how the law could be added because of transgressions that already existed, when transgressions become such only under law and when defined by law. But Paul did not always use the word *parabasis* (transgression) of disobedience to the Mosaic law (Rom. 5:14; 1 Tim. 2:14), and the law itself is conscious of the rebellious nature of the people before the actual ratification of the Mosaic covenant. Deuteronomy 9:7 says, "From the day you left Egypt until you arrived here, you have been rebellious against the LORD." The rebellion of Israel is evidently viewed as commencing before the exodus from Egypt and was manifested in a series of transgressions that led to the ultimate expression of idolatry in the incident of the golden calf (v. 12). Their rebellion continued after the ratification of the law as well (vv. 22 – 24).

This consciousness of the penchant of the Israelites for disobedience to the divine will is also reflected at the end of Deuteronomy. It says in 31:27, "For I know how rebellious and stiff-necked you are. If you have been rebellious against the LORD while I am still alive and with you, how much more will you rebel after I die!" (See also Deut. 31:19 – 22.)

The evident purpose of the law as expressed in the Book of Deuteronomy is to protect the promise. It calls for obedience which will ensure continued participation in the blessings of the promise (30:15 – 16) and warns that disobedience will sever the people from life in the promise (30:17 – 18).

If Paul's statement is understood to mean "because of existing transgressions" it fits with the concept of the nature of law that finds the broadest expression in the Book of Deuteronomy.

The view suggested here seems to have the greater consonance with the clause "until the Seed to whom the promise referred had come" (v. 19). It is not difficult to understand Paul to say here that the law protected the promise until that promise found its full realization in Christ. When Christ came as mediator of the promise (Gal. 3:16) the promise found its security in the one who was its true guarantor; the law was no longer needed for that function.

Paul concluded that law and promise are not opposed to one another (v. 21), for if law were a valid option for achieving life, then

---

100. E. D. Burton, *A Critical and Exegetical Commentary on the Epistle to the Galatians* (Edinburgh: T. and T. Clark, 1921), p. 188.

life would come by law. Since it does not, the two are not competing sources of life (v. 21). Rather than giving law the function of bestowing life, God has declared the whole world a prisoner (*sunekleisen*) of sin (v. 22). According to Romans 11:32, God did this that he might have mercy on all, so that salvation may be by grace. The same thought obtains in Galatians 3:22. Life does not come by law. On the contrary (*alla*, v. 22), God confined the whole world to sin so that the promise could be realized through faith.

Not only does sin confine, but the law does too (v. 23). It had this function until "faith should be revealed" (v. 23). It was a custodian (*paidagōgos*) to lead to Christ (v. 24). E. D. Burton defines a "custodian" as "a slave employed in Greek and Roman families to have general charge of a boy in the years from about six to sixteen, watching over his outward behavior and attending him whenever he went from home. . . ."[101] If the law is understood to have only the function of defining sin in this context, the function of the "custodian" is not given full expression. However, if the law is understood as the guardian of the people with respect to the promise, watching over them until the full security of the promise was achieved in Christ, not only may the word *custodian* have its full meaning, but it is consonant with the whole context as well.

Paul concluded that now that the promise has been realized in Christ, the law is no longer needed (v. 25).

Paul pointed out the inferiority of law to promise in the fact that law was given through a mediator (vv. 19–20). The strong implication, although unstated, is that the promise was given directly by God. If the foregoing discussion is correct, then Paul argued that the Old Testament law was a temporary structure that guarded the promise until it found its ultimate security in Christ.

The law is thus not opposed to promise (v. 21). It fulfilled a highly spiritual function, but it is not the source of the inheritance. That is the promise.

101. Ibid., p. 200.

The Nature and Function
of Covenant
in the History of Redemption

The previous discussion has attempted to draw a distinction between two types of covenants: promissory and administrative.[1] The promissory covenants elicit the response of trust; there is not a covenanted administration of obedience in them. In the administrative covenants, the mode of human obedience is given covenantal formulation.

Arguments may be found in recent scholarship for a stipulatory element in promise covenant. This conclusion is based on analogy with the suzerain-vassal treaties of the ancient Near East.[2] However, in these treaties the stipulations are generally incorporated within the covenant. This is not so with the Abrahamic covenant. It is true that Abraham could have forfeited the promise, but provision for that possibility is not given covenantal status. It is not a part of the formal covenant language of the promise covenant. George E. Mendenhall observes, "It is not often enough seen that

1. D. J. McCarthy acknowledges the need to posit several different types of covenants. "Covenant in the Old Testament: The Present State of Inquiry," *CBQ* 27 (1965): 219–39.

2. Meredith G. Kline argues that the Abrahamic covenant is like ancient suzerain-vassal relationships and thus contains stipulations. He says, "Moreover, it is clear that by rebellion against Yahweh's word Abraham would forfeit the promise (Gen 22:16, 17a; cf. Deut 28 especially vv. 63ff.)...." *Treaty of the Great King: The Covenant Structure of Deuteronomy* (Grand Rapids: Eerdmans, 1963), p. 23.

no obligations are imposed upon Abraham."[3] In no promissory covenant in the Old Testament do we find formal stipulations on which the fulfillment of the intent depends.[4]

The promise covenant never loses its integrity. It is regarded in Old and New Testament alike as the instrument that obligates God to act on behalf of his people. Although both types of covenantal instruments are designated *bĕrît* in the Old Testament, and both have separate functions in the disposition of the inheritance, they are so inseparably bound that the inheritance cannot be successfully administered if the structure is bifurcated. The promissory covenant states and guarantees the elements of the promise; the administrative covenants set forth stipulations of obedience and, except for the covenant of circumcision, explicate the elements of the promise in terms appropriate to the economies they govern.

We can distinguish the two types of covenants by determining their primary function. The distinction between these covenantal administrations will be considered more fully in the subsequent discussion.

The Nature and Function of the Promise Covenant

The continuing force of the promise covenant is a concept essential to the central thesis of this work. We have observed support for this in the fact that its terms remain intact throughout their expression in the successive covenantal administrations of the promise. But at this point it would be well to carry the argument further.

The promise is called a covenant, and its continuing validity is

3. George E. Mendenhall, "Covenant Forms in Israelite Tradition," *BA* 17, no. 3 (1954): 62.

4. Kline alludes to Gen. 22:16–17a and Deut. 28 to support his argument that it was possible to forfeit the promise. In Gen. 22:16–17a God reaffirmed the promise after Abraham demonstrated his willingness to sacrifice his son. But Abraham was not required by covenantal stipulation to sacrifice his son. The promise covenant bestows its gracious inheritance when one responds in faith to the covenanted word. In Scripture Abraham's offer of his son is regarded as an eminent example of faith. James said of Abraham, "His faith was made complete by what he did" (2:22). It is true that the divine approbation immediately follows the oath formulation in Gen. 22:16–17, but the text says, "because you have done this," not, "you shall do this." Obedience is not a covenanted stipulation. In Deut. 28 the stipulations for attainment of the promise of the land are part of the Mosaic covenant, which is not a promissory covenant.

affirmed in a number of passages in both the Old and New Testaments. In Exodus 2:24, "God ... remembered his covenant with Abraham, with Isaac and with Jacob" (see also Exod. 6:4−5). In Deuteronomy 4:31 we are told that God will not forget his sworn covenant made with the forefathers (see also 8:18). Judges 2:1 reiterates that God's covenant with the fathers would never be broken. Psalm 105:8−10 states that the Lord remembers his covenant with Abraham, Isaac, and Jacob forever (see also Ps. 106:45). Ezekiel said that God will remember his covenant (16:60). And Micah testified, "You will be true to Jacob, and show mercy to Abraham, as you pledged on oath to our fathers in days long ago" (7:20). In the New Testament, Zechariah affirmed that God had remembered the covenant sworn to Abraham (Luke 1:72−73). Paul stated that the law did not annul the covenant previously ratified with Abraham (Gal. 3:15−17).

There are several passages in which Paul affirmed the continuing validity of the promise without designating it a *diathēkē*. But we must remember that he gave the promise the status of a *diathēkē* in Galatians 3:15, 17. Thus, statements of Paul that affirm the continuing validity of the promise assume its continuing integrity as a covenant. He said of the "promise" that it is by grace so that it "may be guaranteed to all Abraham's offspring ..." (Rom. 4:16). He proclaimed to King Agrippa that he stood on trial for hope in the promise made to the fathers (Acts 26:6).

The writer of Hebrews attested to the continuing validity of the oath (*horkos*) God swore to Abraham (Gen. 22:16−17) when he said God made the ancient oath so that "*we* who have fled to take hold of the hope offered to us may be greatly encouraged" (6:18, italics added). He affirmed the current force of the promise (6:13) for New Testament believers.

The unity of grace throughout redemptive history is a covenanted unity. It is the promise covenant, the force of which never fails.[5] It never loses its status as a *bĕrît* or oath. It is thus not subsumed under other covenants or historical economies. The unity of the covenants that govern the people of God is not a vague similarity that each shares, nor simply a reflection of the terms of

5. The unity inherent in the divine economies is discussed from a dispensational standpoint by E. E. Johnson, "Hermeneutics and Dispensationalism," in *Walvoord: A Tribute*, ed. Donald K. Campbell (Chicago: Moody, 1982), pp. 239−54.

the promise. The unity of grace is expressed in the unfailing promise covenant. It is a continuing legal entity.[6]

The promise is stated in two promissory covenants that figure prominently in the history of redemption: the Abrahamic and the Davidic covenants. A unique relationship exists between these covenants. Both are affirmations of the promise,[7] and both lack formal stipulations of obedience. The major difference is the emphasis in the Davidic covenant on the role of David's dynasty in the disposition of the promise.

The covenant with David did not abrogate the Abrahamic covenant; it refined it and served as a gracious reaffirmation of the promise.[8] It expressed the promise in terms that were peculiarly appropriate to David. It is essentially the same promise the Lord swore to uphold in the maledictory oath witnessed by Abraham.[9] It is a reiteration of the promise and it witnesses to the continuing validity of the original promise-oath. Because it expresses the promise, it is appealed to by the writers of Scripture in the same way in which appeal is made to the Abrahamic covenant. Indeed, it was the foundation of the Davidic theology that came into such prominence in the Prophets.

The demise of the Davidic monarchy presented the people with not only a national emergency, but a theological emergency as well. If the earthly Davidic monarchy should fall, what of the promise? The emergency was met by appeal to the promises given to David and Abraham. In Isaiah, both the Abrahamic and Davidic theologies find expression, but from the time of the exile the Da-

6. This structure acknowledges the presence of grace in the Mosaic legislation. The promissory covenant is the repository of grace, whereas the administrative covenants oversee obedience.

7. After he discusses the historical relationship between the Abrahamic and Davidic covenants, John Bright concludes, "But, whatever their historical relationships may have been, it appears that in the course of time the Davidic covenant came to be viewed, in some circles at least, as no less than a renewal and extension of the promises to Abraham." *Covenant and Promise: The Prophetic Understanding of the Future in Pre-exilic Israel* (Philadelphia: Westminster, 1976), p. 71.

8. Recent interpretation of the Davidic covenant is discussed by J. Levenson, "The Davidic Covenant and Its Modern Interpreters," *CBQ* 41 (1979): 205–19.

9. R. E. Clements observes a close connection between the two covenants. He says of the Davidic covenant, "This type of covenant is precisely that which we have found to be reflected in Genesis 15 as the original nucleus of the Abrahamic covenant ... we may reasonably conclude that the form of the Davidic covenant was influenced by the recollection in Jerusalem of the ancient covenant with Abraham." *Abraham and David* (London: SCM, 1967), p. 54.

vidic theology comes into greater prominence.[10] Zechariah, a post-exilic prophet, makes no mention of Abraham, but refers to David in his message of hope (12:7 – 8, 10, 12; 13:1). This was particularly appropriate, for the great spiritual need of the time centered on the promise in its relationship to the earthly Davidic throne. The promise was applied to that need by appeal to an element within it that was most appropriate to the situation. It continued to ring with authority in the midst of despair and theological uncertainty.[11]

Since the promissory covenants are of such great importance in the drama of redemption, it is essential to understand their nature and function. One of the important characteristics of *běrît* observable in the promise covenant made with Abraham is that of the formal statement of the terms of the covenant. God obligated himself by oath to fulfill the terms of the promise. If one swears to fulfill an intent the oath is worthless if the terms of the intent are not stated. The promise covenant of Genesis 15:12 – 21 places the terms of the oath in the formal structure of a covenant. What was a promise in Genesis 12 has become a covenanted oath in Genesis 15.

This function of covenant as the expression of intent may be observed in other promise covenants found in the Old Testament. In Genesis 9:9 – 11 God affirms his intent never again to destroy the earth by a flood. In Jeremiah 33:20 there is reference to the Lord's covenant with day and night. The intent is to maintain the regular pattern of the earth's solar revolution (v. 20b). Hosea 2:18 speaks of a covenant with the beasts of the field. The context goes on to establish God's intent to be that of universal peace and safety (vv. 18b – 20). In 2 Samuel 7, the promise is reiterated to David. God's intent to fulfill his promise through David's line is the central concept of this covenant. It is not based on legal obedience. On the contrary, the perpetuity of the covenant is guaranteed by God: "But my love will never be taken away from him, as I took it away from Saul . . ." (v. 15).

The fact that Davidic kings who were disobedient would be

10. Reference is made to Abraham in Isa. 29:22; 41:8; 51:2; 63:16. The Davidic theology is reflected in 9:7; 16:5; 37:35; 38:5; 55:3.

11. Bright observes, "The promises to Abraham and to David assured [Israel] that, in the final analysis, her future rested ultimately not in what she was—or had, or had not, done—but in the sure, immutable purposes of God which nothing could cancel." *Covenant and Promise*, p. 196.

punished (2 Sam. 7:14) is not a condition on which the purpose of God depended.[12] Indeed, the intent to perpetuate the Davidic dynasty is assured by the promise that disobedient kings would be punished, but not so as to terminate the royal line. Verses 14 – 15 state, "When he does wrong, I will punish him with the rod of men. . . . But my love will never be taken away from him, as I took it away from Saul, whom I removed from before you." The Saulide dynasty had been terminated by God, but the Davidic covenant precluded that possibility for David's line. The purpose of God to give David a dynasty is presented in the form of a promissory covenant. There are no stipulations on which that purpose is conditioned.

Another function of the Abrahamic covenant is to assure the implementation of the expressed intent. This is the function of the oath. The security of the terms depends on the integrity and ability of the one who obligates himself to the oath (see Heb. 6:13 – 20).

Since the promise covenant given to Abraham continues in force, the authority of the oath that backs it has never been vitiated. It remains the sworn intent of God to carry out his purposes for the people of God in all ages.

On the basis of this discussion, we may conclude that the primary function of the promise covenant is to grant the inheritance. This is done unconditionally. The covenant righteousness of the promissory covenants is the positive response of faith. God has affirmed his purpose to give his people an inheritance, and he stated that purpose in covenantal instruments of a specific type. Whether we find it proclaimed to Abraham or to David, the promise is given in unconditional covenants.

The Nature and Function of the Administrative Covenants

The covenants that have the distinct function of administering the terms of obedience in redemptive history are the covenant of circumcision, the Mosaic covenant, and the new covenant. The

12. But see O. Palmer Robertson, *The Christ of the Covenants*, (Grand Rapids: Baker, 1980), p. 247, where this is designated a condition.

covenants of Deuteronomy 29 and Joshua 24 are considered here to be reaffirmations of the Mosaic covenant.[13]

The Nature and Function of Circumcision as an Administrative Covenant

The relationship of circumcision to the subsequent administrative covenants

In this section we shall examine the function of circumcision as a formal administrative instrument for governing an aspect of human obedience. But it must be recognized that the bĕrît of circumcision is not the same in every respect as the administrative covenants that follow. These covenants, the law and the new covenant, are unlike the bĕrît of circumcision in a number of ways. Circumcision was a physical rite; the subsequent administrations were verbal covenant instruments. Circumcision was inextricably bound to the promise covenant in that it was a sign of that covenant;[14] although the Mosaic and new covenants express the elements of the promise, they do not have the same precise relationship to the promise-oath. Circumcision was only one stipulation of obedience. The mode of obedience in the law is far more complex, and obedience in the new covenant is motivated by the Holy Spirit. The immediate context in which circumcision was introduced (Gen. 17:9–14) contains no formal statement of the elements of the promise, whereas both the law covenant and the new covenant express and explicate these elements. It is probably because circumcision was a sign (Gen. 17:11) of the Abrahamic covenant and was thus inextricably bound to it that it is not designated the "first covenant" by the writer of Hebrews. He gives that designation to the law (8:7).

Even though circumcision differs so greatly from the subsequent covenants that oversee obedience, it is considered an administrative covenant in this work only because it shares one function with them, that is, the governing of an aspect of obedience. However, we must not lose sight of its close relationship to

13. The form of the covenant in Josh. 24 and its relationship to the Mosaic covenant are discussed by Mendenhall, "Covenant Forms in Israelite Tradition," pp. 67–70.

14. For a discussion of the significance of circumcision as a sign see Meredith G. Kline, By Oath Consigned: A Reinterpretation of the Covenant Signs of Circumcision and Baptism (Grand Rapids: Eerdmans, 1968), pp. 39–49.

the promise covenant, nor its continuing validity in the law and, in a spiritual sense, in the new covenant.

The distinction between circumcision and the promise covenant

The question of the relationship of the rite of circumcision to the Abrahamic covenant is a difficult one. The position taken here is that circumcision represents a distinct covenantal administration within the complex structure that governed the disposition of the inheritance.

Circumcision is introduced against the background of the promise covenant. This covenant is cited and its terms stated in Genesis 17:2 – 8. There is little doubt that the *bĕrît* mentioned in 17:9 refers to the Abrahamic covenant when it says, "As for you, you must keep my covenant, you and your descendants after you for the generations to come." No other covenant has been introduced into the narrative. There is no warrant for seeing it as a covenant other than the Abrahamic covenant.

This may appear to contradict the conclusion that the promissory covenants contain no stipulations of obedience. But a further reading shows that circumcision is given separate status as a *bĕrît*. It is called such in Genesis 17:10, "This is my covenant with you and your descendants after you, the covenant you are to keep: Every male among you shall be circumcised." If circumcision were one in every way with the promise covenant, there would be no need to introduce it in the way in which it is introduced in the context: "This is my covenant. . . ." We have not encountered this *bĕrît* before. It is true that it is given in close connection with the Abrahamic covenant, but it is given separate status as an administration within that covenant by virtue of its distinct introduction and its designation as a *bĕrît*. The giving of the promise was carried out in a complex structure in which we may observe the interplay of two covenantal functions, both designated *bĕrît*.

Several commentators have understood the application of the term *bĕrît* to circumcision to denote only its function as a sign of the Abrahamic covenant.[15] Thus, it is not given separate coven-

---

15. H. C. Leupold says, "The word 'covenant' must here be used by metonymy for 'covenant-sign,' or 'covenant condition.' " *Exposition of Genesis*, 2 vols. (1942; Grand Rapids: Baker, 1949), vol. 1, p. 520. R. S. Candlish understands it as an elliptical structure. He

antal status. However, several factors support our understanding circumcision as a covenant or administration in its own right.

The words *this is my covenant* introduce a function of *bĕrît* which we have not found in the narrative of Abraham's encounter with God. The words *wĕ'attâ* (as for you) in verse 9 dramatically shift the covenantal obligation from God to Abraham. To this point in the narrative God has obligated himself unconditionally to give Abraham and his descendants an inheritance. When God says, "And as for you, you must keep my covenant," we encounter an aspect of covenant we have not seen before: human obligation. Circumcision is not promissory in nature; hence it differs from the promissory covenant to which God had obligated himself in the earlier accounts. In the promissory covenant God took upon himself the sole obligation to give an inheritance. In the *bĕrît* of circumcision Abraham and his descendants assumed the obligation to observe that rite, and this obedience was a sign of their continued participation in the promise.

We may not understand circumcision to function only as a stipulatory element within the Abrahamic covenant, for how then can we explain its distinct designation as a *bĕrît?* It is true that certain types of treaties in the ancient world had such elements. Conditions of obedience may be found in most. But the conditions were part of the one covenantal instrument. The intent of the covenant depended on a proper observance of the conditions for its realization. It was not so with God's covenanted word. His purpose stands forever. Individuals may forfeit their standing in the promise, but that could not invalidate God's stated purpose.

So, when we read "as for you," we are led to expect an element of obligation. The *bĕrît* of circumcision is not promissory, it is stipulatory. There is no exposition of the promise in the context. It is different from the promise *bĕrît* that God made with Abraham. Since it is given the designation *bĕrît* we should not regard it as a stipulation that is essential to the realization of the promise in history. The promise that salvation would come to the Gentiles did not depend on individual submission to the rite of circum-

concludes, " 'This is my covenant' must be understood as elliptical. . . . It cannot be taken absolutely and literally as it stands; for, in that case, not only is it at variance with all the teaching of Scripture upon the subject, but it has no clear or distinct meaning at all." He understands it as a "token or pledge, a confirmation and assurance of the covenant-transaction. . . ." *Commentary on Genesis* (1868; Grand Rapids: Zondervan, 1956), p. 280.

cision; it depended solely on the purposes of God expressed in the promise. The nature of circumcision as a rite of individual obedience is underscored by the words *and as for you*. The function of the promise covenant as the instrument that obligated God to act on behalf of his people is underscored by the words of God in Genesis 17:4, "As for me. . . ." Since circumcision functions differently from the *běrît* to which God obligated himself, we may understand why it is given this separate status.

Circumcision is designated a *běrît* again in this context in Genesis 17:13, where it is called "my covenant in your flesh. . . ." It was thus a sign of the participation of individuals in the promise. But this function of circumcision as a sign should not lead us to deny its separate convenantal function. It is, after all, called a *běrît*, not an *'ôt* (sign), in this clause.

Circumcision is given its own integrity as a covenant in a New Testament tradition. Acts 7:8 says, "Then he gave Abraham the covenant of circumcision" (*diathēkēn peritomēs*).

The role of circumcision as a *běrît* is thus different from the role of the promissory covenant. The latter is eternal and inviolable, and elicits the response of faith. Circumcision, on the other hand, governs an act of obedience and is thus stipulatory in nature. There is a covenant function involved in circumcision that is different from the function of the promise covenant.

Circumcision may be called a *běrît* because it fits the definition noted earlier. It involves the covenant concepts of relationship, obligation, stipulation, and mutuality. It was disobeyed on pain of separation from the inheritance (Gen. 17:14).

Covenantal language is applied to this use of *běrît*. The covenant of circumcision was to be kept (Gen. 17:9). The Hebrew word translated "kept" is the word *šāmar*, a word frequently applied to the keeping of a covenant (e.g., Exod. 19:5; Deut. 29:9; 1 Kings 11:11; Ps. 78:10). In this respect circumcision as a *běrît* was similar in function to the Sabbath, which was a covenant sign in the Mosaic legislation. In Exodus 31:14 – 17 the Israelites were commanded to "keep" (*šāmar*) the Sabbath. The observation of the Sabbath was a sign between God and the Israelites forever (v. 17). In verse 16 the Sabbath is designated a *běrît:* "The Israelites are to observe the Sabbath, celebrating it for the generations to come as a lasting covenant."

The Sabbath could function as a *běrît* because it established a relationship that involved obligation. The Israelites were "to do" (la'ăśôt) the Sabbath as an everlasting covenant. It could function in its own right because it had a special role within the Mosaic covenant. It was singled out because it was a sign. This special function caused it to stand out from the complex of regulations inherent in the law. Because it was a special function of the law and validly fulfilled the role of běrît, it could be regarded as a běrît in and of itself.

In the Mosaic era both promise covenant and law covenant, each with its own integrity, worked together to effect the granting and maintaining of the inheritance. We should not be surprised to find the same relationship in the Abrahamic era. Thus, we may understand the words *this is my covenant*, with reference to circumcision, in their most basic sense.

It is necessary to observe a further refinement. We have noted that the promise covenant elicited the response of faith and obedience. How then is circumcision different from that obedience? Can we make a valid distinction between its requirement and the obedience of faith called for by the promise covenant? Is not circumcision really a response of faithful obedience as well?

The answer to the last question is an unequivocal yes. Paul affirmed that as well. Speaking of Abraham, he said that circumcision was "a seal of the righteousness that he had by faith while he was still uncircumcised" (Rom. 4:11). But circumcision was a precise stipulation. It thus differed from the broad ethical response called for by the promise covenant. Abraham's faithful obedience was not to be expressed only by circumcision. That rite did not prescribe the range of his response of obedience. His submission to it was a manifestation of his righteousness, but only a small aspect of it.

The function of circumcision was to prescribe obedience in one physical rite. It stipulated one aspect of obedience and that aspect had the distinct function of serving as a sign of Abraham's participation in the promise. In this way circumcision is like the law covenant under which it was later subsumed. Circumcision did not grant the inheritance, nor did the law, but both administered the obedience necessary for participation in it. Both specified the nature of obedience, and those stipulations were given for important reasons in redemptive history. The stipulations of the law served, among other things, to protect the people in their quest for the land. Circumcision had a distinct function too—it was a sign of the Abrahamic covenant. In that sense circumcision is different from the response of faithful obedience to the promise. It is a prescribed response. It is a stipulation that could be broken, and hence it is a *bĕrît*.

The Nature and Function of the Mosaic Covenant as an Administrative Covenant

The explication of the terms of the promise in the Mosaic covenant

A new era dawned when Moses received the covenant at Sinai. This covenant administered the obedience of God's people through its complex legislation. The function of the Mosaic covenant was more extensive than was the simple covenant of circumcision. Not only did the Mosaic covenant administer obedience but also it functioned as a formal expression of the terms of the promise.[16]

The expression of the promise in the Mosaic covenant differs from its earlier expression in the Abrahamic covenant in that the elements of the promise are expressed in terms peculiar to the historical situation that obtained under the administration of the Mosaic covenant. This may be observed in the way these terms are expressed before and after the ratification ceremony recorded in Exodus 19. In the early chapters of Exodus the promise is referred to in terms quite like those of the Abrahamic promise (6:4, 7–8) and, except for the anticipation of inheriting the land (15:17), the promise is viewed in relationship to the patriarchs (3:6, 15; 4:5; 6:2–4). At the ratification of the covenant recorded in chapter 19, the elements of the promise are expressed in language appropriate to the new historical situation. The people are to become a nation, and the elements of the promise are given a more nationalistic cast; the people are to become a kingdom of priests and a holy nation (19:6). We may observe then that a function of the Mosaic covenant was to state the promise in terms appropriate to the economy it governed. The new covenant shares this function as well.

It is important to note that the promise found expression in a covenant that involved mutuality of obligation. Note the condition: "Now if you obey me fully and keep my covenant, then out of all

16. Compare the discussion in chapter 2.

nations you will be my treasured possession" (v. 5). This was followed by a response of ratification: "We will do everything the Lord has said" (v. 8).

The Mosaic covenant was clearly an administrative covenant. Its function was to govern the obedience of God's people. Like the covenant of circumcision, its stipulations had an important function. They served to protect the people as they moved into the hostile environment of Canaan. They defined sin and urged holiness. They provided the basis of a strong social structure. They contributed to the health and welfare of the nation. It was a profoundly moving moment when the people responded as they did.

The expression of the promise for the peculiar circumstances of this covenantal era was given in the form of covenant. It was in covenant form that the refinement of the terms of the promise was stated, and it was by obedience to covenant stipulation that the relationship of the people to the inheritance was guarded. The key to understanding the peculiar application of the promise to the people of Moses' era is covenant.

The confirmatory function of the Mosaic covenant

The Mosaic covenant not only explicated the terms of the promise, but served to confirm them as well. In this way it shares another function of *bĕrît*. We may observe this in numerous places in Exodus and Deuteronomy. We recall such statements as "you will be for me a kingdom of priests and a holy nation" (Exod. 19:6); "the LORD your God has chosen you . . . to be his people, his treasured possession" (Deut. 7:6); "when the LORD your God brings you into the land . . ." (Deut. 7:1).

We must not think that the Mosaic covenant usurps the role of the promise covenant because it has this function. If this were so, we cannot understand why Moses would appeal to that promise as he does. The terms of the promise in the Mosaic covenant are confirmed on condition of obedience; thus its confirmatory function is different from that of the promise covenant. The promise that Israel would be a kingdom of priests and a holy nation (Exod. 19:6) is preceded by the words "now if you obey me fully and keep my covenant . . ." (v. 5). The promise that the people are to be God's treaured possession (Deut. 7:6) is based on the promise to Abraham (Deut. 7:7−8). That promise still retains its integrity.

The confirmatory function of the Mosaic covenant involves the obedience of God's people. It confirms, on condition of obedience, the terms of the promise-oath as those terms apply to the economy it governs. The promise confirms its terms unconditionally and for all time. The Mosaic covenant confirms, within its covenant terms and conditions, the elements of promise as they relate to that era in God's redemptive dealings with his people.

The distinction between the Mosaic covenant and the promise covenant

A study of the Mosaic legislation demonstrates that the promise *běrît* and the *běrît* of law were both regarded as having separate status and function. The promise covenant made with the fathers is called a *běrît* throughout the reign of law. In Exodus 2:24, "God . . . remembered his covenant with Abraham. . . ." In 6:4 God said, "I also established my covenant with them to give them the land of Canaan. . . ." In 6:5 God remembered his covenant. In Deuteronomy 4:31 God will not "forget the covenant with your forefathers. . . ." In 7:12 God will keep the covenant of love he swore to the forefathers. There are many other such references. These are sufficient to show that the *běrît* made with Abraham continued to have force and obligated God to act on behalf of his people.

The law is also called a *běrît* (e.g., Exod. 19:5; Deut. 4:13; 5:2). Thus, two separate administrations governed the inheritance in the Old Testament. Each had its own integrity and function, but they were inseparably bound in the fulfillment of the divine purpose.

Paul affirmed the enduring force of the promise covenant in the era of law (Gal. 3:15 – 17). The law, which he called a *diathēkē* in Galatians 4:24, does not annul the promise, which he also termed a *diathēkē* in 3:15, 17.

The offer of life in the law

We observed this function of the law in our discussion of Romans 10:5 – 13, but if we are to have the full-orbed function of the law before us at this point it would be well to recall what was observed there. According to Leviticus 18:5, the law offers life. But this is not to be understood as eternal life. The law did not grant the inheritance. Life in the law connotes the viability of the relationship of the nation or the individual to the promised inheritance. The law, no matter how well observed, is never presented in Scripture as an option to faith as the means of salvation.

Evidence for this meaning of the word *life* was given in the discussion of Romans 10. Both passages used by Paul in that context set forth that connotation of the word. But we may note the concept set forth in other passages, particularly in Deuteronomy. In 4:1, life is associated with possession of the land which the God of their fathers had already given the Israelites. In 5:33 life is welfare and continued existence in the land (see also 8:1, 3; 16:20). Throughout the Book of Deuteronomy there is the clear consciousness that the land has already been given. The people are to be obedient to the commandments lest they perish as a nation.

The inheritance was granted by promise and its continued enjoyment was guaranteed by obedience. Obedience, in the final analysis, was a validation of a living faith. The law did not grant the inheritance, but disobedience to it would cause the nation to perish. They would be severed from their source of national life and existence. As long as they were obedient to God, both nationally and individually, they were in a vital relationship to him which the Old Testament calls "life."

There is a sense in which life was given to them by promise. It established a living relationship with God. God brought them into existence and endowed them with a glorious future, but the function of law with regard to this relationship was one of maintenance. It served to maintain life through obedience. We may thus speak of life in the law, but we must understand that it is not the granting of life that we speak about. It is the continued viability of the relationship established by the granting of the promise to Abraham and his descendants; this viability is maintained through obedience to the commands of God.

The Nature and Function of the New Covenant as an Administrative Covenant

The present validity of the new covenant

Does the new covenant govern the relationship of God's people to the promise today?[17] Can it properly be called a covenant that administers the response of obedience?

17. For a discussion of the present validity of the new covenant of Jeremiah see Albertus Pieters, *The Seed of Abraham: A Biblical Study of Israel, the Church, and the Jew* (Grand Rapids: Eerdmans, 1950), pp. 60–84; O. T. Allis, *Prophecy and the Church* (Philadelphia: Presbyterian and Reformed, 1945), pp. 154, 155.

A number of works presently available set forth the view that the new covenant is primarily for Israel.[18] Several of these affirm that the blessings set forth in the new covenant have been given to the church, but apart from any covenantal validation.[19] Thus, according to this view, the church is not under the new covenant in the sense that that covenant governs the people of God today.

Several crucial passages must be examined in the consideration of this important question. The first is the familiar statement uttered by Christ at the Last Supper. In Matthew 26:28 and Mark 14:24, the statement is reported in the words "this is my blood of the covenant." Several manuscripts read "new covenant" in these passages.[20] If "new" was not the original reading, the sense is not altered, because the institution of this covenant (which is based on the blood of Christ and not the blood of animals) involves the idea of newness. The word *new* may thus be superfluous in these contexts. In Luke 22:20[21] and 1 Corinthians 11:25 the words are reported in this way, "This cup is the new covenant in my blood." The word *new* in these passages is supported by strong manuscript evidence.[22]

These words, spoken by Christ the night before he died, would

18. Most modern dispensationalists affirm the present validity of the new covenant. However, since a significant amount of literature on the Epistle to the Hebrews reflects the view that the new covenant is distinctly Jewish in nature, that view must be considered. See W. H. G. Thomas, *"Let Us Go On," The Secret of Christian Progress in the Epistle to the Hebrews* (Grand Rapids: Zondervan, 1944); William L. Pettingill, *Into the Holiest* (Findlay, Ohio: Fundamental Truth Publishers, 1939); William R. Newell, *Hebrews, Verse by Verse* (Chicago: Moody, 1947).

19. Thomas says, "But we Christians have the spiritual reality of this covenant, which, while made with Israel, is for our benefit as well ... so we distinguish between the primary interpretation to Israel and the secondary (spiritual) application to the church today." *"Let Us Go On,"* pp. 106, 107. E. S. English says, "The Church, then, is not under the new covenant; the Church is, however, a beneficiary of the new covenant. . . ." *Studies in the Epistle to the Hebrews* (Travelers Rest, S.C.: Southern Bible House, 1955), p. 227.

20. It is generally agreed that the better manuscripts support the omission of "new." The omission is supported, for example, by the combination of ℵ and B. In the case of Matt. 26:28 the cursive 33 as well as p 37 supports the omission. The reading *new* is supported by several witnesses, including A, C, D, W, Latin, and Syriac. It is easy to understand how "new" might find its way into the text under the influence of Jer. 31:31; Luke 22:20; and 1 Cor. 11:25. The omission of "new" thus constitutes the more difficult reading and should be given serious consideration.

21. This verse is omitted from the RSV. The textual authority for omitting the end of Luke 22:19 and all of verse 20 is very weak.

22. The word *new* is supported by p 75, ℵ, A, B, C, K, and other manuscripts. There is no support for a reading other than "new" in 1 Cor. 11:25.

certainly bring to the minds of the disciples the new covenant that is mentioned in Jeremiah. There is only one place in all the Old Testament where the new covenant is called "new"; that is Jeremiah 31. The association of Jesus' words with the new covenant in Jeremiah would be most natural. It was a dramatic moment when Jesus lifted the cup in the dim interior of that room, for his action heralded the establishment of that new covenant with all its blessings—blessings incomparably greater than any the old covenant could have given.

One of the blessings of the new covenant cited in Jeremiah is forgiveness of sin (31:34); in fact, it appears that all the benefits of the new covenant derive from this one element. Forgiveness of sin is specifically cited by Christ as a blessing of the new covenant initiated by his blood (Matt. 26:28).

The second statement to be noted is 2 Corinthians 3:6, "He has made us competent as ministers of a new covenant—not of the letter but of the Spirit; for the letter kills, but the Spirit gives life." In this passage the apostle Paul affirmed that his sufficiency in preaching the gospel was from God and not in himself. God qualified him to be a minister (*diakonos*) of a "new covenant." His competency derived from the nature of this new covenant. This covenant is one that flows with life and promise. It is not a covenant of written law (*gramma*) but of Spirit (*pneuma*); not of burdensome regulations but of the inward, animating force of which Jeremiah spoke when he said that God will "write [the law] on their hearts" (31:33).[23] Paul's statement thus clearly reflects the promise of the covenant in Jeremiah 31.

Paul understood the promise of the new covenant to be in force and affirmed that he was a minister of that covenant. In the light of this it is difficult to hold that the church does not participate formally in the new covenant.

The third group of statements to be considered is perhaps the most important. It is Hebrews 7:1 – 10:18. In this extensive passage the writer of Hebrews discussed the superiority of the high priesthood of Christ over the Levitical priesthood. In chapter 7 he compared the priesthood of Christ with that of Melchizedek. He began

---

23. Philip Edgcumbe Hughes notes, "The distinction here . . . indicates the difference between the law as externally written at Sinai on tablets of stone and the same law as written internally in the heart of the Christian believer." *Paul's Second Epistle to the Corinthians* (Grand Rapids: Eerdmans, 1962), p. 100.

by describing the eminent greatness of Melchizedek (7:1 – 10) and the imperfections of the Aaronic priesthood (7:11 – 14). He then spoke of the superiority of the priesthood of Christ (7:15 – 28). In this latter section he quoted from Psalm 110:4 ("You are a priest forever, in the order of Melchizedek"; v. 17) to support the fact that the power of Christ's indestructible life (v. 16) makes him "a priest forever" (v. 17). Since the change of a priesthood necessitates a change of law (v. 12), there is accordingly an annulment of the old law (v. 18). But the priesthood of Christ introduces a better hope (v. 19). Jesus' induction into an everlasting priesthood was accompanied by an oath (v. 20). Not so the Aaronic priesthood (v. 20). Under the old covenant the priests were not backed by oath, but Christ's priesthood is upheld by an irrevocable oath (v. 21). The oath states that Christ is to be a priest forever, unlike the Aaronic priests; it is this oath that makes Christ "the guarantee of a better covenant" (v. 22). The Aaronic priests were only types of the eternal high priest from whom they derived their efficacy; therefore, unlike them, Christ can save to the uttermost (v. 25).

The argumentation of the writer of Hebrews does not easily lead to the conclusion that the "better covenant" is yet to be placed in force. He did not clearly posit a hiatus following the annulment of the law in which covenantal blessings and institutions are completely lacking. On the contrary, the priesthood of the old covenant has been supplanted by the priesthood of Christ, and the sacrifices of the old covenant have been replaced by the one sacrifice of Christ. It is most natural to understand this to be saying that although the Levitical priesthood and the sacrifices of the old covenant have been annulled, they have been replaced by incomparably greater institutions—an eternal priesthood and a once-for-all sacrifice. The continuing existence of the covenantal institutions of priesthood and sacrifice strongly implies the immediate continuation of a covenantal context for these institutions. This is the implication of 7:12, where the writer argued that a change of priesthood brings about a change of law. The priestly ministry of Christ has not only effected the annulment of the law, but also put in force a new law, the law of Christ.

In Hebrews 8:1 – 13 the writer related the high priesthood of Christ to the concept of covenant. He argued that the priestly ministry of Jesus is as superior to the ministry of the Aaronic priests as the covenant which he mediates is superior to the old covenant. He quoted the passage in Jeremiah (31:31 – 34) extensively to prove that the old covenant was rendered ineffectual by the people and was to be replaced (Heb. 8:7).

It has been asserted that the quotation of Jeremiah 31:31 – 34 in Hebrews 8:8 – 12 does not prove that the new covenant of Jeremiah is now in force for the church. Several reasons have been advanced for this. One is that the quotation from Jeremiah says only that the old covenant had to be replaced; it does not say that the new covenant is now in force.[24] Another is that the new covenant of Jeremiah is not presently in force because there are two "new covenants," one for the church and one for Israel.[25] Since the new covenant of Jeremiah was made specifically with the houses of Israel and Judah (Jer. 31:31), it awaits its fulfillment in the time of Israel's future conversion.

It is true that Jeremiah 31:31 – 34 is used in this context to support the fact that the old covenant was to pass away, but the quotation relates to more than simply verse 7, which indicates that the old covenant was annulled. If the author of Hebrews wished to prove only this by the quotation, he could have stopped at Jeremiah 31:32, for the rest of the passage goes on to set forth the promises of the new covenant. The quotation of the whole passage is significant, for the author of Hebrews never elsewhere quoted a passage beyond its appropriate limits. Quoted passages are generally brief catenas that support his arguments. No extraneous material is quoted. One is warranted in looking to the preceding context to see if anything there is given support by the full quotation.

In verse 6 the author speaks of the better promises of the new covenant and argues on the basis of these promises for the superiority of the covenant that Jesus mediates. The quotation of all of Jeremiah 31:31 – 34 supports not only the argument that the law has been annulled, but also the argument that the covenant which Christ mediates is founded on better promises. The writer

24. John F. Walvoord, *The Millennial Kingdom* (Findlay, Ohio: Dunham, 1959), p. 216.

25. C. C. Ryrie, *The Basis of the Premillennial Faith* (New York: Loizeaux, 1953), pp. 119 – 24. But see *The Ryrie Study Bible* on Heb. 8:6: "The covenant Christ mediates is a better covenant ... Christians are ministers of it (2 Cor 3:6); and it will yet have an aspect of its fulfillment in relation to Israel and Judah in the millennium...." See also J. D. Pentecost, *Things to Come: A Study in Biblical Eschatology* (Findlay, Ohio: Dunham, 1958), pp. 124, 125 and Walvoord, *The Millennial Kingdom*, pp. 218, 219.

of Hebrews demonstrated the superiority of the new covenant (v. 6) and argued for the need of a new covenant (v. 7). The argument is a cohesive one which extends through verses 6 and 7, for verse 7 begins with the words *ei gar* (for if), indicating a continuation of thought.

Since the quotation from Jeremiah 31 is used in support of the writer's argument, it is most natural to understand it as a support for all that he contended in this unbroken argument. Both the promises and the need for a new covenant are expressed in the quotation.

It is difficult to argue that the present mediatorial office of Christ spoken of in verse 6 guarantees only a future covenant that relates to Israel alone. If Jeremiah 31:31−34 is quoted in its entirety to support both the annulment of the old covenant and the "better promises" of the preceding argument, it appears as though the writer saw the new covenant of Jeremiah as predicting the ministry of Christ, a ministry that he has already received and which he now mediates. The point of the writer's argument is that we now have a high priest in Christ (8:1) whose ministry is described throughout the chapter. There is no clear evidence that the new covenant is not now in force. The writer of Hebrews called his readers to the "better promises" of that covenant.

In 9:15−17 the writer spoke of the new covenant: "For this reason Christ is the mediator of a new covenant, that those who are called may receive the promised eternal inheritance—now that he has died as a ransom to set them free from the sins committed under the first covenant. In the case of a will, it is necessary to prove the death of the one who made it, because a will is in force only when somebody has died; it never takes effect while the one who made it is living."

It is clear from this great statement of the gospel that Christ's death made him the mediator of the new covenant. The new covenant was put in force by the death of Christ. The realities, of which the Old Testament covenantal institutions were but copies, are here.

This reference to the ratification of the new covenant by the death of Christ is regarded by some as referring to the new covenant for the church, not the new covenant for Israel. The contention that there are two "new covenants," one for Israel and one for the church, deserves consideration. According to this view, the new covenant for the church, apart from the references in the

Gospels, is alluded to in 2 Corinthians 3:6; Hebrews 8:6; 9:15; 10:29; 13:20. The new covenant for Israel is mentioned in Romans 11:27 and Hebrews 8:7 – 13; 10:16 – 17.[26]

If something as monumental as a new covenant for the church— distinct from Israel's new covenant—had been instituted in the economy of God, one wonders why there is no record of its initiation, and why it is cited with no clear distinction from the new covenant of Jeremiah 31. When reading a context like Hebrews 8:6 – 13, one goes immediately from a reference to the better covenant, ascribed to the church in this view, to the covenant of Jeremiah 31, ascribed to Israel. The absence of any definitive contextual delineation of the allegedly different covenants is, to say the least, confusing and suspicious. The most natural reaction of the reader is to identify the two covenants as one.

However, the greatest difficulty is in the context of Hebrews 10:11 – 17. It is held that Hebrews 10:16 – 17 refers to the covenant with Israel. These verses are a quotation from Jeremiah 31:33 – 34. They function in the context as authoritative support for the preceding argument (Heb. 10:11 – 14). The purpose of this argument is to demonstrate that Christ has made one final sacrifice and has sat down at the right hand of God to await his ultimate triumph. The writer then concluded, "Because by one sacrifice he has made perfect forever those who are being made holy" (v. 14). Christ, by his once-for-all sacrifice, has brought to completeness those who are being sanctified. The words *those who are being made holy* are in a present passive participial construction (*tous hagiazomenous*) connoting present action. The sanctifying ministry of Christ is one that he is now carrying on. It cannot be construed as a reference to a future ministry.

The writer then quoted Jeremiah 31:33 to substantiate his argument:

The Holy Spirit also testifies to us about this (*Marturei de hēmin kai to pneuma to hagion*):

"This is the covenant I will make with them
after that time, says the Lord.
I will put my laws in their hearts,
and I will write them on their minds." [Heb. 10:15 – 16]

26. Ryrie, *The Basis of the Premillennial Faith*, pp. 115 – 25; Pentecost, *Things to Come*, p. 124.

The author affirmed by this quotation that the Holy Spirit spoke beforehand in Jeremiah 31:33 of the gracious benefits of the one sacrifice of Christ. This verse speaks of the fact that God will implant his laws in the hearts of his people, giving them the will to obey them. The prophecy of the new covenant in Jeremiah envisioned a holy people. The author quoted this to support the fact that the sacrifice of Christ effected that holiness. The next verse quoted, Jeremiah 31:34, says, "Their sins and lawless acts I will remember no more." This affirms that the sins of the people under the new covenant would be wholly forgiven, and this is the point of the argument that God "has made perfect forever those who are being made holy" (Heb. 10:14).

This perfection is bound up with the new covenant of Jeremiah. That covenant anticipated the blessings of the present atoning and sanctifying work of Christ. Since the sanctifying work of Christ is depicted as a present ministry (by use of the present participle *hagiazomenous*), the quotation of Jeremiah 31:33 − 34 cannot be applied only to future Israel. The quotation demonstrates that the Holy Spirit had already witnessed to that work of Christ in the Old Testament Scriptures. The new covenant of Jeremiah promised what Christ now fulfills.

It should also be noted in this connection that where Jeremiah said, "This is the covenant I will make with the house of Israel . . ." (31:33), the writer of Hebrews said, "This is the covenant I will make with *them* . . ." (italics added). The logical referent of "them" in this clause is the subject of the participle *tous hagiazomenous* (those who are being sanctified). The reference to Israel is applied to the experience of all the people of God, not simply national Israel.

The new covenant is now in force—it is in no way bifurcated. There is one new covenant. It was ratified by the death of Christ and it mediates the gracious blessings of justification and holiness for all who are under that covenant.

One passage remains to be considered. It is Romans 11:27, "And this is my covenant with them when I take away their sins." These words, preceded by the formula *as it is written*, are regarded by many as coming from Isaiah 59:20 − 21.[27] Others see it as a quo-

---

27. William Sanday and Arthur C. Headlam, *The Epistle to the Romans*, ed. Charles J. Ellicott (1903; Grand Rapids: Zondervan; 1957), p. 336; Everett F. Harrison, *Romans*, vol. 10,

tation from Jeremiah 31:33 – 34.[28] At any rate, it is a covenant that guarantees Israel's complete forgiveness, and this can be none other than the new covenant.

This verse need not be understood as teaching that the new covenant of Jeremiah is not now in force because it must be ratified in the future when the nation of Israel is converted.[29] In the previous verses Paul referred to that event. He wrote, "Israel has experienced a hardening in part until the full number of the Gentiles has come in. And so all Israel will be saved." It is the nation of Israel which is in view here. The covenant is now in force, but one day Israel will be admitted to that covenant. It will be ratified with the people, and they will enjoy the blessings of complete forgiveness and unfeigned obedience.[30] This passage does not clearly indicate that the new covenant will be ratified only in the eschaton.

Covenantal nomism in the New Testament

If the new covenant is in force today, Christianity is a covenantal religion and obedience is covenantal obedience. But when we examine the teaching of the New Testament, there appears to be no apparently conscious exposition of covenantal nomism, no calling of mankind to a binding covenantal relationship with God. As a matter of fact, Jesus used the word *covenant* (*diathēkē*) on only one occasion, and Paul used it only nine times in very different ways.

J. Guhrt suggests that the lack of numerous occurrences of the word *diathēkē* (covenant) in the New Testament is because "the underlying thought has been taken over in the sayings about the kingdom of God. Linguistically we can see this perhaps most clearly

the *Expositor's Bible Commentary* (Grand Rapids: Zondervan, 1976), p. 124; F. Godet, *Commentary on the Epistle to the Romans*, trans. A. Cusin (Grand Rapids: Zondervan, 1956), p. 411.

28. F. F. Bruce, *The Epistle of Paul to the Romans: An Introduction and Commentary* (Grand Rapids: Eerdmans, 1963), p. 222; John Murray, *The Epistle to the Romans*, New International Commentary on the New Testament series (Grand Rapids: Eerdmans, 1960), pp. 98, 99.

29. Ryrie, *The Basis of the Premillennial Faith*, pp. 122 – 24.

30. An opposing viewpoint regarding Israel's future is presented by O. Palmer Robertson, "Is There a Distinctive Future for Ethnic Israel in Romans 11?" in *Perspectives on Evangelical Theology: Papers from the Thirtieth Annual Meeting of the Evangelical Theological Society*, ed. Kenneth S. Kantzer and Stanley N. Gundry (Grand Rapids: Baker, 1979), pp. 209 – 27.

in [Luke] 22:29 in the phrase *diatithemai ... basileian,* appoint a kingdom, which exactly expresses the formula *diatithemai diathēkēn.* The new covenant and the kingdom of God are correlated concepts."[31]

Gordon Wenham speaks to the same question. He says, "An understanding of first-century Jewish thinking about the covenant and the law puts the teaching of Jesus and Paul in a clearer perspective. That they rarely mention the covenant does not prove they regarded it as unimportant. It could be that just like the rabbis they assumed it was fundamental, and therefore required no discussion. This latter possibility is confirmed, I believe, by an examination of the teaching of Jesus and Paul."[32]

The apparent absence of a formal covenantal nomism in the New Testament should not be regarded as an anomaly, particularly in view of the previous study of Jeremiah 31:31 − 34. There it was apparent that the new covenant was not to be a covenant involving obedience to an external code of laws, but an obedience prompted by an inner working of the Holy Spirit—a heartfelt response to God. This is just what the ethic of the New Testament is. We are to respond in loving obedience to the sovereign work of grace done on our behalf.

The New Testament writers stress the work of the Holy Spirit in the heart. They call us to obedience because Christ has died on our behalf. The prediction of Jeremiah 31 envisioned a time when the people of God would obey God's *tôrāh,* not out of fear or under duress, but because they had renewed hearts. The New Testament says that time has been realized. The nature of obedience in the New Testament is precisely the same as that described in the new covenant of Jeremiah. The obedience called for by the New Testament is thus covenantal obedience—the same type of obedience that Jeremiah said would characterize the new covenant.

There is a sense then in which a covenantal nomism does exist in the New Testament. The Torah is to be obeyed, according to Jeremiah, but God will impart enablement for that obedience. If the requirements of obedience are not set forth in the form of a strict legal code in the New Testament, it is because they are

---

31. J. Guhrt, "Covenant," *NIDNTT,* vol. 1, p. 369.

32. Gordon Wenham, "Grace and Law in the Old Testament," *Law, Morality and the Bible: A Symposium,* ed. Bruce Kaye and Gordon Wenham (Downers Grove, Ill.: Inter-Varsity, 1978), p. 19.

prompted by a work of grace and motivated by the indwelling Spirit of God. They reflect the changing order of God's economy when the old covenant gave way to the new.

This is a point of emphasis in the Pauline theology. Paul's attitude toward the law was governed by his realization of the fact that a new era had dawned. The Holy Spirit now gives the enablement necessary for obedience to the divine will set forth earlier in the structure of the law (Rom. 8:1 – 4; 2 Cor. 3:4 – 6, 18).

The same principle obtains in the Petrine theology. In 1 Peter 2:9, Peter reiterated the covenantal promises that the offspring will be a holy nation and that the Lord will be God to his people. The context deals principally with obedience. The ethical response with which he dealt is not presented as a set of stipulations on which their relationship to the promise is conditioned. Rather, the relationship is assumed as having been established (1:2), just as it is in the Mosaic covenant. The major difference between the obedience called for in 1 Peter and obedience under the Mosaic covenant is that the obedience is facilitated by the Holy Spirit. Peter wrote that believers are "chosen and destined by God the Father and sanctified by the Spirit for obedience to Jesus Christ . . ." (1:2, RSV).

The distinction between the new covenant and the promise covenant

It is commonly held that the new covenant is a renewal or extension of the Abrahamic covenant.[33] This is based on its gracious character and its clear expression of the terms of the promise. There is another possibility; that is, that the new covenant functions as do the previous administrative covenants. In this view the new covenant is distinguished from the promise covenant and is understood as a covenantal instrument in its own right that explicates the terms of the promise and administers the response of obedience for the people of God. The administration of obedience is effected by the placing of the law within the heart and by the gracious work of the Holy Spirit. It does not present the believer with complex stipulations as does the law, but it does place in covenantal formulation the means by which tôrāh could

---

33. Mendenhall, "Covenant Forms in Israelite Tradition," p. 75. See also Walter C. Kaiser, Jr., *Toward an Old Testament Theology* (Grand Rapids: Zondervan, 1978), p. 234.

be obeyed more effectively than under the law. The covenantal formulation of this concept is contained in the words "I will put my law in their minds and write it on their hearts."

The new covenant governs the obedience of the people under its administration. It does not function precisely as do the promissory covenants. They state the terms of the promise; they do not express stipulations of obedience or administer obedience in covenantal terminology. We can find no statement in the promissory covenants in which the promised intent stands or falls on any condition. It may be negated for an individual who fails to respond in faith to the promise, but we cannot conclude that the covenanted administration of obedience is a formal part of this type of covenant. That is not to deny that the Abrahamic covenant had its own covenantal righteousness (it did—it was the righteousness of faith), but there is no formalized provision for that response and there are no covenantal stipulations that find expression in the contextual limits within which the promise covenants are given formal expression.

On the other hand, the new covenant is concerned with obedience.[34] It is given against the background of the failure of the people to obey the old covenant. Jeremiah said of the new covenant, "It will not be like the covenant I made with their forefathers when I took them by the hand to lead them out of Egypt, because they broke my covenant, though I was a husband to them, declares the LORD" (31:32). Provision for this failure is given covenantal force in the words " 'This is the covenant I will make with the house of Israel. . . . I will put my law in their minds and write it on their hearts' " (v. 33).

It is important to note that the context does not indicate that the new covenant was understood to be an extension or a renewal of the Abrahamic covenant. True, it contains elements of that promise covenant, but as we have observed, the Mosaic covenant does as well, and a clear distinction is drawn in the Old Testament between that covenant and the Abrahamic covenant; each maintains its own force and integrity. The presence of elements of the promise within the new covenant does not prove that it is a renewal of the Abrahamic covenant.

34. The new covenant in Ezekiel has the same concern. We read in Ezek. 36:27, "And I will put my Spirit in you and move you to follow my decrees and be careful to keep my laws."

The context supports another relationship—the new covenant replaces the old. It makes up for the failure of that covenant in that the legal content of the old covenant (i.e., *tôrāh*) is internalized. The new covenant is vitally concerned with ethical obedience—*tôrāh* is to be obeyed—that is the nature of *tôrāh*. However, in that covenant *tôrāh* is not an inflexible taskmaster that demands unswerving obedience to an external code of rigid demands. It is made a part of the process of cognition. It is one with the emotions that run deep in the human heart. It is the ethical motivation from which spring word and deed. It is the source of ethical response to God.[35] In this way the great Deuteronomic ideal is realized. That ideal, a vital aspect of *tôrāh*, is thus perpetuated by the new covenant. The major distinction between it and the old covenant is its provision for the realization of that ideal.

The new covenant does not fit the definition of promissory covenant adopted in this work. The promissory covenants do not involve stipulations. Nor do they covenantally administer obedience as the new covenant does. We should not allow the magnificent work of grace by which the law is placed within the heart to blur the fact that the new covenant administers obedience. Its mode of administration is of incomparably greater glory and grace than the mode of obedience in the old covenant, but it is a *tôrāh* covenant.

Jeremiah placed the new covenant on the same level with the old covenant.[36] It replaces that covenant with its own gracious provision. The fact that separate roles are given to the Abrahamic and Mosaic covenants in Deuteronomy should caution us against the possibility of blurring a distinction that may have been intended in the context of Jeremiah 31:31 – 34. The new covenant is an instrument of grace, the terms of which are designed to aid the people under its administration to secure a spiritual inheritance. It is most natural to understand the words of Jeremiah to refer to a new covenant that answered to the old, hence a new covenant that governed human obedience.

---

35. Hughes says, "In other words, the law ... now becomes internal ... and a delight to fulfill...." Philip Edgcumbe Hughes, *A Commentary on the Epistle to the Hebrews* (Grand Rapids: Eerdmans, 1977), p. 300.

36. Bright observes, "One sees at once that, though this is called a 'new' covenant, neither in its form nor in its content does it differ from the old." *Covenant and Promise*, p. 195.

The new covenant seeks to secure the kind of obedience necessary to ensure the eternal relationship of God's people to the promised inheritance. For this reason it may be designated an administrative covenant.

The new covenant in the prophecy of Jeremiah does not invalidate the role of promise nor rob it of its integrity. Both administrative covenant and promise covenant work together in the broad structure of his theology, just as they did in the Mosaic covenant. In Jeremiah 33, the prophet based his messianic expectation on the promise covenant reiterated to David. He said, "The days are coming, declares the LORD, when I will fulfill the gracious promise I made to the house of Israel and to the house of Judah. In those days ... I will make a righteous Branch sprout from David's line ..." (vv. 14 – 15). It is the sovereign purpose of God to establish a Davidic king. The passage rings with sovereign affirmations: "This is what the LORD says"; "If you can break my covenant with the day and ... night, ... then my covenant with David ... can be broken ..."; "I will make the descendants of David ... as countless as the stars of the sky ..."; "I will restore their fortunes and have compassion on them." It functions as a true promissory covenant, for no stipulations of obedience are cited.

The Davidic covenant continues in force in Jeremiah's theology. He asserted that it can never be broken. The new covenant of Jeremiah 31:31 – 34 explicates the terms of the promise in a new and more wonderful way than did the Mosaic covenant. In that regard it can be said to correspond in function to the Mosaic covenant. The new covenant administers obedience and, in that sense also, it shares a function with the Mosaic covenant. But the Davidic covenant in Jeremiah is a sovereign declaration. It is the ancient promise to David (33:14). We may observe again the covenanting of both promise and obedience in a complex of administrations.

An interesting interplay exists between the Abrahamic promise and the new covenant in the Epistle to the Hebrews. In 6:13 – 20 the writer established the continuing validity of the oath sworn to Abraham. He said of that oath that it was made so that "we who have fled to take hold of the hope offered to us may be greatly encouraged" (v. 18). We observed earlier that "we" in this verse included the writer as well as the believers he was addressing. The Abrahamic promise has a continuing force. Its function as a promissory covenant is confirmed by the fact that it is based solely on the sovereign oath of God. It is not dependent on human obedience. He then went on to discuss the new covenant and quoted the passage from Jeremiah twice (8:8 – 12; 10:16 – 17). There is nothing in his discussion to indicate that he understood the new covenant to be only an extension of the Abrahamic promise.

The new covenant was placed on the same level with the old covenant by the writer of Hebrews. This is the same alignment that we observed in the prophecy of Jeremiah. He established that alignment by demonstrating that the magnificent institutions of the law are perpetuated in the "new" or "better" covenant (7:22). He spoke of the high priesthood (8:1 – 7), the tabernacle (9:1 – 10), and the blood of animals (9:11 – 14); these all prefigured the realities of the new covenant (9:23 – 28). The new covenant administers incomparably greater institutions. The relationship between these two covenants does not easily support the view that the new covenant is a renewal of the Abrahamic covenant. These are all institutions of the Mosaic covenant. Again we find an instance in which the new covenant answers to the old.

The same relationship between these covenants may be observed in the theology of Paul. He affirmed the continuing validity of the Abrahamic promise (Rom. 4:16), but when he expounded the nature of the new covenant, it was in terms of its relationship to the old. The new covenant is the ministry of the Spirit, not of the letter. It is more glorious than the old covenant. It is a lasting covenant, not passing like the old, and it is a covenant in which the transforming power of Christ's glory is seen in a way in which it was not seen under the old covenant (2 Cor. 3:7 – 18).

This structure of the administrative covenants enables us to understand Jeremiah's use of "new" (ḥădāšâ) not as "renew," a meaning it does not frequently have in Hebrew, but as "new" in the strictest sense of the word. The new covenant is a new administration of obedience for the people of God. It is not the covenant of circumcision required of Abraham nor the complex structure of legal statutes given through Moses. It marks a new covenantal era in which the promise-oath is expressed in terms that mark the outpouring of grace in an unparalleled way.

Several concepts in the texts we have examined lend support to this connotation of ḥădāšâ. In Jeremiah 31:32 it says that the new covenant "will not be like the covenant I made with their forefathers. . . ." The view that understands the new covenant to be a renewal of the promise is far too complex for this simple statement and intrudes a concept into the text that has little contextual warrant. If a covenant, called "new," is to be unlike the old covenant (*lō' kabbĕrît*), the most natural interpretation is that it is not a renewal of an unspecified covenant but a new covenant with reference to the old. In 8:13 the writer of Hebrews said of the new covenant, "By calling this covenant 'new,' he has made the first one obsolete" (*pepalaiōken tēn prōtēn*). In this context the meaning of the word *new* (*kainos*) is determined by linear relationship with the word *obsolete*. It is "new" in relationship to an obsolete covenant, not in relationship to the promise.

The new provision for the obedience of God's people renders this covenant a new covenant. It achieves what the law could not. Brevard S. Childs says of the new covenant that "it is not simply a renewal of the Sinai covenant as occurred in the yearly festivals. . . . The new covenant, unlike the old which the fathers broke, will be inviolable. . . . The newness manifests itself in the perfect realization of God's original plan. The law had been accommodated in its form to the sinful condition of the people. It is at this point that the qualitatively new is accomplished."[37]

We must be careful that we do not dichotomize this structure so as to totally isolate the new covenant from the promise. This would be unwarranted. The new covenant expresses the promise. Both are covenantal administrations that function together in a structure that has one purpose. We may observe their separate functions, but we must observe their systematic coordination as well.

The writer of Hebrews set forth the close relationship between the new covenant and the promise in 9:15 – 22. He said in verse 15, "For this reason Christ is the mediator of a new covenant, that those who are called may receive the promised eternal inheritance. . . ." His use of "receive" here must be understood against the background of the failure of the people to enter the land because of disobedience. He cited that failure at the outset of his argument in 3:7 – 19.

In 9:16 he spoke of the promise as a will or testament and said

---

37. Brevard S. Childs, *Myth and Reality in the Old Testament*, 2d ed. (London: SCM, 1962), p. 80.

that for a will to be valid the testator must have died. Such a death has occurred under the new covenant (v. 15); it is the death of Christ (v. 14). But a death occurred under the old covenant as well (v. 18); it is to be found in the symbolic shedding of the blood of animals (vv. 19 — 22). Since a will is a sovereign expression of intent, and thus answers to the promise, we may conclude that the writer affirmed the existence of promise in the old covenant. Death is necessary for the validation of the promise testament, and a legally binding death occurred in connection with both covenants. Under the new covenant, the blood of Christ establishes the "better promises" enacted by his death (9:28). We may thus observe the close interworking of promise covenant and law covenant in the context of Hebrew 9:15 — 22.

The use of *diathēkē* (covenant, testament) in this context is broad and inclusive. The writer used it of a formal covenant in verse 15, where it refers to the new covenant. This type of covenant necessitates a mediator (*mesitēs*); hence there is an element of mutuality involved. He used the term in the same way in verse 15 to refer to the old covenant. However, in verse 16 it connotes a will or testament, not a formal covenant like the old and new covenants.

Several scholars do not agree that this latter use of *diathēkē* connotes a testament.[38] But it is difficult to understand how it could mean anything else. It is put into effect by the death of the testator (v. 16). A mutual covenant is hardly put in force in this way; it would be nullified by the death of one of the parties. The context describes this *diathēkē* as unilateral; hence it is best understood as a testament which, in turn, answers to the promise covenant.

The unilateral nature of this covenant is set forth in the expression *the one who made it* (*tou diathemenou* [v. 16], *ho diathemenos* [v. 17]). It is a *diathēkē* made by one individual which requires the death of the individual for its validation.[39] It is most natural to

38. See, for example, Robertson, *The Christ of the Covenants*, pp. 138 — 44.

39. The phraseology of Heb. 9:17 is appealed to by Robertson in his argument for the meaning *covenant* rather than "testament" in this context. He adopts the view that the words *epi nekrois* (over dead bodies) refer to "a multiple of dead bodies." He says, "Many beasts are slain to symbolize the potential of covenantal curse." *The Christ of the Covenants*, p. 142. However, this expression may be understood to refer to the disposition of an inheritance through successive generations. Or it may simply connote the necessity of death for the ratification of a will. Note the translations *only at death* (RSV) and *when somebody has died* (NIV).

understand it as a testament. Since the author was speaking of the inheritance in this context (v. 15), the allusion to a will is consonant with the thrust of his argument.

The writer can thus move freely within the range of *diathēkē.* He can use the term in the same context to apply to the functions of mutual covenant as well as to testament. This is the same broad range observed in the Old Testament usages of *bĕrît.* Since the concept *testament* is consonant with the promissory type of covenant, we may observe a close interplay of several types of covenants uniting to effect the disposition of the inheritance.

The explication of the terms of the promise in the new covenant

Like the old covenant, the new covenant sets forth the terms of the promise in a way that is appropriate to the new and different era of redemption that it governs. We may observe this especially in the exposition of the function of the new covenant in the prophecy of Jeremiah. There, the elements of the promise are unmistakably present. The promise of the offspring; the land; the new relationship of God to his people; the broad constructs in which God affirmed that he would act in redemptive history—all find expression. God has not forsaken his promise. But the richer content given to the elements of the promise in the new covenant, and the marvelous way in which the Deuteronomic ideal is facilitated by it, witness to the fact that it has an explanatory function. It is a vehicle for the expression of the promise for an age in which God's gracious activity on behalf of his people undergoes dynamic change.

The confirmatory function of the new covenant

The new covenant, like the Mosaic covenant, is confirmatory in nature. It rings with authority when it says, "This is the covenant I will make . . ." (Jer. 31:33). It confirms the elements of the promise that follow in the context. But this does not mean that it is one with the promise in its nature or function. Just as the Mosaic covenant confirmed the promise in the context of its particular administrative function, which was the oversight of obedience, so the new covenant confirms the promise in the context of its administration, which is the change in human hearts that God will effect at its ratification.

The promissory covenant made with Abraham confirmed the

promise as well by virtue of its authoritative oath, but it is unconditional affirmation. The Mosaic covenant affirmed the terms of
the promise, but only insofar as its conditions were met. We find
one of many examples of this in Exodus 19:6, "you will be for me
a kingdom of priests and a holy nation"; but it is conditioned on
keeping the covenant (v. 5). The confirmatory function of the law
was limited by its nature, for it was a conditional covenant and
could not state the terms of the promise with the absolute authority of the promissory covenants.

The new covenant also confirms the promise within its own
terms. It assures the unfailing appropriation of the terms of the
promise by its facilitation of obedience on the part of the people
of God.

The Function of the Administrative Covenants
Relative to the Promise

To this point, the study of the administrative function of the
Mosaic and new covenants has led to the conclusion that they are
not unrelated to the promise. They function with regard to the
promise in that they apply its terms to the people under their
jurisdiction and facilitate the obedience by which their relationship to the promise may be maintained.

There is another function of these convenants that has been
touched on only briefly. It is the amplification of certain terms of
the promise in the course of their expression in the sequence of
administrative covenants. The first of these to be considered is the
promise of the offspring. In the original expressions of the Abrahamic covenant this promise is stated in terms quite appropriate
to the historical circumstances. Abraham had no children, but
God promised him a posterity. There is little interest in anything
else about them. It was enough for Abraham and his descendants
to know that God had provided for their spiritual welfare and had
confirmed his promise by a solemn oath.

When the people became a nation, the elements of the promise
covenant found expression in the administrative covenant given
through Moses. The Mosaic covenant retains the promise of the
offspring, but it has undergone change. It is expressed in terms
appropriate to a national entity; the people are a "kingdom of
priests."

In the new covenant the promise of the offspring appears in the affirmation that the Lord would be God to his people (Jer. 31:33); but the way in which this promise is accomplished in the New Testament and the addition of the people of faith to the descendants of Abraham represent a concept different from the expression of that promise under the preceding covenants. The promise of offspring is intact, but it is expressed in terms that are appropriate to the reign of grace instituted by the death and resurrection of Christ.

We may observe a modification in the expression of this element of the promise that may be described best as expansion. The concept of the offspring develops from its fulfillment in Isaac to include the physical descendants of Abraham, and then the myriad of those who emulate Abraham's faith. This expansion was incipient in the early statements of the promise, for Abraham was promised that his offspring would be as numerous as the stars, but the administration of the promise in the successive administrative covenants enables its realization.

The promise of the land is never abrogated in the covenants, and it too undergoes expansion. In the formal statements of the Abrahamic and Mosaic covenants it is the land of Canaan that is promised. But as the prophets foretold the reign of Messiah, even though they ministered under the old covenant, they envisioned his dominion and the dominion of the people of God as extending far beyond the boundaries of Palestine to include the whole world (Isa. 2:1 – 4; 11:1, 4, 10; Mic. 4:1 – 4; Zech. 14:4, 9). The new covenant, or New Testament, gives formal covenantal validation to this expansion in Romans 4:13, where the apostle Paul referred to the Abrahamic statement of the promise of the land as "the promise that he [Abraham] would be heir of the world."[40]

Thus, the elements guaranteed by the promise covenant undergo amplification and enrichment in their expression in the major administrative covenants.

The Relationship of the Administrative Covenants to the Promise

The basic thesis of this work is that the people of God, from the time of Abraham on, are under two covenantal administrations:

40. See the discussion of this verse in the first chapter.

the promise-oath and the particular administrative covenant in force at the time.[41] Thus, a bicovenantal structure governs the disposition of the inheritance for God's people.

In each era governed by an administrative covenant we have found that the promise covenant was also in force. Circumcision is called a *bĕrît*, but it operates in conjunction with the promise *bĕrît* sworn to Abraham. The law is called a *bĕrît*, but Moses refers as well to the *bĕrît* sworn to Abraham, Isaac, and Jacob. The new covenant is called a *bĕrît*, but both Jeremiah and the writer of Hebrews acknowledge the continuing force of the promise *bĕrît* and *horkos* (oath). In every age God acts on the basis of his eternal promise.

However, there is a period of Israelite history in which it appears that the Abrahamic promise is not the primary basis of divine motivation for the restoration of the people to the land. This is the period initiated by the collapse of the Judahite monarchy. The Abrahamic covenant does not appear to have the importance it did earlier.[42]

This observation raises serious questions about the bicovenantal administration of the inheritance suggested in this work. If God did not bring the people back to the land primarily because he said he would, what are we to surmise about the importance of the promise-oath in the structure of the divine activity in this period?

There is a clear strand of material in this period that indicates that the Lord's compassion for his people and his concern for the vindication of his name include loyalty to his covenanted promise. In Jeremiah 33:6 – 9 Yahweh's compassion for his people is evident in his gracious promise of healing and forgiveness. The basis on

41. Bright observes a similar concept, but from a perspective different from that of this work. He says, "The church, therefore, like Israel, lives under both patterns of covenant. We have received from Christ sure, unqualified promises to which no conditions are attached. . . . These promises we are called to receive in faith, and to live in absolute trust that the outcome of God's purpose in history does not depend on us . . . it rests in his promise and his faithfulness alone. But we have also received grace. And the reception of grace involves us in binding obligation . . . 'If you love me, you will keep my commandments. . . .' " *Covenant and Promise*, p. 197.

42. Elmer A. Martens observes, "If one examines the announcements of the return in the books of Jeremiah and Ezekiel and asks for the motivations of the return, one discovers that not once is the earlier covenant with Abraham cited as a reason for the announcement." *God's Design: A Focus on Old Testament Theology* (Grand Rapids: Baker, 1981), p. 240.

which the restoration to the land (v. 11; cf. v. 16) will be effected is the "gracious promise" made to David (vv. 14–16). We have observed that this promise is essentially the same promise the Lord swore to Abraham.

The Lord's fealty to his covenantal obligation is so strong that he compares it with his covenant with day and night (v. 20); if the succession of day followed by night can be broken, then the Lord's covenant with David can be broken (v. 21). The extension of the divine compassion to the promise may be observed in the designation of the promise as "good" (ṭôb; NIV, "gracious") in verse 14. The connection of the promise to Abraham is reflected in the reference to the descendants of Abraham, Isaac, and Jacob in verse 26. Thus, the prophet Jeremiah pictured God as acting on the basis of his covenanted promise in this period and as expressing his desire to fulfill it.

The interplay of two covenantal administrations may be implicit in Jeremiah 7:5–7, where obedience to the ethical requirements of the law is the condition for their dwelling in the land the Lord gave to their fathers. While the gift of the land is not called specifically "covenant" or "promise" in this context, it is difficult to see how it could be divorced from those concepts, since the land was given to the people in both a promissory mode and a covenantal mode. The concept of the land as a gift is tied to the sworn oath of God in Deuteronomy 1:8. This Deuteronomic concept would not be unknown in Jeremiah's day. It appears then that there exists within the prophecy of Jeremiah a recognition of the sovereign promise of God, upon which he in his compassion is obligated to act.

The Contribution of Hebrews 8:6 to the Nature and Function of the Administrative Covenants

Hebrews 8:6 says, "But the ministry Jesus has received is as superior to theirs as the covenant of which he is mediator is superior to the old one, and is founded on better promises."

The word *founded* (*nomotheteō*) means to "sanction by law."[43] In other words, the new covenant is given legal force or sanction

---

43. Joseph H. Thayer, *Greek-English Lexicon of the New Testament.* "Ordain by law," H. Liddell and R. Scott, *A Greek-English Lexicon.*

by virtue of promise. The new covenant would be only an empty vessel if it did not contain something to guarantee or facilitate and hence put in force.

The new covenant is enacted on "better promises." These are not different promises. God has not abolished the promise of offspring, land, and Gentile inclusion. They are "better" because of their new expression in Christ, the mediator of the new covenant.

The promise of rest in the land continues under the new covenant, according to the writer of Hebrews, but it is a spiritual rest that he affirmed (4:1 − 11). The offspring of Abraham is a continuing concept in his theology, but the offspring are comprised of a people who have a steadfast hope because Christ is their high priest forever (6:17 − 20). The new covenant of Jeremiah 31:31 − 34 is a vehicle of the same elements of the promise given to Abraham, and the writer of Hebrews said these promises are now in force (8:6 − 13). As a matter of fact, the "better promises" of Christ are contained in Jeremiah's statement of the new covenant (Heb. 8:6; cf. vv. 10 − 12). The writer of Hebrews affirmed the present realization of the better promises portrayed by the prophet. We may conclude from this that the administrative covenants do not determine the changing expressions of the promise but are enacted upon them.

What determines the changes in the expression of covenant? It would appear to be one thing; that is, the changing historical circumstances that warrant renewed expression of the divine will. A group of nomad clans, united only by a covenant made long years ago with an ancestor, stands on the borders of a new land. These people are to become a nation. Another covenant is made to govern them and guard the promise. It was the Mosaic covenant. But a new age dawns. It is an age characterized by a new relationship of the Holy Spirit to believers. This age calls for a new covenant that expresses the spiritual realities of the types and shadows of the old. This new covenant is ratified by the blood of Christ and dispenses to its constituents the inheritance that prophets could only dream of and long for. It is salvation history that determines the application of promise. It is the sworn oath of God that guarantees it and provides the adherents of the covenant with "hope as an anchor for the soul, sure and secure" (Heb. 6:19; cf. v. 17).

The new covenant is enacted by "promises," according to the

writer of Hebrews. Again, the interplay of two covenantal administrations is observable. It is promise that is necessary for the force and validity of the new covenant. They are "better promises" because of their expression in this new age, foreseen by the prophets, but realized when Christ entered the arena of human history.

Conclusion

The basic conclusion of this work is that the disposition of the inheritance is effected within a complex of covenants. We have designated this a bicovenantal structure. Both promise covenant and administrative covenant function as valid covenantal instruments because the range of *běrît* in the Old Testament is broad in compass.

Both types of covenants must function together for the successful administration of the inheritance to the people of God. To divorce one from the other is to commit the fatal error of which Paul spoke in Romans 9:30 – 10:13. The administrative covenants are enacted on the promise covenant, the expression of which grows richer with each successive era until it finds its most glorious expression in the ministry of Christ.

The administrative covenants explicate the terms of the promise. We would not know of the amplification of the promise in the Mosaic era or the era governed by the New Testament apart from covenantal pronouncement. It is insufficient to appeal only to history for a knowledge of the changing expression of the divine promise, for it is covenanted expression. We must work back from that covenantal expression to determine the historical outworking of the promise. The great redemptive eras are not simply initiated by covenant; they are governed by it. Covenant is the key to the understanding of redemptive history.

Since the promise is expressed in administrative covenants, covenant is the theological approach to promise. The promise cannot be interpreted apart from its authoritative and definitive expression in covenant. The theology of redemption is covenant theology. We must address the question of the application of the terms of the promise by appealing to their covenanted expression.

The promise covenant finds its richest expression in the new covenant, for there we find the epitome of grace. Sovereign grace is dispensed not only in the promise *bĕrît*, to which the New Testament writers continue to make appeal, but in the new covenant which enables attainment of that sovereign disposition at the highest level.

We must be reminded again that the two covenantal instruments are not to be unduly bifurcated. They are regarded in this work as separate administrations or functions within the covenantal structure by which the inheritance is granted and its continued validity guaranteed.

The new covenant differs from the preceding administrative covenants in that it enables the dispensing of the promise to God's people in the context of sovereign grace. It can never be surpassed in this regard, and thus it is called an "everlasting covenant." John Murray notes the new covenant differs from the old "because it brings to the ripest and richest fruition the relationship epitomized in that promise." The promise of which he speaks is, "I will be your God, and you shall be my people."[44]

This structure enables us to observe the continued validity of the promise. In this way we can give valid theological expression to its eternality and continued integrity. At the same time we may observe the changing nature of the administration of obedience which culminates in the outpouring of grace in the ministry of the Holy Spirit and the renewal of the heart.

44. John Murray, *The Covenant of Grace: A Biblico-Theological Study* (London: Tyndale, 1953), p. 31.

4

The Promise Covenant
as a Theological Category

In this chapter we shall consider one of the foundational aspects
of covenant theology, the accord between the Father and the Son.
This is called the covenant of grace or the covenant of redemption
in covenant theology. It is suggested here that this theological
concept is best understood and defended when it is viewed from
the theological construct of the promise covenant. We shall also
examine the continuing integrity of the elements of the promise
and the implications of that internal unity for the theology of
redemption.

The covenant of grace is a concept that deserves a place of
eminence in any theological system that is constructed on the
canonical texts. It is not a theological category necessary only to
a particular system. It has strong scriptural support. It is the
source from which springs the believer's inheritance in Christ.
Because it is of such great importance, the theological expression
of the covenant of grace warrants continued examination and refinement, for its theological expression must be in exact accord
with the scriptural data if the terms of the promised inheritance
are to be understood with precision and the sovereign grace that
motivated it fully appreciated.

It is not unwarranted to seek refinements of the traditional concepts of covenant theology. John Murray observes:

It would not be, however, in the interests of theological conservation or theological progress for us to think that the covenant theology is in all respects definitive and that there is no further need for correction, modification, and expansion. Theology must always be undergoing reformation.... However architectonic may be the systematic constructions of one generation or group of generations, there always remains the need for correction and reconstruction so that the structure may be brought into closer approximation to the Scripture and the reproduction be a more faithful transcript or reflection of the heavenly exemplar. It appears to me that the covenant theology, notwithstanding the finesse of analysis with which it was worked out and the grandeur of its articulated systematization, needs recasting. We would not presume to claim that we shall be so successful in this task that the reconstruction will displace and supersede the work of the classic covenant theologians. But with their help we may be able to contribute a little towards a more biblically articulated and formulated construction of the covenant concept and of its application to our faith, love, and hope.[1]

It is in the spirit of this statement that this chapter is written.

The Redemptive Relationship Between the Father and the Son

The Theological Terminology for the Relationship

The discussion in the previous chapters has attempted to show that soteriology in Scripture is covenant soteriology. The promise that God will be God to his people, from which the great concepts of salvation flow, is affirmed in covenant, and the variegated expression of the promise to the people of God through the ages is given in the form of covenant.

Although covenant theology in its traditional expression stresses the covenant of grace, the subsequent discussion will show that no universal agreement as to the structure and nature of this concept exists. A brief examination of the conclusions of a few theologians will illustrate the lack of uniformity in the designation covenant of grace in covenant theology.

1. John Murray, *The Covenant of Grace: A Biblico-Theological Study* (London: Tyndale, 1953), pp. 4–5.

Hermannus Witsius defines the covenant of grace: "In order the more thoroughly to understand the nature of the covenant of grace, two things are above all to be distinctly considered. 1st, the covenant which intervenes between God the Father and Christ the Mediator. 2dly, that testamentary disposition, by which God bestows an immutable covenant, eternal salvation, and every thing relative thereto, upon the elect. The former agreement is between God and the Mediator: the latter, between God and the Elect. This last pre-supposes the first, and is founded upon it."[2]

Witsius understood the covenant of grace to include both the relationship of God to Christ the mediator and the relationship of God to his people as the giver of salvation. This twofold relationship was later refined by Charles Hodge, who posited both a covenant of grace and a covenant of redemption. The former is the covenant of God with his people and the latter is the covenant of the Father with the Son. This, he felt, avoided the confusion reflected in the description of the covenant of grace in the Westminster standards. Hodge says, "The Westminster standards seem to adopt sometimes the one and sometimes the other mode of representation."[3]

Hodge says of these two administrations within the covenant of grace that they ought not to be confounded, as both are clearly revealed in Scripture, and moreover they differ as to the parties, as to the promises, and as to the conditions.[4]

Murray differs from some earlier scholars in that he understands the covenant of grace as the sovereign disposition of grace by God to man. He questions whether the proper starting point for the understanding of the covenant of grace is to be found in the idea of "mutual compact."[5]

These citations reveal the difficult problems involved in expressing the complexity of relationships within the covenant of grace and the nature of the covenant within which those relationships exist.

2. Hermannus Witsius, *The Economy of the Covenants Between God and Man*, trans. William Crookshank, 2 vols. (1677; Edinburgh: Thomas Turnbull, 1803), vol. 1, p. 169.

3. Charles Hodge, *Systematic Theology*, 3 vols. (1871–73; Grand Rapids: Eerdmans, 1952), vol. 2, p. 358.

4. Ibid., p. 358.

5. Murray, *The Covenant of Grace*, p. 8.

Representative Theological Explanations of the Redemptive Relationship Between the Father and the Son

Witsius marshals extensive biblical support for the concept of the covenant of grace. However, like those of a number of early theologians, some of his conclusions are questionable in the light of modern exegetical standards.

Witsius appeals to Hebrews 7:22, where it says of Christ that he is "surety of a better covenant."[6] He observes, "It is necessary, we conceive of some covenant, the conditions of which Christ took upon himself; engaging in our name with the Father, to perform them for us. . . ."[7] The "suretiship," Witsius concludes, consists of the fact that Christ "himself undertook to perform that condition . . . without which . . . the grace and promises of God could not reach unto us. . . ."[8]

It is difficult to find an element of condition in this context. As a matter of fact, the function of Christ as the guarantor of the new covenant is based on an unchanging oath (vv. 20 – 21). It is a sovereign disposition which underlies the "suretiship" of Christ.

The "better covenant" of Hebrews 7:22 is the new covenant of Jeremiah 31, not a covenant specifically ratified in eternity past among the members of the Godhead. Note how the argument concerning the priesthood of Christ continues until it finds its climax in the quotation of the passage from Jeremiah 31:31 – 34 (Heb. 8:8 – 9; cf. 8:1). This passage does not provide substantial evidence for a compact between the Father and the Son that principally involved conditions undertaken by Christ.

Witsius appeals also to Psalm 119:122, "be surety for thy servant for good." He likewise cites Isaiah 38:14 in this connection: "I am oppressed, undertake for me."[9] He regards these verses as containing "explicit mention" of the "suretiship of Christ."[10] However, it is unlikely that many scholars today would apply these verses to Christ.

Appeal is also made to Zechariah 6:13, which refers to a "counsel of peace . . . between them both." Witsius applies this to "the

---

6. Witsius, *The Economy of the Covenants*, p. 170.
7. Ibid.
8. Ibid.
9. Ibid., p. 171.
10. Ibid.

man, whose name is the Branch, and Jehovah...."[11] Modern scholarship understands this statement to connote the amicable relationship that will exist between the kingship and the priesthood under the aegis of the Branch, not a covenant between members of the Godhead.[12]

References are cited by Witsius in which Christ calls God his God. These are seen as reflections of the ancient promise that God would be God to his people.[13] Whether the connection is certain is questionable, but, at any rate, there is no reference to a compact or agreement. It is the sovereign promise that is in view.

Witsius also appeals to Luke 22:29, "And I engage by covenant unto you a kingdom, as my Father hath engaged by covenant unto me."[14] He concludes that this refers to "some covenant or disposition...."[15] The word translated "engage by covenant" is the word *diatithēmi*. Some scholars question whether it has a covenantal connotation in this passage.[16] But even if it does have that connotation, the context gives stronger support to the concept of sovereign disposition than it does to contractual agreement. The two major clauses are connected by *kathōs* (just as): "I confer on you a kingdom, just as my Father conferred one on me." There is no hint in the context of mutuality of agreement that involved the disciples. It is a sovereign disposition of the kingdom.

Witsius also appeals to Galatians 3:17, where "Paul mentions a certain covenant, or testament, that was confirmed before of God in Christ."[17] Witsius identifies the *diathēkē* (covenant) as "some covenant or testament, by which something is promised by God to Christ."[18] Witsius cannot be denied here. If other aspects of his exegesis are questionable to modern scholars, this is not. A *diathēkē* exists between God and Christ.

11. Ibid.

12. H. C. Leupold, *Exposition of Zechariah* (1956; Grand Rapids: Baker, 1971), pp. 124 – 25; Joyce G. Baldwin, *Haggai, Zechariah, Malachi: An Introduction and Commentary*, Tyndale Old Testament commentaries (Downers Grove, Ill.: Inter-Varsity, 1972), pp. 136 – 37.

13. Witsius, *The Economy of the Covenants*, p. 174.

14. Ibid., p. 170.

15. Ibid.

16. "The verb is used with reference to testamentary appointment, but not so here where it is used with the disciples as well as with Jesus as the object; 'appoint' is enough." R. C. H. Lenski, *The Interpretation of St. Luke's Gospel* (Minneapolis: Augsburg, 1961), p. 1060.

17. Witsius, *The Economy of the Covenants*, p. 170.

18. Ibid., p. 171.

Witsius observes that Christ has the dual roles of "executor" and recipient within the covenant transaction. He does not give these roles separate designations. It is this complexity that Hodge regarded as a matter of confusion in the Westminster standards.

Hodge's arguments for the existence of a covenant of grace are based on the facts that Scripture presents the plan of salvation as having the nature of covenant, that the divine plan of redemption existed before the foundation of the world, that promises were made to Christ before his coming into the world, that he came in fulfillment of a commission, and that as God entered into a covenant with Adam, so he did with Christ (Rom. 5:12 – 21).[19]

Hodge gives the strongest scriptural support to the argument that Christ came in fulfillment of a commission. In connection with this he argues that whenever one assigns work to another on condition of reward, "there is a covenant."[20]

Hodge cannot be faulted on this; the relationship between the Father and the Son does fall within the broad range of *bĕrît*. But, like Witsius, Hodge posits a conditional covenantal arrangement. He says, "We have, therefore, the contracting parties, the promise, and the condition."[21]

Louis Berkhof argues for the existence of a covenant of redemption along lines that are somewhat similar to those of Hodge. He points to the inclusion of the plan of redemption in the "eternal decree or counsel of God," and cites several verses that speak of the redemptive purposes of God expressed in time past.[22] The element of "covenant" in these verses is seen in the interaction of the members of the Godhead—"a voluntary agreement among the persons of the Trinity."[23]

Berkhof cites verses in which Christ expresses his obedience to a commission given to him by the Father.[24] He also argues that wherever contracting parties, promises, and a condition exists there exists a covenant.[25] In support of this he appeals to Psalm 2:7 – 9, a messianic passage where "the parties are mentioned and

---

19. Hodge, *Systematic Theology,* vol. 2, p. 360.
20. Ibid.
21. Ibid.
22. Louis Berkhof, *Systematic Theology,* 2d rev. ed. (Grand Rapids: Eerdmans, 1941), p. 266.
23. Ibid.
24. Ibid.; see John 5:30, 43; 6:38 – 40; 17:4 – 12.
25. Ibid.

a promise is indicated."[26] He appeals also to Psalm 40:7 – 9, where Christ expresses his obedience to the Father.[27]

Berkhof argues for a covenant of redemption from Psalm 89:3 and Isaiah 42:6, which, he says, "connect up the idea of the covenant immediately with the Messiah."[28] He points also to Messiah's reference to God as "his God," and argues that this is "covenant language, namely Ps. 22:1, 2 and Ps. 40:8."[29]

Exegetical Validity of the Relationship
Between the Father and the Son

The study of Witsius's argument for the covenant of grace presents a number of problems to the modern exegete. Berkhof must say of Witsius's appeal to Zechariah 6:13, "This was clearly a mistake, for the words refer to the union of the kingly and priestly offices in the Messiah."[30]

It appears that Witsius's efforts to find in Scripture a covenant between the Father and the Son that was of a specifically contractual nature led him to passages that did not necessarily support that concept. However, the argument based on Galatians 3:17 is exegetically valid. A relationship described by Paul as a *diathēkē* exists between God and Christ. But it must be noted that in the context this is a sovereign disposition. It is the giving of the promise that is in view. It must be placed within the category of promissory covenant, not conditional covenant.

The distinction between the covenant of grace and the covenant of redemption, posited by Hodge, is unnecessary when the relationship between the Father and the Son is understood to be based on the category of promise. Galatians 3:16 states that the promises were made to Abraham and to Christ. Both stand in the same relationship to the disposition of the promise; Abraham functioned as both mediator and recipient. Since Christ is principal heir along with Abraham, the two functions must be exercised by him as well. We need not bifurcate the construct. It is enough to note that the nature of the promise given to Abraham

26. Ibid.
27. Ibid.
28. Ibid.
29. Ibid., pp. 266 – 67.
30. Ibid., p. 266.

was such that he sustained a complex relationship to it. He was given certain promises, but because his descendants share elements of the promise, he functioned as mediator as well.

Since we do not give independent status or formal designation to the roles of recipient and mediator enjoyed by Abraham, we need not do so in the case of the relationship of Christ to the promise, unless it is in the interest of theological refinement. The promise, by its very nature, contained elements that were intended for Christ as the recipient. He is promised a great name, royal honor, and offspring. Because blessing is promised to the offspring, Christ also sustains the role of mediator relative to the promise. It is the nature of the promise that determines the unique relationship of Christ and Abraham to it; we need not posit two covenants to describe that relationship.

The elements of obedience cited by Hodge are not incompatible with the promise relationship, because such faithful obedience was expected of Abraham. Indeed, he responded to God in faith even before the promise was given covenant form (Gen. 12:1–4).

Much of the evidence cited by these theologians fits best with the sovereign promise viewed as a distinct theological category. It is clear that Galatians 3:15–18 is foundational to the concept of a covenantal relationship between the Father and the Son. However, we must not think it is the only passage in Scripture that supports this concept. We found that there is Old Testament support for the fact that the promises were made to Christ, and much of the evidence in the theologians cited is supported by Scripture. But this passage is the crux of the matter and must be given careful consideration.

Commentators are divided over the meaning of *diathēkē* in Galatians 3:15, 17. The view taken here is that the word connotes a will or testament. Support for this may be found in the Old Testament passages in which we found the promises made to Christ in his roles of Messiah and servant. The granting of the promises is a sovereign disposition in those passages and not clearly conditioned on obedience. Isaiah 53:10 is sometimes appealed to in support of a compactual arrangement between the Father and the Son,[31] but its precise meaning is uncertain. The verse sets forth

31. See, for example, Albert Barnes, *Notes on the New Testament: Hebrews*, ed. Robert Frew (Grand Rapids: Baker, 1949), pp. 202–3.

the promise of the offspring to the servant and may be translated, "if he gives himself as an offering, he will see his seed. . . ." The promise of offspring to the servant seems to be conditioned on obedience. But the word *'im* (if) need not be understood to express a condition. It is true that the word may connote condition, but it may also introduce a temporal clause, that is, "when he gives himself as an offering. . . ."

It is quite out of keeping with the sovereign expression of God's will in the first clause of verse 10 to translate the second clause "if he presents himself as an offering"; according to the first clause, it was the will of God to bruise him. Thus, the translation of the Revised Standard Version ("when he makes himself an offering for sin") seems best.

That is not to say that the obedience of the servant is inconsequential. It is a matter of emphasis. His obedience is assumed. It is obedience within the limits of a sovereign disposition of God.

The concept of "testament" in Galatians 3:15, 17 has exegetical support within the immediate context. Of particular importance is the fact that Paul follows the allusion to the *anthrōpou . . . diathēkē* (an individual's will or a human will) with a reference to the promises. He defines the *diathēkē* as the promise. The act of giving the promise to Abraham was a sovereign disposition, and this fits best with the concept of will or testament.

The point of Paul's argument is that a *diathēkē* is not annulled or amended once it has been ratified. No matter what view one takes of the meaning of *diathēkē*, that assertion must not be lost. The promise covenant was not invalidated by the law.

What then is the nature of the arrangement between God and Christ on the basis of this discussion? It is the same relationship that Abraham sustained to God when the oath was sworn to him. The oath was a sovereign expression of the divine will, with no conditions stated, no demands imposed; obedience was assumed.

This is the theological category that best expresses the divine relationship. At least, one must start from the category. If one wishes to see other covenantal elements in the relationship, such as conditions of obedience, that is one's prerogative. Galatians 3:15 – 18 certainly emphasizes a relationship of promise and provides a starting point that is exegetically sound. On the basis of this passage and the Old Testament passages cited earlier, the concept of a divine arrangement is exegetically unassailable. Redemption is covenantal redemption. It stems from a disposition or arrangement among the members of the Godhead.

Much of the argumentation of the scholars discussed in the previous section assumes that covenant necessarily involves condition. Their discussion does not differentiate types of covenants. We have concluded that promissory covenants contain no stipulations of obedience; other types of covenants necessitate them. In Galatians 3:15 – 18 the *diathēkē* relationship between the Father and the Son is placed by Paul in the category of promise covenant. The covenant of grace is thus a sovereign administration of grace. We are not to find the central motivating factor in the idea of contractual obligation, but in sovereign disposition.

It is surprising that the importance of the covenant of grace is not universally acknowledged. It is the fundamental concept of redemption: the divine decree that set in operation the promise which spans all of human history.

The Function of Promise in the History of Redemption

The Unity of the Promise

The promise-oath continues unchanged in essence throughout the history of redemption. It is thus the vehicle that expresses the unity of the divine redemptive purpose. For example, God's people are guaranteed the land in every covenantal era. Landedness is an aspect of the inheritance even for those who are under the new covenant, for the writer of Hebrews sets forth the realization of the Deuteronomic concept of "rest" as an aspect of the heritage of all who are under the new covenant (Heb. 3 – 4). It is the "rest" of the finished work of salvation. But it is clearly related to the promise of the land, for the writer of Hebrews placed it over against the failure of God's ancient people to enter the land (3:7 – 19) and affirmed that the rest of which he spoke is available in the gospel (4:1 – 16).

The promise of the offspring is still a valid promise. Paul appealed to that concept in his references to Abraham's model of faith. Gentiles have been included within the people of God. They have become a kingdom of priests. God has become their God. The ancient promise has not been nullified. It is an eternal promise, sworn to by God so that his people may have hope and confidence.

Theological Implications of the Unity of the Promise

An element essential to any theological system based on the canonical texts of Scripture is the standard by which the continuity of the redemptive acts of God may be defined and incorporated into theological description. The promise covenant functions as this category, for it crystallizes for all time the unchanging aspects of the inheritance God promised to his people.

Since God covenanted an eternal promise—a promise that is unchanging in essence—his people thus share a common inheritance. It is therefore difficult to posit a radical distinction between Israel and the church. The common inheritance of promise, shared by the people of both testaments, creates a bond that transcends the covenantal eras. The people of God comprise a continuum throughout history. They are the people to whom the Lord has covenanted his redeeming love in the form of promise.

The consciousness of the common heritage of promise permeates the New Testament. The promise that the Lord will be God to his people is echoed in 2 Corinthians 6:16; Hebrews 8:10; and Revelation 21:3, 7. The concept of a royal people is found in 1 Peter 2:9 and Revelation 1:6; 5:10. The promise of the offspring figures prominently in Romans 4:16; Galatians 3:29; Titus 2:14; Hebrews 11:18; 1 Peter 2:9 – 10; and Revelation 12:17; the function of Christ as the offspring appears in Galatians 3:16. The promise of the land may be found in Hebrews 4:1 – 10 and Romans 4:13. Gentile inclusion in the promise is set forth by Paul in Romans 9:24 – 25.

Paul affirmed the continuity between the ancient promises and the gospel in Titus 1:2, and his affirmation that faith is the condition of salvation in every age establishes a common ground for the people of Old and New Testament alike. Paul could quote freely from the Old Testament in support of his exposition of the nature and privilege of the church. He found reference to the calling of the Gentiles in Hosea 2:23 (Rom. 9:25 – 28), and he freely applied a blessing promised to Israel in Isaiah 54:1 to the church (Gal. 4:27).

We have seen that the writer of Hebrews applied the promise of Jeremiah 31:31 – 34 to New Testament believers even though it was specifically directed to the houses of Israel and Judah (v. 31). The use of the Old Testament in this fashion acknowledges a commonality between the two peoples and makes the positing of a radical distinction between them questionable.

This experience, shared equally by the believing remnant of the Old Testament and the body of New Testament believers, is vividly pictured by Paul in Romans 11:17 – 21, where the church is represented as sharing in the spiritual life and privilege that was distinctly that of the people of the Old Testament.

The writer of Hebrews spoke of the oath made by God with Abraham and his descendants (6:13 – 15). As he developed his argument he said the oath confirmed God's purposes to the "heirs of what was promised" (v. 17). Then, with no observable transition, he included himself and his readers in the group he called the heirs of the promise. He affirmed that the same oath provided them with "hope as an anchor for the soul" (v. 19). He wrote, "We who have fled . . . have this hope . . ." (vv. 18, 19). He confirmed here an organic union with believers under the old covenant.

The promise covenant finds expression in the theology of the New Testament as well as the Old. It is a vital theological category, for not only does it guarantee the inheritance, but also the continuing integrity and validity of its constituent elements determine the broad parameters within which God has obligated himself to act on behalf of his people for all time.

The Extent of Promise in the History of Redemption

It is clear from this study that God acts on the basis of promise from the time of Abraham to eternity. But what of the time before Abraham?

In Genesis 3:14 – 19 there is a statement of the promise of the offspring. It affirms that God acted on the basis of promise before it was given expression to the patriarchs. The passage is addressed to the serpent. In verse 15 it says, "And I will put enmity between you and the woman, and between your offspring and hers; he will crush your head, and you will strike his heel."

There is a conflict between two offspring in this passage: the offspring of the serpent and the offspring of the woman. The seed of the woman is to inflict great harm on the seed of the serpent.

The harm appears to be mortal, for the head of the serpent is crushed. The serpent wounds only the heel of the woman's seed.

Many interpretations have been given of this verse. It is not necessary to consider all of them. For the purpose of this discussion it will be assumed that the serpent represents Satan, and his offspring are those who follow him. The seed of the woman represents the godly line.[32]

The translation *he will crush your head* represents the Hebrew clause *hû' yešûpkā rō'š*. The pronoun *hû'* finds its referent in "offspring" in the previous clause. In view of the corporate nature of the concept of the offspring it is doubtful that the word *he* (*hû'*) can refer only to an individual. It seems best to understand the referent to be the godly line.

Paul understood the verse in this way, for in Romans 16:20, in an apparent allusion to this passage, he said to the church, "The God of peace will soon crush Satan under your feet."

It is not wrong to see Christ here, for the development of the concept of the offspring throughout Scripture makes it clear that it included an individual offspring within its corporate structure. But the primary reference of Genesis 3:15 is to the people of God.

In that dark day in human history, God acted on the basis of the promise. The promise did not have its inception with Abraham. It figured importantly in the beginning of human history. It can be said to span all of redemptive history.

Conclusion

The covenant of grace is a sovereign disposition in which a glorious inheritance is bestowed on the people of God through the mediatorial work of Christ. It is best to see this covenant as having been forged in heaven before the foundation of the earth (Eph. 1:4; Titus 1:2).

---

32. "To take the word 'seed of the woman' at this point at once in the sense of an individual and so as a definite and exclusive reference to Christ the Savior is wrong and grammatically impossible ... the second part of the verse points to an enmity established by God and involving on the one side the posterity or children of the evil one, and on the other side the posterity or children of the woman, those who share her definite opposition to the evil one." H. C. Leupold, *Exposition of Genesis*, 2 vols. (1942; Grand Rapids: Baker, 1949), vol. 1, pp. 165 – 66.

Its continued integrity is witnessed to in both Old and New Testaments. The Abrahamic covenant is the historical expression of that heavenly exemplar. Christ, in his role as servant, was promised offspring. The offspring are guaranteed an inheritance along with Christ. The Abrahamic covenant expresses the nature of that inheritance in concrete terminology. It has become a part of the heritage of the offspring. It is the testament of the family of God. It is the statement of the intent of God to bestow eminent blessing on those who trust and obey him.

The covenant of grace was not clearly observed by God's ancient people in the time of law, but Paul affirmed that its blessings could have been appropriated by faith and mediated by Christ. Paul saw Christ in the era of law. Under the new covenant, the covenant of grace may be observed with greater clarity because its mediator has appeared in history; the veil has been lifted by the Holy Spirit, and what were but shadows have become realities.

That is not to deny the continuing validity of the Abrahamic covenant. We observed that its force is not negated in the New Testament. It continues to be the family testament. But the glories it guarantees are presented under the new covenant against the background of the death and resurrection of Christ. The covenant of grace is the instrument that determines the nature of the inheritance given to God's people as expressed in the Abrahamic covenant and guarantees its facilitation for all time.

The unchanging nature of the covenantal expression of the inheritance to Abraham and his offspring provides the means by which we may determine and define unity in God's redemptive acts. We are provided with theological direction and stability. A continuity is established by the promise that has profound implications for theology. It guards against an undue division of the testaments and confirms the unity of God's people throughout the redemptive eras.

5

The Administrative Covenants as Theological Category

The promise covenant expresses the unity of God's dealings with his people. But what of the diversity apparent in the description of his acts in both testaments? The suggestion of this work is that the administrative covenants give covenantal shape and authority to that diversity.

The writer of Hebrews posited the oath made by God to Abraham as an instrument that functions as an expression of the "unchanging nature" of God's purpose (6:17). This purpose is identified with the promise (6:13). But his lengthy discussion of the new covenant (chaps. 7–10), designated in this work as an administrative covenant, had as its purpose the explanation of the great changes that are effected under its administration. The administrative covenants provide us with a category in which, by covenantal authority and disposition, we are given a description of the major refinements within the scope of God's redemptive purposes.

Covenant as Theological Category

The question of categorization in biblical theology is an important one. It is an issue that has not found agreement, however. Walter Brueggemann states, "I have no doubt that those of us engaged in theological study are in a crisis of categories."[1] Theological categorization today runs the gamut from the traditional conservative modes of dispensation and covenant to psychological and sociological modes. The concept of category is vital to theological reasoning, for it provides the theologian with the unifying and evaluative criteria necessary for logical coherence. In this section the implications of the function of the administrative covenants as theological categories will be explored.

A number of important theological questions emerge when covenant is posited as a theological category. Is any part of the promise abrogated by the precise categorization of covenant form? What are the hermeneutical implications of the close associations of promise covenant and administrative covenant? It is necessary to consider these important issues if the role of covenant is to be explored thoroughly.

The dramatic events of the covenant ratification ceremony in Genesis 15 marked not only the making of a covenant with Abraham, but also the initiation of an era—an era in which the promise would be administered perpetually by covenant forms bearing the specific designation běrît or diathēkē. Since the administrative covenants have the function of defining the terms of the promise for the eras they govern, covenant becomes an important theological category. If one is to understand the application of the terms of the promise for a given covenantal administration, one must examine the covenantal expression of the promise in that administration. When Abraham's immediate descendants wished to know of their spiritual heritage they looked directly to the Abrahamic covenant, but under the Mosaic covenant the terms of the promise were explicated in complex legislation. The people understood that they were to be a holy nation, a royal priesthood, and God's treasured possession. They knew this because the covenant expressed those aspects of the promise and set forth the conditions under which they could be maintained. Today, the people of God learn of the significance and meaning of their ancient heritage and the ethical response that God desires in the new covenant or the New Testament. Covenant is the theological approach to promise.

Because the covenant of circumcision differs so radically in

1. Walter Brueggemann, *The Land: Place as Gift, Promise, and Challenge in Biblical Faith* (Philadelphia: Fortress, 1977), p. xvi.

function from the Mosaic and new covenants, we shall consider only the latter administrative covenants and their relationship to the terms of the promise.

The major changes of application of the promise and the expansion of its terms are not actualized at arbitrary points in history but at the ratifications of the administrative covenants. The promise covenant is so inextricably bound up with the administrative covenants that it cannot be interpreted apart from them. There is thus a unity of promise elements but a diversity of their expression in the progress of revelation that is involved in a study of covenant as a theological category.

Unity and Diversity in the Administrative Covenants

An examination of the two major administrative covenants reveals both unity and diversity in their expression of the terms of the promise. Unity is not expressed solely by the promise covenant. The elements of the promise are unchanging—crystallized for eternity. But in the administrative covenants we have unity in diversity. The magnificent institutions of the Mosaic covenant are not wanting in the new covenant. This is the point of the Book of Hebrews. Yet they are vastly different from their Old Testament counterparts. There is a linear relationship between the Mosaic covenant and the new covenant, but it is at the same time startlingly diverse in its expression of the nature of these institutions.

One of the tests of a theological system is its ability to delineate and define elements of diversity in God's dealings with mankind. Diversity is there: that is apparent. There are areas in which God deals differently with his people from the way in which he did in the past. If a theological system is to give a precise description of God's redemptive acts it must not only observe them, but also make an effort to understand and explain them. That is the function of theology. It is the science of understanding God.

The promise reigned from Adam to Abraham with no apparent change in its expression. At the giving of the law we meet with the first restatement of the elements of the promise. The changing historical circumstances have given rise to a reapplication of the terms of the promise. This reapplication is given in covenant and thus is determined by it. The major themes of the promise will be considered here in their covenantal categorization.

The Offspring as the People of God

In the earliest expressions of the Abrahamic covenant, the people of God appear to include only the physical descendants of Abraham. It is not specifically stated that Gentiles will be part of the offspring. We know only that divine blessing will come to them. This, of course, strongly implies that they will inherit equally with Abraham's lineal descendants. Abraham may have known much more about the spiritual dimension of the promise than the patriarchal traditions indicate (Heb. 11:10), but we are limited to the statements of the covenant in those traditions and cannot go beyond what they permit.

In the Mosaic covenant we observed a pronounced expansion in the expression of the promise of offspring. This change was geared to the new circumstances that surrounded their independence and growing national consciousness. To be sure, the concept of nationhood was inherent within the Abrahamic covenant (Gen. 12:2), but its perspective was future and that covenant does not set forth the constitutional and legal forms of government found in the Mosaic covenant.

The new covenant uses terminology similar to that of the old covenant in its description of the privileges of the people of God. In the New Testament they are called God's treasured possession and a kingdom of priests, but the diversity inherent in the application of these designations sets forth a new perspective and places the incomparable glory of the new covenant in vivid contrast to the earlier covenant. One aspect of that diversity is the spiritual nature of the concept of nationhood. The people of God under the new covenant are conceived of as a nation. They are called such (1 Peter 2:9)—once they were not a people; now they are (v. 10)—but they are also a "spiritual house" (v. 5). The major difference between the two covenants is the historicoreligious circumstances that lie behind them. The Mosaic covenant had as its perspective a national entity, a people who lived within definable borders. The new covenant governs a spiritual people who fulfill the Levitical regulations in a spiritual way (1 Peter 2:5).

This observation boldly underscores that the shadows of the old covenant have faded before the realities. The types have given way to their counterparts. A new kingdom with a new constitution has now been realized. That constitution is ratified by the blood of Christ and sealed by the Holy Spirit.

Another aspect of covenantal diversity in the concept of the people of God is the means of obedience. The New Testament makes much of this. It is vital to Paul's understanding of "spirit." The new covenant calls its adherents to obedience because of the relationship established in Christ and encourages us to yield to the promptings of the Spirit.

The Christian is not to obey out of legalistic motives (nor was the believer under the Mosaic covenant), but the presence of the Holy Spirit in the believer's heart today creates the proper motives. The Holy Spirit must be seen as working in hearts in the Old Testament, but not to the same degree as he does now. Joel envisioned the time when all, regardless of sex, age, or station, would possess the Holy Spirit (2:28 – 29) and Jeremiah spoke of the time when believers would experience the initimate knowledge of God inherent only in the mediatorial functions of priest and prophet (31:34).

This diversity enables us to observe certain distinctions in the status and privilege of God's people under the two major administrative covenants. These distinctions must be given consideration, if for no other reason than that their covenantal expression warrants it.

The spirit of the New Testament is one of awe as it beholds the inception of the church in God's program. A new age has dawned, a people of God have been formed whose spiritual privileges cause the privileges of the people of the Old Testament to pale before them. The church is formed of people who possess the motivating presence of the Holy Spirit in their hearts in a way that was foreshadowed in the Old Testament but not realized. They are a people whose sins are not remembered and who possess a superior covenant.

Paul saw the church as a body unlike the people under the old covenant in the sense that both Jew and Gentile have become one organic whole. This was accomplished by Christ, who "has made the two one and has destroyed the barrier, the dividing wall of hostility . . ." (Eph. 2:14). We cannot say that the people of God in the Old Testament era were constituted in precisely the same way as Paul described the church in Ephesians 2:14. This new "body," in which Jew and Gentile enjoy equal status, was formed by Christ's "abolishing in his flesh the law with its commandments and regulations" (v. 15). In other words, this organism, called by Paul "one body," was formed only when the old covenant was abolished and the new covenantal era dawned. It was the abolishing of the law that constituted the people of God in this new fashion, for when the law was abolished the "dividing wall of hostility" was destroyed. The people of God could not have existed in the fashion described by Paul as long as they were under the covenant of law. Indeed, the new constitution of God's people demanded a new covenant, for the new body was formed when the two groups were reconciled by the cross. Thus, an old era died, and the new era, the era of the new covenant, ratified by the blood of the cross, witnessed the manifestation of God's people in a form that did not and could not characterize them under the old covenant. This distinction between the church and God's ancient people is determined by covenantal administration.

In 2 Corinthians 3 Paul spoke of his ministry under the new covenant. In the course of his discussion of the glory of that ministry he made certain statements about the status of believers under that covenant. He spoke of the constant growth of believers in the likeness of Christ; this growth is accomplished by the Spirit (v. 18). It is a dispensation in which life is given by the Spirit (vv. 4 – 6). These are privileges which were not known to the same extent by believers who lived under the Mosaic covenant.

The writer of Hebrews also described the privileges of those who are under the new covenant. He spoke of the perfection of God's people because of the one sacrifice of Christ (Heb. 10:14). This perfection, he said, is covenanted by the new covenant of Jeremiah (Heb. 10:16 – 17).

Peter wrote that Christians are "a royal priesthood, a holy nation" (1 Peter 2:9). This language reflects promises of the old covenant. But he posited a difference between them and the Old Testament people, for he called them "a spiritual house," a priesthood that offers "spiritual sacrifices" (v. 5).

Both unity and diversity may be found in this study. The unity of elements transferred from the old covenant to the new covenant confirms the linear relationship between the two covenants that we sought to affirm earlier. The new covenant does not totally supersede the Mosaic covenant. It enables the realization of the great ideals of that covenant. The promise covenant presents us with an absolute unity; the administrative covenants present us with unity in diversity.

Gentile Inclusion in the Promise

The fact that Gentile inclusion in the promise is not clearly formulated in the Mosaic covenant, but continues to be affirmed by prophets who served under its administration, attests to the independent function of promise as a sworn oath. It is a *bĕrît* that is eternally valid. If Gentile inclusion was not given specific covenantal formulation under Moses it is because covenant serves to express the promise in terms that are meaningful and appropriate to the people under its administration.

This function of the new covenant is observable in several ways. First, the new covenant affirms the realization of this promise in Christ. Isaiah proclaimed that ancient promise in 49:6, and Matthew and Luke echoed it and saw its fulfillment in Christ (Matt. 12:18; Luke 2:32). Second, the new covenant explicates the promise to those who are under its administration. Paul referred to the promises to the patriarchs in Romans 15:7 – 13 and then went on to quote Isaiah 11:10 to support his contention that Gentiles are welcome to the gospel (Rom. 15:12).

In Galatians 3:6, Paul quoted from Genesis 15:6, concerning Abraham who "believed God, and it was credited to him as righteousness." He argued in this passage that faith is the means of salvation for all, whether Jew or Gentile. Thus, the ancient promise is explained for the new covenantal jurisdiction initiated by Christ.

When Christ came he set into operation the constituent elements of the new covenant. He established a new era. The New Testament relates to the new covenant in that it records the historical outworking of its elements of promise, explicates its terms, and authoritatively affirms the validity and application of those terms.

The Promise of the Land

The concept of the land has received a good deal of attention in recent years, and deservedly so.[2] Its importance cannot be

2. Brueggemann, *The Land;* W. D. Davies, *The Gospel and the Land: Early Christianity and Jewish Territorial Doctrine* (Berkeley: University of California Press, 1974); M. Dion, "Yahweh, Dieu de Canaan, et la terre des hommes," *CJT* 13 (1967): 233 – 40; D. E. Gowan, "Losing the Promised Land: The Old Testament Considers the Inconceivable," in *From Faith to Faith: Essays in Honor of Donald G. Miller on His Seventieth Birthday,* ed. Dikran Y. Hadidian, Pittsburgh Theological Monograph Series, no. 4 (Pittsburgh: Pickwick, 1979),

minimized. It has even been suggested that this concept may serve as an organizing principle of biblical theology.[3]

Perhaps the most profound questions raised by the theological function of covenant are in relation to this aspect of the promise. The promise of the land is an eternal promise, yet the New Testament seems to contain not one unequivocal affirmation that the promise of the land will be fulfilled for the Jewish people within the definable boundaries of Palestine. In fact the New Testament expands that promise to include the whole world (Rom. 4:13). In Ephesians 6:2−3 Paul quoted from Deuteronomy 5:16; he said, " 'Honor your father and mother'—which is the first commandment with a promise—'that it may go well with you and that you may enjoy long life on the earth' "; the promise in Deuteronomy refers to the land. Matthew 5:5 contains an apparent reference to Psalm 37:11, where the hope of inheriting the land ('ereṣ) is set forth; it employs the Greek word gē in its familiar reference to the meek who "will inherit the earth."

These verses raise serious questions concerning the perpetuity of the promise of the land. They have been answered in a variety of ways.

Representative solutions to the problem of the fulfillment of the promise of land

One approach to this problem is to affirm that Israel did see the fulfillment of the promise in its history, but forfeited eternal pos-

pp. 247−68; Walter C. Kaiser, Jr., "The Promised Land: A Biblical-Historical View," BS 138 (1981): 302−12; Elmer A. Martens, God's Design: A Focus on Old Testament Theology (Grand Rapids: Baker, 1981), pp. 97−115, 175−89, 237−48, 252−53, 258−60; P. Miller, "The Gift of God: The Deuteronomic Theology of the Land," Interp 22 (1969): 451−65; Gerhard von Rad, "The Promised Land and Yahweh's Land in the Hexateuch," in The Problem of the Hexateuch, and Other Essays, trans. E. W. Trueman Dicken (New York: McGraw-Hill, 1966), pp. 79−93; H. E. von Waldow, "Israel and Her Land: Some Theological Considerations," in A Light Unto My Path: Old Testament Studies in Honor of Jacob M. Myers, ed. Howard N. Bream, Ralph D. Heim, and Carey A. Moore, Gettysburg Theological Studies, no. 4 (Philadelphia: Temple University Press, 1974), pp. 493−508; Hans-Rudi Weber, "The Promise of the Land: Biblical Interpretation and the Present Situation in the Middle East," Study Encounter 7 (SE 16 1971): 1−16; M. Wilson, "Zionism as Theology: An Evangelical Approach," JETS 22 (1979): 27−44; G. Ernest Wright, "Israel in the Promised Land: History Interpreted by a Covenant Faith," Encounter 35 (1974): 318−34.

3. Brueggemann says, "Land is a central, if not the central theme of biblical faith. Biblical faith is a pursuit of historical belonging that includes a sense of destiny derived from such belonging.... I suggest that land might be a way of organizing biblical theology." The Land, p. 3.

session of the land because of disobedience. The promise is thus viewed as conditioned on Israel's obedience. Louis Berkhof says, "It is very doubtful, however, whether Scripture warrants the expectation that Israel will finally be reestablished as a nation, and will as a nation return to the Lord. Some Old Testament prophecies seem to predict this, but these should be read in the light of the New Testament. Does the New Testament justify the expectation of a future restoration and conversion of Israel as a nation? It is not taught nor even necessarily implied in such passages as Matt. 19:28 and Luke 21:24, which are often quoted in its favor. The Lord spoke very plainly of the opposition of the Jews to the spirit of his kingdom, and of the certainty that they, who could in a sense be called children of the kingdom, would lose their place in it. . . ."[4]

Berkhof's reference to the New Testament underscores a serious question in the use of covenant as a category. Does covenant abrogate the promise in any way? Does the New Testament somehow vitiate the promise of the land with reference to Israel?

A somewhat similar approach affirms the historical fulfillment of the promise of the land but maintains the eternality of the promise in its fulfillment in the spiritual realities of the Christian faith. Philip Edgcumbe Hughes says, "This covenant promise was fulfilled in an external and this-worldly sense, as the Israelites themselves freely acknowledged when they obtained possession of the land under the leadership of Joshua and subsequently became a great and numerous nation. . . . Yet because of the transitory nature of earthly possessions and the mortality of man which makes certain his separation sooner or later from the acquisitions of this life, it was impossible that an 'everlasting covenant' promising an 'everlasting possession' and an 'eternal inheritance' could find the completeness of its fulfillment in the present order of things. The physical land and the posterity that in due course inherited it were in effect sacramental in character: they constituted a sign, visible and passing, which pointed beyond itself to a reality, as yet invisible, which would be permanent."[5]

Another approach is to see the promise as eternal and still valid.

4. Louis Berkhof, *Systematic Theology,* 2d rev. ed. (Grand Rapids: Eerdmans, 1941), p. 699.
5. Philip Edgcumbe Hughes, *A Commentary on the Epistle to the Hebrews* (Grand Rapids: Eerdmans, 1977), pp. 367–68.

It is to be fulfilled literally for Israel. John F. Walvoord says, "The united testimony of the prophets is all to the same point, that Israel will yet be regathered from the nations of the world and reassembled in their ancient land. The beginnings of this final regathering are already apparent in contemporary history with almost two million Jews . . . now living in Palestine."[6]

Several recent works have set forth strong arguments for a territorial doctrine in the New Testament. George W. Buchanan states, "Reimarus' claim that Jesus as well as his Jewish contemporaries expected the near establishment of the political nation of Palestine as the kingdom of God has received more support in this chapter. This does not mean that all New Testament teaching about the kingdom of God has this meaning, but the percentage of references for which the nationalistic meaning was clear was high enough to justify further consideration of sabbatical eschatology in relationship to a certain geographic area in the Near East as the Kingdom of God."[7] And W. D. Davies asserts that the Old Testament teaching about the land appears in several strata in the New Testament. One of these strata regards the promise of the land positively. Davies says of this stratum, "The emergence of the Gospels . . . witnesses to a historical and therefore geographic, concern in the tradition, which retains for the *realia* their full physical significance. The need to remember the Jesus of History entailed the need to remember the Jesus of a particular land."[8] He concludes, "In sum, for the holiness of place, Christianity has fundamentally, though not consistently, substituted the holiness of the Person; it has Christified holy space."[9]

6. John F. Walvoord, *The Millennial Kingdom* (Findlay, Ohio: Dunham, 1959), p. 182.

7. George W. Buchanan, *The Consequences of the Covenant* (Leiden: Brill, 1970), p. 90. See also A. Wainright's study of Luke's interest in the future of Israel in "Luke and the Restoration of the Kingdom to Israel," *ET* 89 (1977): 76–79. He concludes that "the allusions which [Luke] makes to the future of Israel and Jerusalem are best explained by the assumption that he shared a large measure of traditional Jewish expectation, and that although he believed that God had rejected Israel, he did not believe the rejection to be final" (p. 79).

8. Davies, *The Gospel and the Land*, p. 366.

9. Ibid., p. 368. In a recent article which makes reference to Davies's thesis, Elmer A. Martens, while acknowledging a figurative use of the promise of land by the New Testament writers, cautions that "general usage of Old Testament material [in the New Testament] does not allow us to say dogmatically that this figurative usage exhausts the Old Testament promise. We must be open to the possibility of the historical restoration of Israel to the land" ("The Promise of the Land to Israel," *Direction* 5 [1976]: 12). In "Israel

In his study of the land in the Pauline epistles, Davies discusses the Pauline counterpart to the Old Testament temple, a reference he finds in 2 Corinthians 6:14 − 7:1.[10] In 6:16 Paul said of Christians, "For we are the temple of the living God" (*hēmeis gar naos theou esmen zōntos*). Davies concludes, "The Church is for Paul the fulfillment of the hopes of Judaism for the Temple: the presence of the Lord has moved from the Temple to the Church, which now bears the dangerous holiness once associated with the former, and the life of the Church replaces the temple cult through its own spiritual sacrifices (Rom 12:1ff.) and the foundation of the new temple (Eph 2:20). It is easy to conclude that there was a deliberate rejection by Paul of the Holy Space in favor of the Holy People—the Church."[11]

Davies sees no explicit rejection of the Jerusalem temple by Paul, however, and draws our attention to 2 Thessalonians 2:3 − 4, where the temple remains "for Paul a centre of eschatological significance."[12]

It is very significant that the atmosphere of 2 Corinthians 6:14 − 7:1 is one of promise. There is first a direct allusion to the promise in the words "I will be their God, and they will be my people" (v. 16; cf. Gen. 17:7 − 8; Exod. 6:7; 29:45; Lev. 26:12; Jer. 31:33). Second, in 7:1 Paul referred to his previous argument and said, "Since we have these promises (*epangelias*). . . ." The promise that God would be present with his people has been fulfilled in the church. There is not a territorial dimension to the concept of the temple, but the promise has not been abrogated. It continues on in the new covenant, but its realization in this context is spiritual, not temporal. This is only one of the many motifs explored by Davies. It is a sufficient illustration of his concept of Christification of holy space.

Brueggemann acknowledges a debt to Davies's work, but says that the concept of land in the New Testament "has not been so

as a Theological Problem in the Christian Church," *Journal of Ecumenical Studies* 6 (1969): 329 − 47, Dutch Reformed theologian Hendrikus Berkhof says, "We believe that in one way or another we have to consider them [Israel] *as the other half of God's people*" (p. 337, quoted in Martens, p. 13, n. 11), and "many prophecies were fulfilled in Christ, but they never apply this expression to the promises of the land" (p. 341, quoted in Martens).

10. Davies, *The Gospel and the Land*, pp. 185 − 94.

11. Ibid., p. 188.

12. Ibid., pp. 193 − 94.

fully spiritualized" as Davies concludes.[13] He points to several passages that speak of being "heirs" (Rom. 4:13 – 14; 8:17; Gal. 3:14, 18; 4:7, 28) and says, "It is central to Paul's argument that the promise endures. The heirs in Christ are not heirs to a new promise, but the one which abides, and that is centrally land."[14] To Brueggemann, "landedness" in the New Testament is to be found in community with Christ—membership in his kingdom.

Unity and diversity in the promise of the land

Does covenant theology demand a cessation of the promise of a literal land? Several factors in the use of covenant as a theological category may seem to point in that direction. First, since covenant gives concise definition to the promise in its varied administrations, the lack of a clear affirmation of the prospect of a literal fulfillment of this promise in the New Testament may indicate that it has been annulled in the present economy. The expansion of the promise of the land in the New Testament to include the whole world may indicate that this promise has given way to the more sweeping promises of the new covenant. Second, the New Testament affirms that many historical institutions and events of the Old Testament are "fulfilled" in a spiritual sense in the Christian experience and do not retain their literal significance. The Old Testament priesthood, for example, finds its counterpart in the New Testament in the more spiritual concept of the priesthood of believers. Does the promise of a literal land fade in the blazing light of the believer's spiritual inheritance in Christ? Does it find its fulfillment only in the concept of "place" inherent in the doctrine of the believer's position "in Christ"?

It must be noted first that there is a clear consciousness of a territorial promise in the New Testament and a clear affirmation that it will be fulfilled in a physical sense. One passage that reflects this consciousness is Romans 4:13. This important verse is a test case for the question of the perpetuity of the promise of the land. In it Paul refers directly to that promise as given to Abraham. But the inheritance that Abraham's descendants are to receive, according to Paul, is the world. He does not specify the land. This expansion of the promise of the land should not be allowed to obscure the fact that the territorial aspect of that promise has not

13. Brueggemann, *The Land*, p. 170.
14. Ibid., pp. 177 – 78.

been abrogated in the New Testament. There is the expectation of a fulfillment of the promise in the physical realm. The promise is expanded, but expansion is not synonymous with abrogation. The continuity of this promise is affirmed by the new covenant.

We have observed that Davies posits a development in Pauline thought in which certain factors led Paul "not so much to look away from the land of his fathers as to discover his inheritance 'in Christ'—the land of Christians, the new creation. . . ."[15] He does find a concern with geographical entity in 2 Thessalonians 2:3–4, in the Jerusalem temple which is "a centre of eschatological significance" for Paul, but says of 2 Thessalonians that it "must be regarded as a very early epistle, the thought of which his other epistles attest, he outgrew."[16] Davies thus posits in Paul's thinking a movement away from a primary concern with geographical-eschatological concerns to the more spiritual concepts of "place" in Christ.

Romans 4:13 renders this development somewhat less precise, however, for it demonstrates a clear territorial emphasis in Pauline thought which is not limited only to the sphere of spiritual experience. Davies gives only scant attention to this verse, but its importance cannot be minimized for an understanding of the Pauline application of the promise.

Paul's thought in Romans 4:13 is not out of keeping with the Old Testament, for there is certainly a universalistic element in the Abrahamic covenant in the extension of divine blessing to all nations. He is in keeping with the Old Testament messianic tradition, for in Psalm 2:8, the nations and the ends of the earth are promised as the inheritance (nahălâ) and the possession of the recipient. Who was that recipient? Although it may be considered tenuous to interpret Paul by Acts, there is a strong tradition there that supports the fact that Paul understood Psalm 2 messianically (Acts 13:33). The prophets also envisioned the entire world under the aegis of Messiah. Micah saw the influence of the messianic king extending to the ends of the earth (5:4 [3]). Once again Paul saw the perspective of the whole Old Testament as it unfolded before him. He saw within this concept all of the richness with which the progress of revelation has invested it.

15. Davies, The Gospel and the Land, p. 219.
16. Ibid., p. 194.

Brueggemann argues that even though Davies is correct in saying that "the inheritance has been boldly redefined" we cannot eliminate the concept of land from Pauline passages dealing with inheritance (*klēronomos, klēronomia*) such as Romans 4:13 – 14; 8:17; Galatians 3:14, 18; 4:7, 28.[17]

Is the believer's inheritance only a redeemed earth? Hardly. This is not consonant with Pauline thought. The inheritance of Galatians 3:15 – 18 is not a literal land or a renovated earth. It is all that faith in Christ can give. It is spiritual "landedness." Paul said in verse 21 that the law could not give life, and the implication is that the promise can and does. Life in the land was promised to the covenant people in the Old Testament if they were obedient. The inheritance of the Christian is primarily spiritual life; at-home-ness in Christ. The blessing of Abraham, according to Galatians 3:14, comes in Christ (*en Christōi*) "so that by faith we might receive the promise of the Spirit." There is thus a diversity in the concept as well. According to Ephesians 1:3 believers are blessed "in the heavenly realms with every spiritual blessing in Christ." Again, the concept of place is evident.

The writer of Hebrews reflects a clear land consciousness in chapters 3 and 4. The rest that would have come to the Old Testament people if they had been obedient is still available (4:1). The "rest" spoken of in this context is no longer the land. It is the promise of land (note "promise" in 4:1), but the promise now has a spiritual perspective; it is the gospel (v. 2).

This unity and diversity in the New Testament's understanding of the land demands explanation. Is it to be resolved by positing a development in Pauline thought? How can the two exist side by side in the New Testament? Indeed, how can they exist in the writings of one man?

The answer lies in the fact that the gospel is not entirely otherworldly. It permeates the *kosmos* as the spirit permeates the body. The kingdom is now invisible but it will one day embrace a redeemed earth. The gospel is a spiritual message, but it is a message that beckons individuals who belong to distinct geographical localities within the *kosmos*. The redemption of the sons of God entails the redemption of a cursed creation. "The meek will inherit the earth."

---

17. Brueggemann, *The Land*, pp. 177 – 78.

The believer enjoys spiritual blessings within the sphere of his relationship to Christ. But the gospel includes more. It involves a negation of the curse on the physical world. It witnesses to the complete conquest of Christ over all the work of Satan.

But what of a literal restoration of the land to Israel? If the New Testament does not clearly go that far, does covenant theology demand a cessation of that aspect of the promise? The answer may be found in part in a principle that is emerging from this study. That is, the promise undergoes expansion, but it never suffers observable abrogation. The use of covenant as a vehicle of the promise does not demand abrogation of any of the terms of the promise. All the constituent elements of an aspect of the promise, no matter how much that aspect is expanded in the covenants, may continue in force.[18] If the New Testament does not emphasize a literal restoration of Israel to the land it may be because the Gentile church is largely in view in the New Testament.

It is at best arguing from silence to deny a continuing promise of land for Israel because of a lack of emphasis in the New Testament. D. Flusser says, "It is true that in the extant Gospels Jesus does not speak directly about God's promise of the Land to Israel, but it is equally true that in the Mishnaic Tractate 'The Sayings of the Fathers', Israel's links with its Land are never mentioned."[19]

18. Compare C. Klein, "The Theological Dimension of the State of Israel," *Journal of Ecumenical Studies* 10 (1973): 700−715, who states that "Rom. 9, 4f. affirms categorically the permanent validity of the promises to Israel, which, from the very beginning of its history, have included the gift of Land" (p. 702) and further comments, "The problem ... turns on the concepts of election and covenant. If one is prepared to accept that these have not been abrogated [cf. Rom. 11:29], then it follows that the bond which links Israel to the land has to be accepted as still in force. And here is the rub!" See further the position of Weber, "The Promise of the Land," p. 15, and Wainwright's study of "Luke and the Restoration of the Kingdom to Israel."

19. S. Talmon and D. Flusser, "The Gospel and the Land: Early Christianity and Jewish Territorial Doctrine," *Christian News from Israel* 25 (1975): 137. Also relevant is B. H. Amaru's investigation into the land theology of Josephus ("Land Theology in Josephus," *JQR* 71 [1981]: 201−29). Amaru notes the lack of references to the land as promised or covenanted land (pp. 205−26), observing that "Josephus weakens, if not breaks, the link—the land promise to the patriarchs is not covenanted; ..." (p. 227) and concludes, "Given this portrayal of the future, Josephus' rendition of covenanted land with all his deletions and additions begins to make sense. He deleted the theology of covenanted land because he did not want the land to be a focal point, as it was for Davidic messianism, with all its revolutionary implications in Josephus' day. Josephus feared and despised the messianism of the Zealots, and he structured his account of the Jewish origins and beliefs in such a way as to remove the theological basis for that messianism" (p. 229). Political circumstances and Josephus's purposes thus determined his presen-

It has been observed that the promise of Gentile inclusion is almost entirely absent from the statements that formalized the Mosaic covenant, yet that promise was never abrogated. Prophets who lived under that administration could proclaim the inclusion of Gentiles in the promise even though that concept never found concrete covenantal expression.

Just as the birth of Isaac was an earnest of the promise that Abraham would be the father of multitudes, so the presence of the Jewish state in Israel today may be regarded as an earnest of the future conquest of the world by Christ. It is a reminder that God has not forgotten his promise. He is at work in the events of world history, governing the affairs of mankind as they move toward the eventual triumph of Christ and his eternal reign.

The prospect of landedness is expressed in the Old Testament Prophets in a twofold perspective. There is the expectation of restoration to the land of Palestine, but there is also the prospect of a world conquered and ruled by Messiah. The hope of landedness is expressed within the broad confines of a world subject to the benign rule of Messiah.

The New Testament affirms that Christ will conquer the world (Rev. 11:15; 12:5; 19:15). Nations will be subject to him. The land will become the territorial possession of God's people by virtue of the conquest of Christ over a sinful world—a world now in opposition to him. The new heavens and the new earth will be free of sin because of a righteous rule imposed upon them.

The land will belong to the people of God because it is part of the larger triumph of Christ. Perhaps the definable borders of Canaan will no longer be important under the rule of David's son, but the promise of land as a territorial heritage need not be considered as abrogated if one approaches the promise through covenant. The twofold perspective of the prophets may still obtain under the new covenant.

The prospect of territorial landedness is only part of the Christian's experience within the promise. We are indebted to Davies, Brueggemann, and others for demonstrating the spiritual aspects of that promise. Christians are a landed people. The promise of

tation about the promise of the land; any claim that he did not share the Jewish view concerning the land as promised or covenanted land because of his omissions would certainly be precarious. The same is true of any argument from silence concerning the New Testament writers.

"rest" and "landedness" should be an important part of the Christian's realization of all that he has as his inheritance in Christ. This is what the writer of Hebrews affirmed.[20]

The new covenant thus functions as a typical administrative covenant in this respect. It affirms the continuing validity of an element of the promise covenant, but it explicates that element in a way that is appropriate to the people under its administration. We have found that these are a "chosen people" (1 Peter 2:9) with a spiritual inheritance. But it also amplifies the promise. It affirms its application to the "new earth" and demonstrates its spiritual application to God's people. The land has been won! God has not forgotten his promise for his people under the new covenant.

The Promise of a Divine-Human Relationship

The promise that the Lord would be God to his people is reaffirmed by the new covenant. Diversity in the expression of this promise may be found specifically in the way in which the promise is secured in the new administration.

In 2 Corinthians 6:16 that promise is quoted by Paul. He said, "For we are the temple of the living God. As God has said: 'I will live with them and walk among them, and I will be their God, and they will be my people.'" The unity of this promise throughout the covenantal eras is obvious.

The diversity is found in the concept of the believer as the temple of God. God is united with his people in fulfillment of that which the Old Testament temple foreshadowed. The ancient covenants witnessed God manifest his presence to the patriarchs. Later he guided them by his presence and then revealed his spiritual presence in the tabernacle and the temple. Now God dwells in his people. They are a spiritual temple (1 Peter 2:5).

The union of God with his people is effected by one of the most important accompaniments of the new covenant in the Pauline theology—the indwelling of the Holy Spirit in believers. In 1 Corinthians 3:16 Paul said, "Don't you know that you yourselves are God's temple and that God's Spirit lives in you?"

20. See especially A. T. Lincoln, "Sabbath, Rest, and Eschatology in the New Testament," in *From Sabbath to Lord's Day: A Biblical, Historical, and Theological Investigation*, ed. D. A. Carson (Grand Rapids: Zondervan, 1982), pp. 205–14.

The promise appears again in Hebrews 8:10. It is part of the "better promises." It is presented in covenantal formulation, for it is secured by the new covenant foreseen by Jeremiah. The promise reaches its climax when the eternal state is realized (Rev. 21:3, 7). The old covenant did not witness the realization of the promise, but the promise is realized now in the covenanted blessing of the Holy Spirit.

Conclusion

God has covenanted his promise in several ways. The administrative covenants in particular provide the theologian with an authoritative instrument by which diversity in theological expression may be made a vital part of the descriptive function of the theologian's task. Christ, in whom the realities of the new covenant are actualized, affirmed the need for the recognition of change in God's dealings with his people. He gave authority to that change, abrogating a portion of the law and declaring another a concession. He thus prepared us for the new administration of grace when the old covenant passed away and its splendor faded before the splendor of the "better promises" of the new covenant.

We must look to the expression of the new covenant to determine the nature of the rule under which the Christian lives. That rule was first expressed in covenantal formulation and its broad outline given in covenantal language by the prophet Jeremiah. The New Testament writers reveal that they are conscious of that covenant. They express its promise in the realities of the Christ event.

The expression of the new covenant in Jeremiah authoritatively sets forth the fact that one day aspects of the old covenant will no longer be valid and they will be replaced by incomparably greater privilege and blessing. That fact is determined by covenant. That is where its authoritative delineation lies.

The administrative covenants may permit abrogation of aspects of the old covenant, but they do not abrogate the elements of the promise covenant that are universal in their application. They explicate, redefine, and confirm the promise elements, but the function of abrogation cannot easily be assigned to these covenants.

The lineal relationship between the Mosaic and new covenants allows for a continuity to be observed in their promises. But this is not to be understood as an absolute continuity. If it were, there would be no need for the new covenant. The new covenant gives a perspective to the old institutions that is centered in the "better promises." The ministry of the Holy Spirit enables the facilitation of obedience under the new covenant, and the believer's inheritance under the new covenant "can never perish, spoil or fade" (1 Peter 1:4).

6

The Extent of Covenant as Theological Category

The administrative covenants oversee the disposition of the promise-oath from Abraham to the consummation. The covenant that was established between the Father and the Son when God gave the promises to Christ extends from eternity to eternity and is the divine authority that gives force and validity to the covenantal expression of the promise.

Covenant theology posits another covenant: the covenant of works.

The Covenant of Works in Traditional Covenant Theology

The covenant of works is a covenant made between God and Adam. The term *covenant of works* is not favored by a number of scholars. Meredith G. Kline questions the traditional designation because "it fails to take account of the continuity of the law principle in redemptive revelation and therefore is not a sufficiently distinctive term."[1] In its traditional expression, the covenant of

1. Meredith G. Kline, *By Oath Consigned: A Reinterpretation of the Covenant Signs of Baptism and Circumcision* (Grand Rapids: Eerdmans, 1968), p. 32.

works consisted of a covenant between God and Adam, in which Adam was promised life on condition of obedience.[2]

Efforts to find direct exegetical support for designating this relationship a covenant have generally yielded questionable results. John Murray, an eminent covenant theologian, makes this significant statement about the Adamic administration:

> This administration has often been denoted 'The Covenant of Works.' There are two observations. (1) The term is not felicitous, for the reason that the elements of grace entering into the administration are not properly provided for by the term 'works.' (2) It is not designated a covenant in Scripture. Hosea 6:7 may be interpreted otherwise and does not provide the basis for such a construction of the Adamic economy. Besides, Scripture always uses the term covenant, when applied to God's administration to men, in reference to a provision that is redemptive or closely related to redemptive design. Covenant in Scripture denotes the oath-bound confirmation of promise and involves a security which the Adamic economy did not bestow.
>
> Whether or not the administration is designated covenant, the uniqueness and singularity must be recognized. It should never be confused with what Scripture calls the old covenant or first covenant (cf. Jer 31:31–34; 2 Cor 3:14; Heb 8:7, 13). . . . The view that in the Mosaic covenant there was a repetition of the so-called covenant of works, current among covenant theologians, is a grave misconception and involves an erroneous construction of the Mosaic covenant, as well as fails to assess the uniqueness of the Adamic administration.[3]

The Adamic administration was characterized by God's sovereign declarations, according to Murray. He says, "It was not a contract or compact."[4] He points out that "the principle of representation underlies all the basic institutions of God in the world—the family, the church, and the state."[5]

---

2. Charles Hodge defines the covenant of works: "God having created man after his own image in knowledge, righteousness, and holiness, entered into a covenant of life with him, upon condition of perfect obedience, forbidding him to eat of the tree of knowledge of good and evil upon the pain of death." *Systematic Theology,* 3 vols. (1871–73; Grand Rapids: Eerdmans, 1952), vol. 2, p. 117.

3. John Murray, "The Adamic Administration," in *Collected Writings of John Murray,* 4 vols. (Edinburgh and Carlyle, Penn.: Banner of Truth Trust, 1976), vol. 2, pp. 49, 50.

4. Ibid., p. 50.

5. Ibid., p. 51.

The passage most frequently appealed to in support of the application of the term *bĕrît* to the Adamic administration is Hosea 6:7. The New International Version translates the verse, "Like Adam, they have broken the covenant—they were unfaithful to me there." The Revised Standard Version translates it, "But at Adam they transgressed the covenant; there they dealt faithlessly with me." The problem is apparent. The name *Adam* may be understood in two ways: the first man, as well as a place. A site named Adam is known from Joshua 3:16.

The Hebrew text reads *kĕ'ādām 'ābrû bĕrît šām bāgdû bî*, literally, "as Adam they transgressed the covenant, there they were unfaithful to me." The interpretation of *kĕ'ādām* as a place name does not necessarily require an emendation.[6] F. I. Andersen and David Noel Freedman observe, "The best conclusion, we believe, is that Adam is a place and *kĕ'ādām* means 'as in/at Adam,' although Adam is not the only place where such things occur. For the same syntax, see *kmdbr*, 'as in the wilderness' (2:5), although the *k* could also be explained as asseverative."[7] The word *šām* (there) is often appealed to in support of a locative connotation for the word *Adam*. James Luther Mays notes this, but uses it as an argument for emending the *kĕ* (as) to *bĕ* (at).[8] O. Palmer Robertson, who supports "Adam" as a proper name, explains *šām* as representing "a dramatic gesture toward the place of Israel's current idolatry. . . ."[9]

In spite of the uncertainty in the interpretation of this verse, a good case can be made for the translation *like Adam*, referring to the first man. There is no record of a specific transgression committed at Adam, unless that site is understood to represent the whole wilderness experience.

The word *šām* (there) in the text is the most important bit of evidence supporting a geographical location. But it may occur in Psalm 14:5 in a nongeographical sense. In verse 4 the psalmist spoke of evildoers "who eat up my people as they eat bread" (RSV). In verse 5 he continued, "There they shall be in great terror, for

---

6. O. Palmer Robertson, *The Christ of the Covenants* (Grand Rapids: Baker, 1980), p. 22; James Luther Mays, *Hosea: A Commentary* (Philadelphia: Westminster, 1969), p. 100.

7. F. I. Andersen and David Noel Freedman, *Hosea*, the Anchor Bible (New York: Doubleday, 1980), p. 439.

8. Mays, *Hosea*, p. 100.

9. Robertson, *The Christ of the Covenants*, p. 22, n. 2.

God is with the generation of the righteous" (RSV). The word *there* (*šām*) in verse 5 may be a vague reference to the place of judgment, or a reference to the state of transgression they are in when God judges them. The latter seems more likely. If this is how we are to understand Hosea 6:7, then the prophet is saying that the Israelites transgressed the covenant, as did Adam, and in that act of transgression they dealt faithlessly with God.

The translation *as in/at Adam,* connoting a place, has no clear referent for the comparative *kĕ* (as). The translation *like Adam* renders the verse a complete unit, making it consonant with the terse statements that characterize this section.

Understood in this way, Adam's transgression was a violation of a *bĕrît* made with him by God to maintain his state of fellowship with God. This is the function of the covenant made with Israel.

Although the latter interpretation may have the better support, it is by no means certain. This verse may not be appealed to as conclusive evidence for a covenant of works.

Another passage that is used to support the extension of the concept of covenant to the pre-Noahic period is Jeremiah 33:20–26.[10] This refers to God's covenant with nature that secures an unbroken succession of days and nights. The passage states that just as the procession of time is incapable of being interrupted, so the promises made to David cannot be broken. However, the covenant of Jeremiah 33 is not a covenant with mankind and may reflect the use of hyperbolic language to express an observable phenomenon of nature.

Even though these passages do not yield conclusive exegetical support for a covenant between God and Adam, covenant theologians should not be faulted for applying the term *covenant* to the Adamic probation. It has been observed that the term *bĕrît* is very flexible, describing many different kinds of relationships. Robertson has rightly observed that "nowhere in the original account of the establishment of God's promise to David does the term 'covenant' appear. . . . Subsequent Scripture specifically speaks of God's 'covenant' with David (cf. 2 Sam. 23:5; Ps. 89:3)."[11] And Walther Eichrodt observes, "The crucial point is not—as an all too naive criticism seems to think—the occurrence or absence of the Hebrew

10. Ibid., p. 19.
11. Ibid., p. 18.

word *bĕrît.*"[12] Since the word *bĕrît* can connote a loose relationship such as the sovereign intent of God to impose certain strictures on his created world, the relationship with Adam may be called such, if one wishes. It certainly was a relationship that involved strictures.

Why then is it not called such in the early chapters of Genesis? What does the literary shape of those chapters tell us about the absence of the term *bĕrît?* The question is a difficult one, but the intent may be that we are not to understand the relationship with Adam to be a *bĕrît* in the same sense that the word has in its other occurrences in the Book of Genesis. In the other instances where the word is used of a divine-human relationship, it connotes the assurance of a divine promise of blessing that the human participant did not previously possess. This is true of the covenant with Noah. It assured him and his posterity that the world would never again be destroyed by a flood. The word *bĕrît* has a similar function in the case of the promise given to Abraham.

The Adamic relationship, on the other hand, assured the maintenance of a condition that already existed. The prohibition against partaking of the tree of the knowledge of good and evil marked the path to the loss of the state Adam already enjoyed. He was told, "In the day that you eat of it you shall die" (Gen. 2:17, RSV). The relationship established by the proscription was not a redemptive relationship, nor a relationship of promise. One may object to using the term *covenant*, but the recognition that a sovereign disposition of God on mankind, governing human relationships and institutions, was established with Adam is an important theological concept.

The covenant of works has not been limited only to the Adamic administration by theologians. Its influence has been extended to the law and even into the New Testament. The Westminster Confession of Faith states with regard to the covenant of works, "This law, after [man's] fall, continued to be a perfect rule of righteousness; and, as such, was delivered by God upon Mount Sinai in ten commandments, and written in two tables...."[13] It says further, "Although true believers be not under the law as a cove-

---

12. Walther Eichrodt, *Theology of the Old Testament*, trans. J. A. Baker, 2 vols. (Philadelphia: Westminster, 1961), vol. 1, pp. 17, 18.

13. Philip Schaff, *The Creeds of Christendom*, 3 vols. (Grand Rapids: Baker, 1966), vol. 3, p. 640.

nant of works, to be thereby justified or condemned; yet it is of great use to them, as well as to others; in that, as a rule of life, informing them of the will of God and their duty, it directs and binds them to walk accordingly. . . ."[14]

Charles Hodge says, "Even the New Testament, as we have seen, contains a legal element, it reveals the law still as a covenant of works binding on those who reject the gospel; but in the Old Testament, the law predominated over the gospel."[15]

Neither of these statements can be understood to regard the law as an option for salvation or a rival of sovereign grace. But, if the covenant of works is regarded as an instrument that held out a valid offer of life, its extension into the law may possibly be construed as giving to the law the function of granting life or salvation on condition of perfect obedience.[16]

Does the covenant of works offer life on condition of obedience? The affirmation that it does is so well entrenched in Reformed theology that one asks the question with trepidation. Yet, it is in the interest of theological progress to rethink our categories.

The suggestion given here is that the covenant of works does not offer life, but functions as does the law, that is, to maintain a relationship to God that was already established. In the case of the law the relationship was established by promise and maintained by obedience.

An examination of the conditions of the covenant of works in Genesis 2:15—17 shows that the prospect of death, not life, was set before Adam. It says, "In the day that you eat of it you shall die" (v. 17, RSV). The conclusion that life was offered to Adam is, at best, an inference. We may understand the condition of the covenant of works, taken at face value, to offer only one thing, that is, death—the cessation of the relationship that Adam enjoyed with God.

Obedience to the stipulation of the covenant maintained the relationship to God and his world that was established by virtue of Adam's creation. That relationship was one that involved the

14. Ibid., pp. 641—42.

15. Hodge, *Systematic Theology*, vol. 2, p. 376.

16. Daniel P. Fuller comments, "If there really is a mixture of a virtual covenant of works in the decalogue itself with grace in the introduction to it . . . how can anyone then blame the poor Jews for trying to be saved by works . . . ? *Gospel and Law: Contrast or Continuum?* (Grand Rapids: Eerdmans, 1980), p. 53.

knowledge of God, communion with God, the enjoyment of an unsullied creation—this was life. But disobedience would sever that relationship, and this severance is called death.

The covenant of works is a valid legal instrument. It functioned as did the law. It oversaw obedience; it maintained the viability of Adam's relationship to God; it was stipulatory in nature.

It was not a covenant of promise, for Adam was not promised life; he was promised death if he disobeyed. Life flowed to Adam from his privilege as a created being, placed in an environment in which he had direct access to God. The viability of that gracious privilege depended on his obedience. It is difficult to see its promise as the offer of eternal life.

We thus may draw the conclusion that God has always acted on the basis of grace. Mankind was never offered eternal life solely on the basis of legal obedience. The admixture of law and grace that may result from too formal a structuring of the theological construct called the covenant of works may even impinge on the clarity of the gospel. The message of the gospel is that God has accomplished all that mankind needs for redemption. When one sincerely accepts that gift, the Holy Spirit begins to promote valid obedience by changing the motives and desires of the individual. One does not work to achieve merit; that is legalism. One obeys from an unfeigned and humble faith. Obedience witnesses to such a faith and is the mark of a proper relationship to God.

Perhaps Murray's designation *administration* is best for this era in human history,[17] although it must be reiterated that the application of the term *covenant* is not wrong, provided we understand it to be used in its broadest relational sense. The term *administration* recognizes the governance of God over his creation and, at the same time, avoids confusing the relationship between God and Adam with the relationships designated *běrît* that occur later in Genesis.

The Nature of the Adamic Administration

The presence of grace even in this dark time in human history is apparent. It has been observed that God acted on the basis of

17. Murray, "The Adamic Administration," pp. 49, 50.

his eternal promise when he pronounced the curse on the serpent (Gen. 3:14 – 15). The promise to the offspring, which was reiterated to Abraham, is one that is continually operative. We have seen that Paul could appeal to it in his message to the Christian church at Rome. It is the eternal promise which later became a sworn oath.

In the relationship that God established with mankind and the created world, certain strictures were placed on creation that obtain to this day. Thus the emphasis on "creation" rather than "works" in the more recent designation *covenant of creation* is more consonant with the intent of this context. Adam thus functioned as the representative of all mankind as he received the announcement of the divine disposition.

This federal function of Adam was appealed to by Paul in Romans 5:12 – 21. This passage fits within the general discussion to this point as well. There seems to be no absolute demand to designate this relationship a covenant (the federal function of Adam is not diminished if the relationship is designated an administration), yet the relationship falls within the general category of *bĕrît*. Covenant theology should not be rejected on this basis. Paul called the sovereign disposition of the promises to Christ a *diathēkē*. The term is correct provided one does not read into the theological construction of this relationship aspects of the concept of *bĕrît* that are not warranted exegetically. The term *administration* may also be a valid translation for the type of *bĕrît* relationship that obtains here.

Conclusion

The concept of the administrative covenant is not to be limited only to circumcision, the law, and the new covenant. The covenant of works, if understood as this discussion has suggested, falls into the same category. But its function is not exactly consonant with the law and the new covenant. They administer the promise; the covenant of works administers a relationship established by creation. But it administers it through obedience and thus it may be viewed as an administrative covenant.

Its violation by Adam has brought condemnation and death on all mankind. There was thus a need for a Redeemer. Provision for a Redeemer becomes clear in the unfolding of the promise. The inheritance given to God's people is based on the mediatorial work of Christ. This was first established in the covenant of grace made between the Father and the Son. This covenant overcomes the penalty of death established by the covenant of works. Thus, God has dealt with mankind on the basis of covenant from the beginning of time.

7

The Hermeneutical Implications of the Study

A number of important hermeneutical issues emerge from this study of the covenantal administration of the divine redemptive activity. This chapter is an effort to isolate from the preceding discussion the major hermeneutical issues that are explicit or implicit in the covenantal structure. These issues will be summarized and discussed briefly.

Law and Grace

Law and grace are not opposing concepts. Faith and legalism are. If law is regarded as a covenant of works, on the basis of which one may receive eternal life, then law and grace are competing modes of salvation. Both dispensationalism and covenant theology evince concern for the relationship of these two concepts.

The law does not command one to work in order to achieve a relationship with God. It assumes an established relationship. It commands one to obey in order to maintain that relationship. Leviticus 18 makes it clear that disobedience will sever one's relationsip to the promise (vv. 28–29), but the relationship is presumed to have been established. The great statements of the law are preceded by a consciousness of a relationship established solely on the basis of grace. The magnificent cadences of the law should not be allowed to drown out the major theme expressed in such words as, "I am the God of your father, the God of Abraham, the God of Isaac and the God of Jacob" (Exod. 3:6); "I have remembered my covenant . . ." (Exod. 6:5). The relationship was established by a gracious oath on the part of the God. It would be realized regardless of human success or failure. One had only to respond to that affirmation in trust. If that promise was to be realized it had to be protected and obedience had to be encouraged. It was the function of the law to do this. Legal obedience is a manifestation of faith in the promise.

The grace that shines with such magnificence in the new covenant is not different in essence from the grace that obtained throughout the era of law. It guarantees the same promise. It elicits the same faith and it requires obedience for the maintenance of the promise. The major difference is the facilitation of obedience through the gift of the Holy Spirit and the expression of the promise in a way more appropriate to the era initiated by the death of Christ and the ministry of the Spirit.

The Old Testament law should be a delight to the Christian, for he has been freed from its condemning power. Its institutions contain promise of the greater institutions that have been realized in Christ. Its precepts continue to provide wisdom and strength. Its efforts to legislate love and understanding in the social sphere permeate the teaching of the New Testament writers. Jesus did not abolish the law.

The Relationship Between the Testaments

The question of the relationship that exists between the Old and New Testaments has received much attention in recent years.[1] This section will explore the ways in which the covenant structure suggested in this work relates to this important theme.

The Old Testament must remain an essential part of biblical

1. Bernard W. Anderson, ed., *The Old Testament and Christian Faith* (New York: Harper and Row, 1963); James D. Smart, *The Interpretation of Scripture* (Philadelphia: Westminster, 1961); Claus Westermann, *The Old Testament and Jesus Christ*, trans. Omar Kaste (Minneapolis: Augsburg, 1970); R. T. France, *Jesus and the Old Testament* (Downers Grove, Ill.: Inter-Varsity, 1971); R. E. Murphy, "The Relationship Between the Testaments," *CBQ* 26 (1964): 349–59.

theology; indeed, the relationships of promise-anticipation and type-reality give to the Testaments an equal role and affirm an interdependence that is organic in nature. This interdependence renders the Old Testament necessary to the New Testament and the New Testament necessary to the Old. The interdependence is governed to a great extent by the eternal promise.

The law is not an impediment to the unity of the Testaments when viewed from the vantage point of covenant. On the contrary, it contributes to the integrity and unity of the promise covenant by protecting and amplifying it. When the law is regarded as a valid option for achieving life, or as being in opposition to gospel, the unity of the Testaments is threatened, for the sovereignty of grace is threatened.

Rudolf Bultmann's contention that promise in the Old Testament emerges from the miscarriage of Old Testament history may be questioned in light of the continuing force of the promise covenant. Bultmann says, "The miscarriage of history actually amounts to a promise. There is nothing which can count as a promise to man other than the miscarriage of his way, and the recognition that it is impossible to gain direct access to God in his history within the world, and directly to identify his history within the world with God's activity. ... This miscarriage is, of course, to be understood as a promise only on the basis of its fulfillment, that is on the basis of the encounter with God's grace...."[2]

To be sure, promise arises out of failure in the Old Testament. The new covenant replaces a covenant that failed—the ancient people fell far short of the Deuteronomic ideal, and a new people have entered the sphere of redemptive history. But promise in the Old Testament is not one with the Old Testament institutions and Old Testament history. It is always separate from them in the sense that the promise covenant never loses its integrity, and in this sense it remains objective promise in every era.

The failure of the law to maintain the national life of the people confirmed the continuing validity of the promise covenant, for the prophets affirmed it had not been nullified. It was objective promise that the failure of the Mosaic covenant assured, and not only an existential encounter with divine grace. Jeremiah observed the

2. Rudolf Bultmann, "Prophecy and Fulfillment," in *Essays on Old Testament Hermeneutics*, ed. Claus Westermann (Richmond: John Knox, 1963), p. 73.

broken law (31:32) and affirmed the continuation of the ancient promises given to Abraham. It is in this regard that the writers of the New Testament established a unity with the Old Testament.

The sequential structure of the administrative covenants does not negate the validity of the Old Testament as God's word to the present. The Old Testament continues to speak to mankind under the new covenant. If it did not, how else may we explain the numerous references of the New Testament writers to that old covenant? They appeal to it for objective truth, for argumentational support, for comfort, for exhortation. Surely these appeals cannot be explained adequately by the need to accommodate their Jewish readers to whom the Old Testament was the sole repository of God's word. This does not adequately explain Paul's use of the example of Abraham's faith to expound justification. The faith of Abraham was objective fact, derived exegetically from the Old Testament; it was not merely illustrative material that gave a Jewish aura to what was only a Christian concept. The new covenant itself witnesses to the divine authority of the Old Testament and attests to its continuing validity.

There is a twofold direction inherent in the relationship between the Testaments. First, there is a line of authority that moves forward from the Old Testament through the New Testament. But we must also think in terms of the other direction. The very fact that we ask questions of the New Testament and seek to determine its attitude toward the Old Testament indicates that we recognize in it an authority that is, in a sense, distinct from the authority of the Old Testament. John Bright observes, "We must begin with the Old Testament's own theological assertions and concerns, with the Old Testament's own structure of faith; we must follow that ahead through history to see how it was taken up in the New Testament, and then, from that perspective, we may look back and again understand the Old."[3]

One cannot conclude that the New Testament is thus absolute authority in the progress of revelation. On this basis how can we explain the ultimacy in the appeals to the Old Testament that we find in Christ and the New Testament writers? It was an appeal to the divine word; an appeal that shut mouths and convinced

3. John Bright, *The Authority of the Old Testament* (1967; Grand Rapids: Baker, 1975), p. 112.

skeptics. The authority of the Testaments must be refined to take into account all the data.

One aspect of the authority of the New Testament is in its covenantal function of diversification. The new covenant discriminates among the aspects of the divine will set forth in the Old Testament and authoritatively asserts that the promise-oath is still in force. It indicates the aspects of the Mosaic covenant that were not intended for its specific era and shows which aspects have continuing force. In the light of this valid covenantal function, one cannot affirm an authority for the New Testament that supersedes the authority of the Old. The Old Testament speaks to us today with an undiminished force. Even in those areas where the husk has been removed to reveal the true spiritual kernel, the typological and apologetic value of the types and shadows lends a function to the Old Testament that attests to its continuing power and application.

The New Testament limits and redefines elements in the old covenant that do not apply in the same way today. But the Old Testament possesses a similar function in relation to the New Testament. It too defines and limits. It defines the nature of faith. Paul's concept of justification by faith was carefully confined to what the Old Testament revealed. The nature of God is compatible with that concept in the Old Testament, even in his judgmental activity. The Old Testament sets forth the historical ground from which spring such New Testament concepts as the spiritual priesthood and the land.

Because of its relationship to the promise, the Old Testament remains a valid and necessary repository of divine truth. J. Woods says, "There is nothing in the Old Testament that is not linked with the sequence of events in the revelation of the living God, who has bound himself to the witness of this scriptural record and not to some other religious book of the East."[4]

The supreme authority of the Old Testament is ultimately the same as that of the New Testament, that is, Christ. It is Christ, not only in his objective delineation of Old Testament word, but in his living presence in the word. He mediates the promises, according to Paul, not only in the New Testament era, but in the Old Testament era as well, for in some way those promises were made to

---

4. J. Woods, *The Old Testament in the Church* (London: S.P.C.K., 1949), p. 17.

Christ before the new covenant appeared in history (Gal. 3:16). He may be seen by Paul in the Old Testament word just as vividly as he is in the New Testament. Paul could see Christ in Deuteronomy 30, as we observed in our study of Romans 10:5 – 7. In that passage Christ became the facilitating principle of obedience. This was not an objective application of the verse, but it was an objective realization of the relationship of Christ to the promise. This relationship permeates the covenants. It led utlimately to the appearance in history of the one to whom the words were spoken, "I will keep you and will make you to be a covenant for the people . . ." (Isa. 49:8).

Covenantal Religion

On the basis of the conclusions reached in this work we may say that Christianity is a covenantal religion and the obedience of the Christian faith is covenantal obedience. But it is obedience to the new covenant, not the old. The obedience of the new covenant is motivated by the Holy Spirit. But the covenantal nature of obedience may be observed in the fact that obligation on the part of the Christian has not been negated.

The apostle Paul reflected that covenantal obligation in Romans 8:12, where he said, "Therefore, brothers, we have an obligation— but it is not to the sinful nature. . . ." It becomes obvious in the context that the obligation is to the Holy Spirit, who enables us to put to death the deeds of the flesh (v. 13). This is confirmed in 7:6, where Paul wrote that after our release from the law, "we serve in the new way of the Spirit, and not in the old way of the written code."

The obligation of which Paul spoke is to the Holy Spirit, who administers obedience under the new covenant. Thus, obedience is manifestly important to the believer, for it is his covenantal obligation.

The importance of obedience must be recognized. The teaching of Jesus is filled with commandments that he expected his followers to obey. If these are treated lightly, or if the believer's obligation to obey them is not clearly understood, we may be in danger of bifurcating the covenantal relationship as did the Pharisees of Paul's day.

Obedience witnesses to a valid faith. It does not save. It cannot grant the inheritance. But by virtue of its attestation of a living faith it is a precious commodity for the believer. Not only is it his obligation; not only does it bring eminent satisfaction; but also it relates to faith in that it demonstrates that the believer's faith is true saving faith. It witnesses to a change in the believer that has turned his heart toward God. "Therefore, brothers, we have an obligation...."

The Relationship of the Church to God's Ancient People

The unity of the people of God in all ages is more than a simple commonality in the way of salvation. It is an organic unity fashioned by the one promise covenant that is their common heritage. This unity has important hermeneutical implications, for it means that the blessings of the inheritance promised to the remnant in the Old Testament are blessings shared by the church. It is a rich experience for the believer to realize that his roots go back through the ancient people to Abraham. We share the same faith—the same hope—as the believing Jews of the old era.

A hermeneutical unity that broadens the avenue of our approach to the statements of promise and blessing in the Old Testament becomes apparent. The followers of Christ share a hope similar to that of the remnant of the Old Testament. We shall one day reign under the aegis of Messiah, as Micah said the remnant would (4:7). We shall experience the ultimate triumph of Christ (Mic. 2:12–13).

Yet the new-covenant believer observes a greater glory in his experience and greater privilege than did his Old Testament counterpart. The church represents a manifestation of the people of God in a way different from that of the Old Testament. This distinction is observed in the covenantal language of Jeremiah, and the realization of that language in the New Testament.

Implications for Preaching

The preceding section shows that the recognition of the continued force of the promise covenant enables the preacher to communicate the Christian's hope from Old Testament passages that deal with God's ancient people. However, New Testament preaching is the preaching of a new covenant. We must not preach to a new-covenant congregation that which was specifically for another era. This observation raises serious questions for the communication of authorial intent in the texts of Scripture.

It is the responsibility of the preacher to reflect the intent of Scripture. If he does not, he is failing in his responsibility as a herald of God's truth. Yet, our study of the administrative covenants has led us to conclude that certain aspects of the old covenant have been abrogated for the Christian or have taken a spiritual form. This means that aspects of the Old Testament have been recast by the new covenant.

If this is not recognized, portions of the Old Testament are very difficult to preach. One thinks of Psalm 149, where we read of God's people,

> May the praise of God be in their mouths
>   and a double-edged sword in their hands,
> to inflict vengeance on the nations
>   and punishment on the peoples,
> to bind their kings with fetters,
>   their nobles with shackles of iron,
> to carry out the sentence written against them. [vv. 6 – 9]

Since this is not given an eschatological perspective, we must conclude that the author intended this as an expression of hope for his people. But it is not the prerogative of the Christian to disseminate his faith by the sword. This is antagonistic to the nature of the gospel.

However, under the new covenant, the enemies of the "spiritual house" are spiritual enemies (Eph. 6:12). C. H. Spurgeon notes, "In this Israel was not an example, but a type: we will not copy the chosen people in making literal war, but we will fulfill the emblem by carrying on spiritual war. We praise God and contend with our corruptions; we sing joyfully and war earnestly with evil of every kind. Our weapons are not carnal, but they are mighty, and wound with both back and edge. . . . The verse indicates a happy blending of the chorister and the crusader."[5]

5. C. H. Spurgeon, *The Treasury of David*, 7 vols. (New York and London: Funk and Wagnalls, 1881), vol. 6, p. 454.

We must guard against departure from the central thrust of the text. We saw how Paul used the Old Testament passage in Romans 10:6 – 10. He did not depart from its central meaning, but he saw Christ there. The passage was read in the light of the covenant of which Paul was a minister. We may not make an Old Testament passage mean what we wish it to mean. But at the same time we must not impose on our people that which is not their responsibility, privilege, or function.

The Old Testament must be viewed within the grid of the new covenant. The preacher will not want for Old Testament materials if he does this; there is very little that has not come over to the New Testament in some form. He will be guarding his preaching and assuring the correctness of its application to the church. At the same time he will be demonstrating that the roots of the Christian faith are in the Old Testament, and the preponderance of Christian experience may be found there. He will also guard his New Testament preaching by the precepts of the old covenant— Paul did!

Like Paul, the New Testament preacher stands on this side of Calvary and views the unfolding panorama of divine grace in a full-orbed perspective. He may preach Christ from the Old Testament. He sees a linear development in the progress of redemption. The promise covenant guarantees that unity and, since it reflects the covenant of grace, one can see Christ in the Old Testament, administering the promise to his people.

Conclusion

The authority of God's redemptive dealings lies in covenanted word and deed. The bicovenantal structure of the covenants has profound implications for faith and practice.

Basic to this structure is the fact that God made a promise to which he asks only the response of faith. True faith manifests itself in loving obedience which results from a consciousness of the inner motivation of the Holy Spirit. To all who respond to God in faith he gives a glorious inheritance, "an inheritance that can never perish, spoil or fade—kept in heaven for you, who through faith are shielded by God's power until the coming of the salvation that is ready to be revealed in the last time" (1 Peter 1:4 – 5).

Bibliography

Allen, Leslie C. *The Books of Joel, Obadiah, Jonah, and Micah.* New International Commentary on the Old Testament series. Grand Rapids: Eerdmans, 1976.

Allis, O. T. "The Blessing of Abraham." *Princeton Theological Review* 25 (1927): 263–98.

—————. *Prophecy and the Church.* Philadelphia: Presbyterian and Reformed, 1945.

Amaru, B. H. "Land Theology in Josephus." *Jewish Quarterly Review* 71 (1981): 201–29.

Andersen, F. I., and David Noel Freedman. *Hosea.* The Anchor Bible. New York: Doubleday, 1980.

Anderson, Bernard W., ed. *The Old Testament and Christian Faith.* New York: Harper and Row, 1963.

Anderson, H. *The Gospel of Mark.* New Century Bible. London: Oliphants, 1976.

Bacon, B. "Jesus and the Law: A Study of the First 'Book' of Matthew (Mt. 3–7)." *Journal of Biblical Literature* 47 (1928): 203–31.

Baldwin, Joyce G. *Haggai, Zechariah, Malachi: An Introduction and Commentary.* Tyndale Old Testament commentary. Downers Grove, Ill.: Inter-Varsity, 1972.

—————. "ṢEMAḤ as a Technical Term in the Prophets." *Vetus Testamentum* 14 (1964): 93–97.

Banks, R. *Jesus and the Law in the Synoptic Traditions.* Cambridge: At the University Press, 1975.

Barclay, William. "New Wine in Old Wineskins." *The Expository Times* 86 (1974–75): 68–72.

Barnes, Albert. *Notes on the New Testament: Hebrews.* Edited by Robert Frew. Grand Rapids: Baker, 1949.

233

Barrett, C. K. *A Commentary on the Epistle to the Romans*. New York: Harper, 1958.

Barth, Gerhard. "Matthew's Understanding of the Law." In *Tradition and Interpretation in Matthew*. Translated by Percy Scott. Philadelphia: Westminster, 1963.

Barth, Karl. *Church Dogmatics*. Vol. 2, *The Doctrine of God*. Translated by G. T. Thomson. Edinburgh: T. and T. Clark, 1936.

Beecher, Willis J. *The Prophets and the Promise*. Grand Rapids: Baker, 1963.

Berkhof, Hendrikus. "Israel as a Theological Problem in the Christian Church." *Journal of Ecumenical Studies* 6 (1969): 329 – 47.

Berkhof, Louis. *Systematic Theology*. 2d rev. ed. Grand Rapids: Eerdmans, 1941.

Black, Matthew. *Romans*. New Century Bible Commentary. 1973. Grand Rapids: Eerdmans, 1981.

Branscomb, B. H. *Jesus and the Law of Moses*. New York: R. R. Smith, 1930.

Briggs, Charles A. *Messianic Prophecy: The Prediction of the Fulfilment of Redemption Through the Messiah*. New York: Scribner's, 1886.

Bright, John. *The Authority of the Old Testament*. 1967. Grand Rapids: Baker, 1975.

————. *Covenant and Promise: The Prophetic Understanding of the Future in Pre-exilic Israel*. Philadelphia: Westminster, 1976.

————. *Jeremiah*. The Anchor Bible. Garden City, N.Y.: Doubleday, 1965.

Bring, R. "Paul and the Old Testament." *Studia Theologica* 25 (1971): 21 – 60.

Bruce, F. F. *The Acts of the Apostles*. Chicago: Inter-Varsity Christian Fellowship, 1952.

————. *The Epistle of Paul to the Romans: An Introduction and Commentary*. Grand Rapids: Eerdmans, 1963.

————. *The Epistle to the Hebrews*. New International Commentary on the New Testament series. Grand Rapids: Eerdmans, 1964.

————. "Paul and the Law of Moses." *Bulletin of the John Rylands University Library* 57 (1974/1975): 259 – 79.

Brueggemann, Walter. *The Land: Place as Gift, Promise, and Challenge in Biblical Faith*. Philadelphia: Fortress, 1977.

Bryant, D. "Micah 4:14 – 5:14: An Exegesis." *Restoration Quarterly* 21 (1978): 210 – 30.

Buchanan, George W. *The Consequences of the Covenant*. Leiden: Brill, 1970.

Bultmann, Rudolf. "Prophecy and Fulfillment." In *Essays on Old Testament Hermeneutics*, edited by Claus Westermann. Translation edited by James Luther Mays. Richmond: John Knox, 1963.

Burney, C. F. "The Book of Isaiah: A New Theory." *Church Quarterly Review* 75 (1912): 99 – 139.

Burton, E. D. *A Critical and Exegetical Commentary on the Epistle to the Galatians*. Edinburgh: T. and T. Clark, 1921.

Campbell, W. S. "Christ the End of the Law: Romans 10:4." In *Studia Biblica 1978*,

III: Papers on Paul and Other New Testament Authors, edited by E. A. Livingstone. Sixth International Congress on Biblical Studies. Sheffield: JSOT, 1980.

Candlish, R. S. *Commentary on Genesis*. 1868. Grand Rapids: Zondervan, 1956.

Carson, D. A., ed. *From Sabbath to Lord's Day: A Biblical, Historical, and Theological Investigation*. Grand Rapids: Zondervan, 1982.

Cassuto, Umberto. *A Commentary on the Book of Genesis*. 2 vols. Translated by Israel Abrahams. Jerusalem: Magnes Press, Hebrew University, 1961 – 64.

Chafer, Lewis Sperry. *Systematic Theology*. 8 vols. Vol. 5. Dallas: Dallas Seminary Press, 1947 – 48.

Childs, Brevard S. *Introduction to the Old Testament as Scripture*. Philadelphia: Fortress, 1979.

————. *Myth and Reality in the Old Testament*. 2d ed. London: SCM, 1962.

Clements, R. E. *Abraham and David*. London: SCM, 1967.

Cranfield, C. E. B. *A Critical and Exegetical Commentary on the Epistle to the Romans*. 2 vols. International Critical Commentary series. Edinburgh: T. and T. Clark, 1975.

————. *The Gospel According to Mark*. Cambridge: At the University Press, 1959.

————. "St. Paul and the Law." *Scottish Journal of Theology* 17 (1964): 43 – 68.

Dahood, M. *Psalms II*. The Anchor Bible. Garden City, N.Y.: Doubleday, 1966 – 70.

Darnell, D. R. *Rebellion, Rest, and the Word of God (An Exegetical Study of Hebrews 3:1 – 4:13)*. Ann Arbor: University Microfilms, 1973.

Davies, W. D. *The Gospel and the Land: Early Christianity and Jewish Territorial Doctrine*. Berkeley: University of California Press, 1974.

Delitzsch, Franz. *Isaiah*. Commentary on the Old Testament. 2 vols. Reprint. Grand Rapids: Eerdmans, 1980.

Dion, M. "Yahweh, Dieu de Canaan, et la terre des hommes." *Canadian Journal of Theology* 13 (1967): 233 – 40.

Dodd, C. H. *The Epistle of Paul to the Romans*. London: Hodder and Stoughton, 1932.

Driver, S. R. *The Book of Genesis*. London: Methuen, 1906.

Driver, S. R., and A. Newbauer. *The Fifty-third Chapter of Isaiah According to the Jewish Interpreters*. Vol. 2, *Translations*. New York: Ktav, 1969.

Eadie, J. *Commentary on the Epistle of Paul to the Galatians*. 1884. Grand Rapids: Zondervan, n. d.

Eichrodt, Walther. *Theology of the Old Testament*. Translated by J. A. Baker. 2 vols. Philadelphia: Westminster, 1961.

Ellis, E. Earle. *Paul's Use of the Old Testament*. Grand Rapids: Eerdmans, 1957.

English, E. S. *Studies in the Epistle to the Hebrews*. Travelers Rest, S.C.: Southern Bible House, 1955.

Filson, F. V. *A Commentary on the Gospel According to St. Matthew.* 2d ed. London: A. and C. Black, 1971.

Flückiger, F. "Christus des Gesetzes *telos.*" *Theologische Zeitschrift* 11 (1955): 153−57.

Foulkes, F. *The Acts of God.* London: Tyndale, 1955.

France, R. T. *Jesus and the Old Testament.* Downers Grove, Ill.: Inter-Varsity, 1971.

Fuller, Daniel P. *Gospel and Law: Contrast or Continuum?* Grand Rapids: Eerdmans, 1980.

Godet, F. *Commentary on the Epistle to the Romans.* Translated by A. Cusin. Translation revised and edited by Talbot W. Chambers. Grand Rapids: Zondervan, 1956.

Gowan, D. E. "Losing the Promised Land—The Old Testament Considers the Inconceivable." In *From Faith to Faith: Essays in Honor of Donald G. Miller on His Seventieth Birthday,* edited by Dikran Y. Hadidian. Pittsburgh Theological Monograph Series, no. 4. Pittsburgh: Pickwick, 1979.

Greenberg, Moshe. "Hebrew *segullā:* Akkadian *sikiltu.*" *Journal of the American Oriental Society* 71 (1951): 172−74.

Guhrt, J. "Covenant." In *The New International Dictionary of New Testament Theology,* edited by Colin Brown. Vol. 1. Grand Rapids: Zondervan, 1975.

Guthrie, Donald. *Galatians.* London: Nelson, 1969.

Hamilton, Floyd E. *The Epistle to the Romans: An Exegetical and Devotional Commentary.* Grand Rapids: Baker, 1958.

Harris, R. Laird. *Inspiration and Canonicity of the Bible: An Historical and Exegetical Study.* Grand Rapids: Zondervan, 1957.

Harrison, Everett F. *Romans.* Vol. 10, the *Expositor's Bible Commentary.* Grand Rapids: Zondervan, 1976.

Hendriksen, William. *A Commentary on Galatians.* London: Banner of Truth Trust, 1969.

Hodge, Charles. *Commentary on the Epistle to the Romans.* 1835. Grand Rapids: Eerdmans, 1952.

_____. *Systematic Theology.* 2 vols. 1871−73. Grand Rapids: Eerdmans, 1960.

Howard, G. E. "Christ the End of the Law: The Meaning of Romans 10:4ff." *Journal of Biblical Literature* 88 (1969): 331−37.

Hughes, Philip Edgcumbe. *Paul's Second Epistle to the Corinthians.* Grand Rapids: Eerdmans, 1962.

Jenkins, A. K. "A Great Name: Genesis 12:2 and the Editing of the Pentateuch." *Journal for the Study of the Old Testament* 10 (1978): 41−57.

Johnson, E. E. "Hermeneutics and Dispensationalism." In *Walvoord: A Tribute,* edited by Donald K. Campbell. Chicago: Moody, 1982.

Kaiser, Walter C., Jr. "The Blessing of David: A Charter for Humanity." In *The Law and the Prophets: Old Testament Studies Prepared in Honor of Oswald Thomp-*

son Allis, edited by John H. Skilton. Nutley, N.J.: Presbyterian and Reformed, 1974.

—————. "The Promised Land: A Biblical-Historical View." *Bibliotheca Sacra* 138 (1981): 302 – 12.

—————. *Toward an Old Testament Theology.* Grand Rapids: Zondervan, 1978.

Käsemann, Ernst. *The Epistle to the Romans.* Translated and edited by Geoffrey W. Bromiley. Grand Rapids: Eerdmans, 1980.

Kaufman, Yehezkel. *The Religion of Israel, from Its Beginnings to the Babylonian Exile.* Translated and abridged by Moshe Greenberg. Chicago: University of Chicago Press, 1960.

Keil, Carl F., and Franz Delitzsch. *Biblical Commentary on the Books of Samuel.* Reprint. Grand Rapids: Eerdmans, 1969.

Klein, C. "The Theological Dimension of the State of Israel." *Journal of Ecumenical Studies* 10 (1973): 700 – 715.

Kline, Meredith G. *By Oath Consigned: A Reinterpretation of the Covenant Signs of Circumcision and Baptism.* Grand Rapids: Eerdmans, 1968.

—————. *Treaty of the Great King: The Covenant Structure of Deuteronomy.* Grand Rapids: Eerdmans, 1963.

Knight, G. A. F. *Deutero-Isaiah: A Theological Commentary on Isaiah 40 – 55.* New York: Abingdon, 1965.

Kruse, C. G. "The Servant Songs: Interpretive Trends Since C. R. North." *Studia Biblica et Theologica* 8 (1978): 3 – 27.

Laetsch, Theodore. *Bible Commentary: The Minor Prophets.* Saint Louis: Concordia, 1956.

Lane, William L. *The Gospel According to Mark.* New International Commentary on the New Testament series. Grand Rapids: Eerdmans, 1974.

Lenski, R. C. H. *Interpretation of St. Luke's Gospel.* Minneapolis: Augsburg, 1964.

—————. *The Interpretation of St. Paul's Epistles to the Galatians, to the Ephesians, and to the Philippians.* Minneapolis: Augsburg, 1961.

Leupold, H. C. *Exposition of Genesis.* 2 vols. 1942. Grand Rapids: Baker, 1949.

—————. *Exposition of Zechariah.* 1956. Grand Rapids: Baker, 1971.

Levenson, J. "The Davidic Covenant and Its Modern Interpreters." *Catholic Biblical Quarterly* 41 (1979): 205 – 19.

Lightfoot, J. B. *The Epistle of St. Paul to the Galatians.* 1865. Grand Rapids: Zondervan, 1962.

Lincoln, A. T. "Sabbath, Rest, and Eschatology in the New Testament." In *From Sabbath to Lord's Day: A Biblical, Historical, and Theological Investigation,* edited by D. A. Carson. Grand Rapids: Zondervan, 1982.

Longenecker, Richard N. *Biblical Exegesis in the Apostolic Period.* Grand Rapids: Eerdmans, 1975.

—————. " 'Son of Man' Imagery: Some Implications for Theology and Discipleship." *Journal of the Evangelical Theological Society* 18 (1975): 3 – 16.

Luther, Martin. *Lectures on Romans*. Translated and edited by Wilhelm Pauck. Philadelphia: Westminster, 1961.

McCarthy, D. J. "Covenant in the Old Testament: The Present State of Inquiry." *Catholic Biblical Quarterly* 27 (1965): 217–40.

_____. *Treaty and Covenant*. New ed. Rome: Biblical Institute Press, 1978.

McComiskey, Thomas E. "Idolatry." In *International Standard Bible Encyclopedia*, edited by Geoffrey W. Bromiley. Vol. 2. Grand Rapids: Eerdmans, 1982.

_____. "*qādaš*." In *Theological Wordbook of the Old Testament*, edited by R. Laird Harris, Gleason L. Archer, Jr., and Bruce K. Waltke. Vol. 2. Chicago: Moody, 1980.

Manson, William. *Jesus and the Christian*. Grand Rapids: Eerdmans, 1967.

Marshall, I. Howard. *Luke: Historian and Theologian*. Contemporary Evangelical Perspectives series. Grand Rapids: Zondervan, 1971.

_____. *St. Mark*. London: Scripture Union, 1968.

Martens, Elmer A. *God's Design: A Focus on Old Testament Theology*. Grand Rapids: Baker, 1981.

_____. "The Promise of the Land to Israel." *Direction* 5 (1976): 8–13.

Mays, James Luther. *Amos: A Commentary*. Philadelphia: Westminster, 1969.

_____. *Hosea. A Commentary*. Philadelphia: Westminster, 1969.

_____. *Micah: A Commentary*. Philadelphia: Westminster, 1976.

Mekilta de-Rabbi Ishmael. Translated by Jacob Z. Lauterbach. 1933–35. Philadelphia: Jewish Publication Society of America, 1976.

Mendenhall, George E. "Covenant Forms in Israelite Tradition." *Biblical Archaeologist* 17, no. 3 (1954).

Meyer, H. A. W. *Critical and Exegetical Hand-book to the Epistle to the Romans*. Translated by John C. Moore and Edwin Johnson. Rev. ed. New York: Funk and Wagnalls, 1884.

Meyers, P. "Romans 10:4 and the 'End' of the Law." In *The Divine Helmsman: Studies on God's Control of Human Events, Presented to Lou H. Silberman*, edited by James L. Crenshaw and Samuel Sandmel. New York: Ktav, 1980.

Miller, P. "The Gift of God: The Deuteronomic Theology of the Land." *Interpretation* 23 (1969): 451–65.

Moo, Douglas J. "Jesus and the Authority of the Mosaic Law." *Journal for the Study of the New Testament* 20 (1984): 3–49.

_____. " 'Law,' 'Works of the Law,' and Legalism in Paul." *Westminster Theological Journal* 45 (1983): 73–100.

Morgenstern, J. "The Suffering Servant—A New Solution." Parts 1, 2. *Vetus Testamentum* 11 (1961): 292–320, 406–31.

_____. "The Suffering Servant—A New Solution." Part 3. *Vetus Testamentum* 13 (1963): 321–32.

Murphy, R. E. "The Relationship Between the Testaments." *Catholic Biblical Quarterly* 26 (1964): 349—59.

Murray, John. "The Adamic Administration." In *Collected Writings of John Murray.* 4 vols. Vol. 2. Edinburgh and Carlisle, Penn.: Banner of Truth Trust, 1976.

————. *The Covenant of Grace: A Biblico-Theological Study.* London: Tyndale, 1953.

————. *The Epistle to the Romans.* New International Commentary on the New Testament series. Grand Rapids: Eerdmans, 1960.

Na'aman, N. "The Brook of Egypt and Assyrian Policy on the Border of Egypt." *Tel Aviv* 6 (1979): 68—90.

Newell, William R. *Hebrews, Verse by Verse.* Chicago: Moody, 1947.

Nixon, R. "Fulfilling the Law: The Gospels and Acts." In *Law, Morality and the Bible: A Symposium,* edited by Bruce Kaye and Gordon Wenham. Downers Grove, Ill.: Inter-Varsity, 1978.

North, C. R. *The Suffering Servant in Deutero-Isaiah: An Historical and Critical Study.* London: Oxford University Press, 1956.

Orlinsky, Harry M. "The So-called 'Suffering Servant' in Isaiah 53." In *Interpreting the Prophetic Tradition,* edited by Harry M. Orlinksy. Cincinnati: Hebrew Union College Press, 1969.

Pentecost, J. D. *Things to Come: A Study in Biblical Eschatology.* Findlay, Ohio: Dunham, 1958.

Pettingill, William L. *Into the Holiest.* Findlay, Ohio: Fundamental Truth Publishers, 1939.

Pieters, Albertus. *The Seed of Abraham: A Biblical Study of Israel, the Church, and the Jew.* Grand Rapids: Eerdmans, 1950.

Pusey, E. B. *The Minor Prophets.* 2 vols. Grand Rapids: Baker, 1950.

Rad, Gerhard von. *Old Testament Theology.* Translated by D. M. G. Stalker. 2 vols. New York: Harper, 1962—65.

————. *The Problem of the Hexateuch, and Other Essays.* Translated by E. W. Trueman Dicken. New York: McGraw-Hill, 1966.

Räisänen, Heikki. "Paul's Theological Difficulties with the Law." In *Studia Biblica 1978, III: Papers on Paul and Other New Testament Authors,* edited by E. A. Livingstone. Sixth International Congress on Biblical Studies. Sheffield: JSOT, 1980.

Rhyne, C. T. "Romans 10:4 Once More." In *Faith Establishes the Law.* Chico, Calif.: Scholars, 1981.

Ridderbos, Herman N. *The Coming of the Kingdom.* Edited by Raymond O. Zorn. Translated by H. de Jongste. Philadelphia: Presbyterian and Reformed, 1962.

Robertson, O. Palmer. *The Christ of the Covenants.* Grand Rapids: Baker, 1980.

————. "Current Reformed Thinking on the Nature of the Divine Covenants." *Westminster Theological Journal* 40 (1977—78): 63—76.

_____. "Is There a Distinctive Future for Ethnic Israel in Romans 11?" In *Perspectives on Evangelical Theology: Papers from the Thirtieth Annual Meeting of the Evangelical Theological Society*, edited by Kenneth S. Kantzer and Stanley N. Gundry. Grand Rapids: Baker, 1979.

Rordorff, Willy. *Sunday*. Translated by A. A. K. Graham. Philadelphia: Westminster, 1968.

Rowley, H. H. *The Faith of Israel: Aspects of Old Testament Thought*. Philadelphia: Westminster, 1957.

Ryrie, C. C. *The Basis of the Premillennial Faith*. New York: Loizeaux, 1953.

Sanday, William, and Arthur C. Headlam. *The Epistle to the Romans*. Edited by Charles J. Ellicott. 1903. Grand Rapids: Zondervan, 1957.

Schaff, Philip. *The Creeds of Christendom*. Vol. 3. Grand Rapids: Baker, 1966.

Scharbert, Josef. "Curse." In *Sacramentum Verbi: An Encyclopedia of Biblical Theology*, edited by Johannes B. Bauer. Vol. 1. New York: Herder and Herder, 1970.

_____. In *Theological Dictionary of the Old Testament*, edited by G. Johannes Botterweck and Helmer Ringgren. Translated by John I. Willis. Vol. 2. Grand Rapids: Eerdmans, 1975.

Skinner, J. *A Critical and Exegetical Commentary on Genesis*. International Critical Commentary series. 2d ed. Edinburgh: T. and T. Clark, 1930.

Smart, James D. *History and Theology in Second Isaiah: A Commentary on Isaiah 35, 40 – 66*. Philadelphia: Westminster, 1965.

_____. *The Interpretation of Scripture*. Philadelphia: Westminster, 1961.

Speiser, E. A. *Genesis*. The Anchor Bible. Garden City, N.Y.: Doubleday, 1964.

Spurgeon, C. H. *The Treasury of David*. Vol. 6. New York: Funk and Wagnalls, 1881.

Strack, H., and P. Billerbeck. *Kommentar zum Neuen Testament aus Talmud und Midrasch*. Vol. 3. München: Beck, 1961 – 65.

Suggs, J. "The Word Is Near You: Romans 10:6 – 10 Within the Purpose of the Letter." In *Christian History and Interpretation: Studies Presented to John Knox*, edited by W. R. Farmer, C. F. D. Moule, and R. R. Niebuhr. Cambridge: At the University Press, 1967.

Swetnam, James. "Some Observations on the Background of צדיק in Jeremias 23:5a." *Biblica* 46 (1965): 29 – 40.

Talmon, S., and D. Flusser. "The Gospel and the Land: Early Christianity and Jewish Territorial Doctrine." *Christian News from Israel* 25 (1975): 132 – 39.

Thomas, W. H. G. *"Let Us Go On," the Secret of Christian Progress in the Epistle to the Hebrews*. Grand Rapids: Zondervan, 1944.

Thompson, J. A. *The Book of Jeremiah*. New International Commentary on the Old Testament series. Grand Rapids: Eerdmans, 1979.

Tucker, G. M. "Covenant Forms and Contract Forms." *Vetus Testamentum* 15 (1965): 487 – 503.

Wainright, A. "Luke and the Restoration of the Kingdom of Israel." *Expository Times* 89 (1977): 76−79.

Waldow, H. E. von. "Israel and Her Land: Some Theological Considerations." In *A Light Unto My Path: Old Testament Studies in Honor of Jacob M. Myers*, edited by Howard N. Bream, Ralph D. Heim, and Carey A. Moore. Gettsyburg Theological Studies, no. 4. Philadelphia: Temple University Press, 1974.

Walvoord, John F. *The Millennial Kingdom*. Findlay, Ohio: Dunham, 1959.

Weber, Hans-Rudi. "The Promise of the Land: Biblical Interpretation and the Present Situation in the Middle East." *Study Encounter* 7 (SE 16 1971): 1−16.

Weinfeld, M. "The Covenant of Grant in the Old Testament and in the Ancient Near East." *The Journal of the American Oriental Society* 90 (1970): 184−203.

Wenham, Gordon. "Grace and Law in the Old Testament." In *Law, Morality and the Bible: A Symposium*, edited by Bruce Kaye and Gordon Wenham. Downers Grove, Ill.: Inter-Varsity, 1978.

Westermann, Claus. *The Old Testament and Jesus Christ*. Translated by Omar Kaste. Minneapolis: Aubsburg, 1970.

————. "The Way of the Promise Through the Old Testament." In *The Old Testament and Christian Faith*, edited by Bernhard W. Anderson. New York: Harper and Row, 1963.

Wilson, M. "Zionism as Theology: An Evangelical Approach." *Journal of the Evangelical Theological Society* 22 (1979): 27−44.

Witsius, Hermannus. *The Economy of the Covenants Between God and Man*. Translated by William Crookshank. 1677. Edinburgh: Thomas Turnbull, 1803.

Wolfe, R. E., and H. A. Bosley, *The Book of Micah*. Vol. 6, the *Interpretor's Bible*. New York and Nashville: Abingdon, 1956.

Wolff, H. W. "The Kerygma of the Yahwist." *Interpretation* 20 (1966): 131−58.

Woods, J. *The Old Testament in the Church*. London: S.P.C.K., 1949.

Wright, G. Ernest. "Israel in the Promised Land: History Interpreted by a Covenant Faith." *Encounter* 35 (1974): 318−34.

Index of Subjects

Abishai, 40

Abraham: faithful obedience of, 36, 38, 40, 64 – 65, 119; personal blessing of, 38 – 40; righteousness of, 107

Abrahamic promise covenant, 15 – 66; of blessing/curse of others, 41 – 42; of blessing for Abraham, 38 – 40; continuing validity of, 166 – 67; of divine-human relationship, 57; of enhanced reputation, 40; establishing of, 64; eternality vs. conditionality of, 17, 64 – 66; faithful obedience and, 64 – 65; of Gentile inclusion, 55 – 57; of land, 42 – 55; nature and function of, 15 – 17, 142 – 44; new covenant and, in Hebrews 6:13 – 20, 166 – 67; of offspring, 17 – 38; reaffirmation of, 61; restoration of Israel and, 173 – 74; self-maledictory nature of, 60, 61; statement of, 16 – 17; as sworn oath, 61 (see also Promise-oath); terms of, 16

Adam: federal function of, 220; as place name, 215 – 16

Adamic administration, 213 – 21; nature of, 219 – 20. See also Covenant of works

Administrative covenants: circumcision as, 145 – 50; nature and functions of, 144 – 76; promise and, relationship between, 171 – 76; sequential structure of, 226; as theological category, 193 – 211; unity and diversity in, 195 – 210. See also Circumcision, covenant of; Mosaic covenant

Allis, O. T.: on Gentile blessing, 56

Amaru, B. H.: on land theology of Josephus, 207 n. 19

Andersen, F. I.: on "Adam" in Hosea 6:7, 215

Anderson, H.: on Matthew 12:5, 95 n. 33

Babylon, 80, 81

Bacon, B.: on Jesus and law, 77 n. 21

Baldwin, Joyce G.: on meaning of "righteous Branch," 27 n. 17

Banks, R.: on fulfillment of Old Testament, 104; on typology (Jesus and David), 96 n. 36

Barrett, C. K.: on inheritance of promise, 53

Barth, Karl: on righteousness, 123

Beecher, Willis J.: on tôrāh, 22 n. 10

Berkhof, Hendrikus: on Israel as people of God, 203

Berkhof, Louis, 201; on covenant of redemption, 184 – 85

Black, Matthew: on Romans 7:25, 110

Blessing, meaning of, 39 – 40, 41 – 42, 55 – 57

Index of Scripture

Index of Greek and Hebrew Words

Hebrew

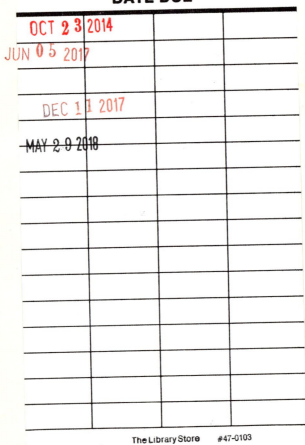